Native
Religions
and
Cultures
of North
America

From the Series Anthropology of the Sacred
Edited by Julien Ries and Lawrence E. Sullivan

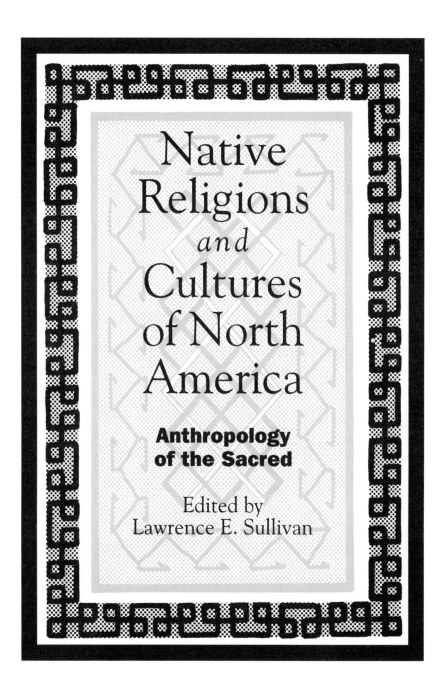

Native
Religions
and
Cultures
of North
America

**Anthropology
of the Sacred**

Edited by
Lawrence E. Sullivan

Continuum • New York and London

2000

The Continuum International Publishing Group Inc
370 Lexington Avenue, New York, NY 10017

The Continuum International Publishing Group Ltd
Wellington House, 125 Strand WC2R OBB

Printed in the United States of America

Library of Congress Cataloging-in-Publication Data
Native religions and cultures of North America / edited by Lawrence E. Sullivan.
    p.   cm. – (Anthropology of the sacred)
    Includes bibliographical references and index.
    ISBN 0-8264-1084-7
    1. Indians of North America – Religion. 2. Indians of North America – Social life
and customs. I. Sullivan, Lawrence Eugene, 1949–   II. Series.
E98.R3 N39 2000

                                                                        99-049012

Contents

Introduction   1
    Lawrence Sullivan

1. Renewal as Discourse and Discourse as Renewal   33
in Native Northwestern California
    Thomas Buckley

2. Traditional Ways and Contemporary Vitality: 53
Absaroke/Crow
    John A. Grim

3. Rebalancing the World in the Contradictions of History: 85
Creek/Muskogee
    Joel W. Martin

4. Wiping the Tears: Lakota Religion in the   104
Twenty-first Century
    William K. Powers

5. The Continuous Renewal of Sacred Relations: 121
Navajo Religion
    Trudy Griffin-Pierce

6. In the Space between Earth and Sky: 142
Contemporary Mescalero Apache Ceremonialism
    Ines Talamantez

7. Synchretism, Revival, and Reinvention: 160
Tlingit Religion, Pre- and Postcontact
    Richard Dauenhauer

8. Eye of the Dance: Spiritual Life of the Central Yup'ik
Eskimos   181
    Ann Fienup-Riordan

9. Images of the Sacred in Native North American Literature   208
    Franco Meli

Contributors   239

Index   241

Contents

Introduction   1
    Lawrence Sullivan

1. Renewal as Discourse and Discourse as Renewal   33
    in Native Northwestern California
    Thomas Buckley

2. Traditional Ways and Contemporary Vitality: 53
    Absaroke/Crow
    John A. Grim

3. Rebalancing the World in the Contradictions of History: 85
    Creek/Muskogee
    Joel W. Martin

4. Wiping the Tears: Lakota Religion in the   104
    Twenty-first Century
    William K. Powers

5. The Continuous Renewal of Sacred Relations: 121
    Navajo Religion
    Trudy Griffin-Pierce

6. In the Space between Earth and Sky: 142
    Contemporary Mescalero Apache Ceremonialism
    Ines Talamantez

7. Synchretism, Revival, and Reinvention: 160
    Tlingit Religion, Pre- and Postcontact
    Richard Dauenhauer

8. Eye of the Dance: Spiritual Life of the Central Yup'ik
    Eskimos   181
    Ann Fienup-Riordan

9. Images of the Sacred in Native North American Literature   208
    Franco Meli

Contributors   239

Index   241

Understanding Native American Religious Lifeways: An Introduction

Lawrence E. Sullivan

I think it is necessary that the younger ones know something about their religion. Their minds are confused, not knowing what they should do. They should know that there are religions, that their people have a religion that is different from other religions, and our religion was given to us Indian people long before our time.
— THOMAS YELLOWTAIL
Absaroke/Crow Sun Dance Chief[1]

All our actions are based on our religion — if that goes, we go as a people.
— BERNARD SECOND
Mescalero Apache Singer[2]

Religion stands at the heart of Native American life. Not the sort of "religion" that is set apart, isolated from other domains in life. Rather, religion in Native American culture is robust, an entire lifeway that engages all that is vital and relates one to everything that matters. This volume contains insightful essays on significant spiritual moments in eight different Native American cultures. These essays are rare gifts from writers who are themselves gifted with rare knowledge of and long intimacy with Native American religious lives. They know the communities, speak the languages, walk the walk. Each essay encapsulates the most central and moving spiritual elements in the cultures described.

1. *Yellowtail, Crow Medicine Man and Sun Dance Chief: An Autobiography*, as told to Michael O. Fitzgerald (Norman: University of Oklahoma Press, 1991), 1, as cited in the article by John Grim below.
2. Bernard Second, Mescalero Apache Singer, as cited in Claire R. Farrer, "Singing for Life: The Mescalero Apache Girl's Ceremony," *Southwestern Indian Ritual Drama* (Albuquerque: University of New Mexico Press, 1980), 125–59; quotation on 125.

The book paints nine pictures of remarkable religious vitality, especially because these communities exist in the face of daunting odds. These are not romantic visions that whitewash the devastating history that Native peoples have endured for five centuries. The trail of broken treaties, the decimations of populations through force of arms and disease, and the disintegration of cultures through hatred, ignorance, and proselytism have provoked spiritual malaise as well as economic and cultural destruction. Truly amazing and admirable, then, is the cultural courage and spiritual fortitude of Native American peoples who have persevered with their religious lives. Even more than holding the line, the steadfast focus on spiritual heritage has instigated remarkable religious innovations, risings of the spirit in the form of new movements as well as creative restatements of traditions long suppressed.

This book addresses all readers interested in religious life, especially those wanting to know more about spiritual life as practiced on the continent of North America. For those of us who live on this continent, it is essential to make ourselves one in understanding the many spiritualities that characterize North America so distinctly. The land bears a material bounty but also a spiritual heritage worked out in intimate religious interactions with it over millennia. The religious practices of Native Americans have consecrated the landscapes of North America, building over time a spiritual endowment which we turn from at our peril. Such escapism is a practiced habit in North America, where the teaching of Native American religions is hardly a serious part of any curriculum at any educational level. Willful blindness has yielded a violent history of relations with Native peoples as well as the scandalous conditions into which peoples of exquisite culture have been plunged since the time of the conquest. For the sake of the peace and well-being that comes only from profound understanding and respect of others, all of us on the continent would do well to take better cognizance of the spiritual aspirations and religious accomplishments of those here present, especially the people of its First Nations.

This respect and understanding as well as the desire to widen spiritual horizons in a way better suited to our day are the aims of this book and its companion volume, which will present the religious life of Mesoamerica and South America. Better knowledge of the most important religious ideas and practices of the world is, in fact, the goal of the entire book series entitled "The Anthropology of the Sacred," which I edit with Julien Ries. Given the interactions, on nearly every plane, of people from diverse religious cultures on the globe today, it is incumbent on us to better understand the religious grounds of one another's cultural behaviors, moral codes, and deepest aspirations. The volume does not claim to be comprehensive or encyclopedic. It opens nine windows on the spiritual practices and religious lifeways of Native North America and offers a way of looking at each with high regard and sympathetic understanding.

We focus on an anthropology of the sacred — by which we mean each culture's understandings of fundamental realities, powers, and processes as well as the religious responses they inspire in individuals and communities. Emphasis falls, therefore, on religious capacities: how each culture sharpens religious sensitivity and cultivates spiritual perception to make life a *different way* of seeing, sensing, and listening.[3] By orienting humans toward transformative powers of the first order, an anthropology of the sacred changes human life, not just in a neutral or value-free fashion, but by impelling us to assume our own place in the world and to achieve our most proper and vital way of relating to all realities.

The spiritualities described in these essays aim to quicken the awareness that life carries more depth than is taken in by glancing at its surface. The aim is to reveal the inner meaning and true significance of appearances. In some cases, even good and evil prove to be chimeras in the end, for little or nothing lies beyond transformation when brought into right relationship with the sources of sacrality. Critical recitation of and reflection on religious narratives, the performance of associated rites, and the subsequent reordering of heart and life transform relationships of all kinds. There is nothing automatic or mechanical about the recitation of myth and the reenactment of ceremony. They are exercises of the mind, heart, and body which may require arduous effort, both inner and outer, and affect many levels: individual psyche, physical form, social standing, and cosmic renewal. When performed

---

3. Vine Deloria, Jr., a Native American philosopher and writer from the Standing Rock Sioux community, argued that diverse religious perceptions generate distinct views of the mysteries of the universe. "The fundamental factor that keeps Indians and non-Indians from communicating is that they are speaking about two entirely different perceptions of the world" (Vine Deloria, *The Metaphysics of Modern Existence* [San Francisco: Harper & Row, 1979], vii). In 1996, in my capacity as president of the American Academy of Religion, I invited Vine Deloria, Jr., to address the plenary assembly of the Academy at its annual meeting. In his address, he emphasized that accounts of Native American religious life have seldom been fair or neutral and that a reappraisal of Native American religious life is essential to reestablishing right relations among peoples on the continent and, indeed, to reestablishing health and well-being.

appropriately, myth and rite unite devotees with the powerful beings who performed them for the first time when they shaped life as it is known. The labors of rite and myth also unite contemporary religious actors with all the ancestors who have performed them since the beginning. The religious learning and actions of interlinked generations, passed down the long chain of time, explain why religious knowledge and reenactment still exist today. As the essays show, each generation and individual makes a unique contribution. We join that chain of transmission through reading this book, among other ways. If we hold ourselves to the task, we must eventually think about how we will take to heart the knowledge passed on to us.

Eyewitnesses to History

Native American peoples are singularly important eyewitnesses to modern history. They are not treated as such, due to prejudices about cultural evolution left over from the nineteenth century. Native ways of thinking were deemed irrelevant, superseded, or passed by as demonstrably wrong-headed in the forward march of progress. The depressions, wars, and failures of the twentieth century, which called the illusory Myth of Progress into question, did not succeed in redeeming the value of Native American reflections on the history we share. The presence of Native Americans in global affairs parallels that of Protestants; European relations with indigenous peoples characterize the human situation in the world over the same span of centuries. Nevertheless, American culture has never turned to Native American religious commentators as they have turned to the Niebuhrs, Paul Tillich, and Martin Marty to understand the spiritual consequences of the Ages of "Discovery," "Colonialism," "World Warfare," "Postcolonialism," and "Development" which shape us all. Native American religious reflection is valuable. It is irreplaceable in order to understand the religious predicaments and possibilities inherent in the history that we share. Learning from the spiritual and material conditions that exist on reservations, for instance, North Americans gain a different picture of the way we act in the world: the destructive consequences of our acts as a civil society and the underlying ignorance and moral attitudes which need to change. We must become convinced of the historical value and the relevance of our Native American contemporaries. It seems as ludicrous as it is still necessary to insist that "they are not . . . the ancient vestiges of an overthrown past. In an epoch concretely dominated by the effects of Western thought, they are moving witnesses to a different way of apprehending the world and others. . . . That is no doubt why they pay such heavy tribute to a History from which, not having been its accomplices, they stand to gain no benefit."[4]

All communities are entitled to reflect on the human situation in the world, within the context of their own culture. Any serious anthropology must take these reflections on the human condition into account. Native American religions are important reflections on the situation of humanity at the turn of the twenty-first century. The truths conveyed by Native American religious practice need not be seen as overly mystical or ancient. They are shrewd interpretations of the very world we inhabit today. Native Americans have always come to the fore as public spokespersons for their own points of view. They have not usually gained a good hearing, as one can read in the sad commentaries on the "trail of broken treaties," the history of Indian-white negotiations over the past centuries.[5]

One thinks, for example, of the stirring testimony of Roberta Blackgoat and Kee Say, traditional Big Mountain Navajo representatives who addressed the Fourth Russell Tribunal in Holland. Big Mountain is the most prominent feature in the JUA, the Joint Use Area, otherwise known as Grazing District 6, inhabited by both Hopi and Navajo peoples. Big Mountain is at the center of the four sacred mountains that define the Four Corners area where Colorado, New Mexico, Arizona, and Utah meet. Sacred to both Navajo and Hopi, Big Mountain is an important source of life-giving energy and healing. Big Mountain is female and is called "Mother." From her body grow all the herbs and medicines that the Navajo and Hopi use in their healing ceremonies. On the Mother are found shrines and springs such as the traditional home of Be'gochidi, the "One Who Created People." Although the traditional home of Be'gochidi is located on Big Mountain, the leaders

---

4. André-Marcel d'Ans, *Le Dit des vrais hommes: Mythes, contes, légendes et traditions des indiens cashinahua* (Paris: Union Générale d'Éditions, 1978), 22.

5. Important testimony from Native American leaders is recorded in Robin M. Wright and José Barreiro, eds., *Native Peoples in Struggle: Russell Tribunal and Other International Forums* (Boston: Anthropology Resource Center, 1982). The testimony of ongoing leadership is gathered and reported by entities such as the Native American Rights Fund in Boulder, Colorado, the Indian Law Resource Center in Washington, D.C., the National Congress of American Indians, the Association of American Indian Affairs, and so on. I have cited important work by these and other groups in previous publications. See, for example, Lawrence E. Sullivan, ed., *Native American Religions: North America* (New York: Macmillan, 1989), ix–xviii.

emphasized that he is found everywhere: the Sun never leaves him, for he is constantly transforming sunlight into wind and into other life-giving realities. Not only do the Navajo and Hopi hold to this view, but the Holy People themselves still live in the area and make it powerful and life-giving. These are the religious underpinnings of life that leaders brought to the Fourth Russell Tribunal to serve as a discussion of concrete issues: crimes against Native American peoples, relocation, resources, and the negative repercussions of policy.

Imaginary Indians and a Variety of Voices

A volume on Native North American religions must wrestle with stereotypes. American Indians have a high recognition factor around the world; their images are as well known as Pepsi, McDonald's, and the cartoon characters of Walt Disney. But the popular images of Native Americans have oftentimes arisen in the fantasies of enemies during conquest or in the fictional accounts and "Wild West" films which bear little resemblance to real life.[6] These "imaginary Indians" are well known but, as Modoc writer Michael Dorris points out, "flesh and blood Native Americans have rarely participated in or benefited from the creation of these imaginary Indians."[7]

One stereotype that needs to be overcome immediately is that of the Vanishing Indian. From the first moment of contact, invaders propagated the disinformation that Indians were vanishing from the continent in order to justify the expropriation of land from peoples allegedly doomed to extinction. Propaganda about the Vanishing Indian played into the cheap cultural science of evolution. The image of the Vanishing Indian trivialized Native American religious ideas as archaic and passé, superstitions left over from earlier evolutionary ages of hunting or neolithic agriculture. Social sciences encouraged the disregard of ideas deemed unfit to survive in the modern world.[8] Native American leaders have remarked on the sense of loss and disturbance suffered

6. Gretchen M. Bataille and Charles C. P. Silet, *The Pretend Indians: Images of Native Americans in the Movies* (Ames: Iowa State University Press, 1980) with a foreword on "American Fantasy" by Vine Deloria, Jr.

7. Michael Dorris, "Indians on the Shelf," in Calvin Martin, ed., *The American Indian and the Problem of History* (New York: Oxford University Press, 1987), 98–105; quotation from 100.

8. Brian W. Dippie, *The Vanishing Indian: White Attitudes and U.S. Indian Policy* (Middletown, Conn.: Wesleyan University Press, 1982); Christopher Lyman, *The Vanishing Race and Other Illusions: Photographs of Indians by Edward S. Curtis* (Washington, D.C.: Smithsonian Institution Press, 1982).

over the last centuries, but the fact is that every state in the Union has a Native American population which, against insurmountable challenges, continues an authentic sense of their role in the world and their place in history. Native Americans today continue the struggle to preserve their land and resources, their biological well-being and material survival, but also to shape their own meaning and destiny. That distinctive destiny and meaning are most clearly depicted in Native American ideas and practices.

A number of recent developments in the study of Native American religions help overcome the fantasies and false facts of the past. One development is the increasing number of presentations of diverse perspectives put forward by Native Americans themselves, speaking in their own voice. These many voices have allowed for a more nuanced understanding of diverse spiritual heritages. It has become clearer that complexity and subtlety exist in any community's religious life. A meeting held in Bismark, North Dakota, in the spring of 1982, for instance, gave rise to the book *Sioux Indian Religion: Tradition and Innovation,* edited by Raymond J. DeMaillie and Douglas R. Parks.[9] In spring 1982, the Sacred Pipe Bundle was put away for seven years as the spirits themselves suggested doing. The gathering became an occasion to reflect on blessings brought by the Pipe. Leaders of many religious orientations contributed to the volume. It is fascinating to read about the sacredness of the Pipe from such a variety of practitioners. Among them are Arval Looking Horse, the nineteenth generation of the keepers of the Pipe, who describes the power of the Sacred Pipe in the community today; Mercy Poor Man, a fundamentalist Christian; Vine Deloria, Sr., a Lakota Episcopal priest from South Dakota and the father of Vine Deloria, Jr.; Emerson Spider, the Oglala bishop of the Native American (Peyote) Church; Robert Stead, a traditional leader and healer; Beatrice Medicine, an anthropologist who discusses the roles of women in the contemporary resurgence of traditional ceremony; and Arthur Amiotte, the contemporary Native artist who illustrated the volume. The guiding interpretations of Native American authors is reshaping the understanding of Native American religious life.[10]

9. Raymond J. DeMaillie and Douglas R. Parks, eds., *Sioux Indian Religion: Tradition and Innovation* (Norman: University of Oklahoma Press, 1987).

10. The input of leading Native Americans in teaching and writing is also reshaping college curricula on the subject. See, for example, Ward Churchill and Annette Jaimes, "American Indian Studies: A Positive Alternative," *Bloomsbury Review* (September–October 1988), which suggests thematic and interdisciplinary courses.

Exchanges That Open New Ground

Benjamin Franklin and others, in their day, drew the framework of government and certain language of the United States Constitution — in some cases, word for word — from federated groups of First Nations in the Americas. "The people united to form a more perfect union" continue to benefit contemporary culture with their sense of art, sports, history, language, and family. In her article on Mescalero Apache female ceremonialism, Inés Talamantez, herself an Apache scholar directing a doctoral program in Native American religious studies at the University of California in Santa Barbara, believes that "Apache ceremony is especially timely as contemporary women question what it means to be a woman at this time in history."[11]

Beatrice Medicine emphasizes the special role that ceremonial life plays in maintaining a creative and balanced relationship between the sexes. Marla N. Powers notes that females appear in myth and ritual as the prime movers of Oglala society. Based on her analyses, she challenges certain feminist theories. "A number of feminist writers view women's productive and reproductive roles as the basis for female subordination.... For the Oglalas, it is just the opposite."[12] The traditional role of Oglala women as wife and mother, she claims, facilitates the assumption of important economic and political roles. Powers asks that Native American women's lives be examined without equating women's productive and reproductive roles with subordination and without assuming the universality of male dominance. She argues that Native American life demonstrates "the possibility of seeing more complex relationships."[13]

The exchange of beliefs and practices between Native peoples and settlers who moved into North America has occurred at almost every

---

11. Talamantez joins a number of authors underscoring the relevance of Native American teaching and practice regarding notions of femaleness as well as attitudes toward sex, marriage, reproduction, and social roles. See, for example, Gretchen M. Bataille and Kathleen Mullen Sands, *American Indian Women: Telling Their Lives* (Lincoln: University of Nebraska Press, 1984); Alice Schlegel, ed., *Sexual Stratification: A Cross-Cultural View* (New York: Columbia University Press, 1979); Alice Schlegel, "Hopi Gendered Ideology of Female Superiority," *Quarterly Journal of Ideology* 8, no. 4 (1984): 44–52; Christine Bolt, *American Indian Policy and American Reform: Case Studies of the Campaign to Assimilate the American Indians* (London and Boston: Allen & Unwin, 1987), 252–69. Important work on the Mescalero girl's puberty ceremony has been published by Claire R. Farrer.

12. Marla N. Powers, *Oglala Women: Myth, Ritual, and Reality* (Chicago: University of Chicago Press, 1986), 6.

13. Ibid., 7.

level: style of dress, tactics of war, agriculture, hunting, foods, governance, and vocabulary loaned to English, French, Spanish, and Portuguese. Early settlers adopted many Native American lifeways. Why did they not more fully convert to Native American religious beliefs and practices? Look, for example, at the case of tobacco use. Before contact, tobacco growing and ceremonial use spread across the American hemisphere from Native communities deep in South America. Virtually all Native groups that opted to grow tobacco preserved the religious character of tobacco as a sacred plant used for ritual purposes.[14] Europeans were eager to use tobacco from the first moments of contact. What is notable, however, is that they transformed the sacred plant into a commodity and the religious ceremony into a pastime, divesting tobacco of its religious character. Moreover, tobacco became a profane substance. Settlers and their descendents failed to understand the religiosity that underlay tobacco consumption in the Native view. For this reason, they failed to perceive tobacco use as relevant to their own sacramental practices and religious lives. Here the conclusions of Vine Deloria, Jr., apply: "The fundamental factor that keeps Indians and non-Indians from communicating is that they are speaking about two entirely different conceptions of the world."[15] This seems as true at the level of tobacco as it is at the level of the Supreme Being.

Though most settlers generally refused to embrace Native religious traditions or knew little about them, large numbers of settlers who had the chance to know Native religious life more intimately did join the Native community. This is a remarkable and little-known story uncovered by James Axtell, *The Invasion Within: The Contest of Cultures in Colonial North America.*[16] Why are these "conversion" experiences not better known and understood, as are other notable religious conversions of the period? Axtell reports on the lives of hundreds of European settlers who were taken to live in Native communities. Later, over the protestations of friends and relatives, they remained with their former "captors" or pined for the communities of Native peoples whom they had come to love. In New England, fully 15 percent of all individuals "captured" by Native Americans before 1782 chose to stay with their

14. Johannes Wilbert, *Tobacco and Shamanism in South America* (New Haven: Yale University Press, 1987).
15. Deloria, *The Metaphysics of Modern Existence,* vii.
16. James Axtell in *The Invasion Within: The Contest of Cultures in Colonial North America* (New York: Oxford University Press, 1985).

newfound Indian families. They became fully acculturated in custom and ceremony and were treated as full-fledged Indians.[17] Unfortunately, these conversions of hundreds of their sons, daughters, and friends provoked no general moment of self-understanding, tolerance, or humility to question the settlers' belief in the superiority of their own mores. This story is a telling lesson for us today.

This volume looks at diverse religious communities in Native North America. Close examination of Native American religions changes preconceptions about the relationship of religion to society, culture, political order, and art. In Native American societies, religion cannot be reduced to a private affair or doctrines believed. On the contrary, religious life pitches one into the vitalities that fill ordinary circumstance and the powers that render the world concrete in the first place. Religious experience opens ground for drama and fine arts, music, poetry, dance, visual design, and architecture. Religious life embraces individual and collective spirituality as well as economic activities and various forms of knowledge. In such circumstances, religion becomes the basis for a correct perception of nature and human nature, as well as land, space, and time. This volume seeks to enrich our understanding of religious life and its function by presenting distinctive examples of the rich religious life of Native North America.

Renewing Deep Longing

In "Renewal as Discourse and Discourse as Renewal in Native Northwestern California," Thomas Buckley looks at the role of religion, especially rituals of world renewal, in the creative life of the Yurok Indian village of Pecwan on the Lower Klamath River in northwestern California. Buckley shows how the Yurok occasionally mend the world by resolving all differences and creating the proper sense of wholeness and balance that cures the world's ills and staves off evil. "Fixing the world" requires special labor on the part of male and female dancers and special cultivation of their spiritual life as individuals and as groups. In this labor, the community works with the tensions that arise between people and endeavors to transform those tensions

---

17. James Axtell, "The Scholastic Philosophy of the Wilderness," in *The School upon a Hill* (New Haven: Yale University Press, 1974), 287 and 333. See also Bolt, *American Indian Policy and American Reform*, 17. See also Kenneth M. Morrison, *The Embattled Northeast: The Elusive Ideal of Alliance in Abenaki-Euramerican Relations* (Berkeley: University of California Press, 1984).

into a yearning for unity — a unity that remains a deep desire only momentarily satisfied in the rites and their aftermath before the longing sets in once again. Like a gymnast poised for a few seconds above the high bar, seconds after swinging high above it and moments before falling back down, the ceremony holds the world's tensions in right relationship for an important moment of poise that occurs every eighteen months or so. The ritual balance restores lost joy and creativity until gravity and momentum topple them again to bring new energy to the next ritual build-up. Buckley contends that a right understanding of world renewal helps correct misunderstandings that have led scholars astray, preventing them from learning how religion works in Yurok life. Buckley looks on his own writing as a kind of ritual dance. Much like the dances performed by the subjects of his study, Buckley dances into print, publishing interpretations that oppose and complement some of the leading scholars of the past in the way that the ritual dance teams contend with one another in the ceremony. His aim is to achieve a broader, more holistic understanding of Yurok religious life.

Buckley wants to emphasize the religious responsibility that the Yurok assign to the individual in the ritual Jump Dance that fixes the world, an individual role largely ignored in the past. Buckley notes that individuals engage in heated debates and dialogues that lead up to the Jump Dance. In 1990, for example, debates centered on the great changes that press themselves onto Yurok society. Individual debaters wondered whether these changes diminished or eliminated the powerful effects of the rites: incorrect dancing, changes in costumes and materials, the presence of Christians, the changed times and locations of the dances, and the participation of non-Indians in the ceremonies. Such questions provoked an original and intense self-scrutiny and an evaluation of the spiritual, intellectual, and political state of affairs in the community. The debates themselves were a spiritually invigorating contestation, seen to be an underlying dynamic empowering the dances and undergirding the structure of the sacred at work in society and in the world. The Immortals described in important religious narratives set the model for this intense effort to discover the correct forms of dance, behavior, and intention. Should today's leadership, aiming at renewal, step forward on the basis of inspiration by the Spirit (through vision or asceticism)? Or should this charismatic approach be set aside in favor of shrewd political leadership?

Buckley pays special attention to the language in which these debates are waged: dance prayers, formulas, formal speeches delivered in Yurok at one time and now more often given in English. What is the proper ritual speech? Buckley shows how Native American intellectuals and artists and other creative people (whose reading during the 1988 dances included Stephen Hawking's *A Brief History of Time*), modeled their debate speeches on a variety of speech forms, ranging from the English of high-court lawyers and high-church preachers to broken English and so-called "Indian English dialects." Buckley explains why these differences matter deeply to the spiritual life, because of the powerful nature of ceremonial dialogue. He holds that a certain amount of factionalism is crucial to creative action, in the Yurok view. Various differences and distances from the ideal must be described and enacted so as to render the dances vibrant and vital. The staged disagreements become the very means through which the dances work.

The Yurok find the dances important because they renew the world — they provoke new ways of speaking, acting, and questioning about all aspects of life important to the community at the moment. The most profound questions have no immediate answers and might be best understood as deep longings that are kept alive through the dance and dialogue process. That is why the process of fixing the world is an ongoing project, the sacred project of Yurok anthropology.

The Embrace of the Tipi
and the Sounds of the Land

John Grim, in his contribution entitled "Traditional Ways and Contemporary Vitality: Absaroke/Crow," shows how spiritual knowledge, which is acquired in a personal exchange between *maxpe* (the sacred) and an individual, embraces deep ethical concerns for the larger community. Grim lays out in clear terms the relationship between individual practice, spiritual knowledge, the spiritual beings who transmit these blessings, and the links to the wider community at all points in the process. This is the comprehensive and complex view that the Absaroke/Crow hold concerning the anthropology of the sacred. John Grim draws upon Thomas Yellowtail's book, published just before his death in 1993 at the age of ninety-seven, to make an important point. Yellowtail turned around the usual understanding of the relationship of the individual to the sacred narratives he or she might recite. The individual is dependent upon the narratives for existence. Yellowtail insisted that the individual comes from the tales, is embedded in the memory and outflow of special religious narratives maintained by the community.

Sound is the prized vehicle that transmits power through oral narrative and musical performance. The Absaroke language is still spoken by about 30 percent of the Crow people and is taught as well in the tribal college. The sonic character of narrative, chant, and song shoot power back and forth between individual, community, and *maxpe*. The communication of *maxpe* through sound never resolves the creative tension that exists between fierce individualism and strong communalism, a tension between poles that ground the Absaroke way of life. The relationships that are important within families, clans, and phratries as well as between the human and material world are established precisely to transfer sacred power between individuals and groups. Sound and song constitute distinctively Crow forms of critical reflection on everything that matters, whether at the level of the individual, community, or the tradition itself. Ritual is the medium of critical inquiry and reflection, which bring one into contact with *maxpe*.

Grim details the connection between sound and land, a deep spiritual bond that becomes the foundation for all life and knowledge. The bond between territory and sacrality in Native American life has escaped many observers, as is evident in American jurisprudence. Grim offers a new approach, brought home to him in a conversation he had with Harry Moccasin during the Crow Fair of 1994, to help us understand this connection, which is synecdochal. For instance, the richly metaphorical structure of the tipi not only indicates a boundary (and therefore a territory or a cosmos), but, more especially, a spiritual matrix of bounded earth that gives life to and embraces the Crow just as a mother does her children. The tipi, which is a sacred metaphor for Absaroke land, enlivens, nourishes, and nurtures this matrilineal people. Sound enters the equation in this way: the life-giving connections between land and sacrality are brought to mind and memory — and, therefore, brought into new embodied life in each generation — through the recitation of mythic narratives that recount the origins of the people and their movement to this land under divine guidance. Grim introduces us to the diverse origin narratives kept in the memories of different bands. He also analyzes the official version of the Absaroke migration story, which is used in bilingual instructional materials. It describes the great spiritual journey of the ancestors to the land. At that time, No-Vitals received a vision from the spirit world which revealed the life that the Crows were to find in a future place where sacred tobacco seeds grew. These narratives have found modern-day applications, for example, in the college catalog of Little Big Horn College, where the account of mythic origins leads off the description of contemporary Crow studies.

The ancient narratives of the Crow describe the journey to the land of Crow country. As the nineteenth-century chief Arapooish expressed it: "The Crow country is exactly in the right place." That is why the land is alive with sacred movement. It is the sacredness of the land, the optimal location between the Sky and the Mountains, Father and Mother, which makes the specific spiritual life practiced by the Crow possible as well as necessary. Stewardship and responsibility toward the land is an integral part of religious life. I might add, as a relevant aside, that the role of land in the economy of religious life is shared by many indigenous peoples. In a meeting of indigenous religious leaders which John Grim organized at the Harvard University Center for the Study of World Religions, the cultivation of religious life was linked to the integrity of the land time and time again. This was a recurrent theme, for instance, in the plenary talk given by Chief Oren Lyons, the faithkeeper of the Haudenosaunee (Six Nations Iroquois), when he spoke at the Harvard meeting and also in the remarks he made in the meeting we held at the United Nations in New York to report our findings.

Individual religious practitioners rethink traditional ways in response to the needs of new generations. In this way, Abasaroke lifeways are maintained and renewed, as are the spiritual lineages that link the present with the past. The process is neither a mechanism nor an abstraction, but one that builds on the understandings achieved through individual experience and cultivation of the spiritual life. Individuals must reflect creatively upon historical realities, exchanges with *maxpe,* and interactions with humans and the land. They must learn to view their experiences as extensions of the exemplary actions occurring in the great narratives. Grim explains in fine detail the spiritual exercises and relationships that lead individuals to see themselves in this way, especially healers and diviners. Through great personal effort and with the help of an older mentor as well as the blessing of traditional spiritual helpers (*Iilapxe,* Medicine Fathers), the individual becomes adopted by a spiritual being. Through dreams and visions, the adopted devotee receives revelations and directions on how to gather a sacred medicine bundle (*xapaalia*). A series of exchanges takes place. Grim details exactly how, in the view of the Absaroke/Crow, spiritual power is cultivated through these exchanges with powerful mentors and through contacts with *maxpe* in myth, ritual, and ethical behavior.

In the Absaroke view, all entities in the world are connected in a meaningful and powerful way, and the human being becomes a link intrinsic to the assembly of life and power: a special role and responsibility. Above all religious roles, the human religious actor performs the great liturgy of the medicine bundle. In fact, Grim helps us understand how medicine bundles (*xapaalia*) are themselves liturgies composed of a symphony of objects whose powers have been revealed to an individual by a Medicine Father spirit. Through the ritual, properly performed both outwardly and inwardly, each object becomes a living evocation of the sacred *maxpe* brought alive through liturgical chants, sounds, and ritual movements that generate special privileges and responsibilities for all.

Having clarified these basic understandings, Grim applies them to disclose the spiritual meaning of the sweat lodge (*awusha*), which provides extraordinarily intimate contact with the spiritual world. The sweat lodge cleanses purposes and renders them sincere. It may be a daily ceremony as well as a ritual performed in preparation for more complex ceremonies held only on occasion. In the sweat lodge, the heat from rocks and the steam from water merge with the air consecrated by the sounds and dreams brought by sacred beings to the participants who pray and cry in response to the powers present there. They ask repeatedly for the fulfillment of their deepest heart's desires. The resurgence of traditional religion among the Absaroke/Crow is signaled by the widespread practice of the sweat lodge ceremony on the Crow reservation.

In addition to applying his insights to the sweat lodge, Grim helps us understand how Crow spirituality has endured in contact with Christian churches over the last two centuries, especially in contact with Baptists, Catholics, and Holiness Pentecostal churches. The Holiness Pentecostal Church has drawn traditional Abasaroke views of the sacred into Christian rituals through speaking in tongues, interpreting in tongues, and prophesying in manners similar to those used in the dramatic recitations of Crow narrative. So too the gifts associated with the power of the Spirit in the Holiness Pentecostal Church, such as healing, miracles, and personal faith, were seen as parallels to the gifts of power that were part of the older "bundle way." Currently there is an upsurge in the number of Crow practicing Absaroke rituals like the sweat lodge and Sun Dance in an ongoing quest for contact with *maxpe*.

Forgiveness and Renewal on the Square Ground

The contribution of Joel W. Martin, "Rebalancing the World in the Contradictions of History: Creek/Muskogee," gives special attention to the history of change, continuity, and survival over the past centuries. The Creek/Muskogee communities maintained a steadfast focus on their common religious goal and responsibility: to alter or restore the balance among contrary powers. Through all the vicissitudes and violence of their contacts with Europeans and Americans, the Creek kept their eyes on the role they should play as responsible religious actors in the world. Traditionally, medicine (*hiliswa*) restored or altered balance, and it was applied in rituals associated with warfare, hunting, menstruation, and childbirth. These events altered the flow of energies in the world and opened human life to marked time, the sacred times of special seasons, events, and relationships which the Creeks observed with ritual. Some ritual cycles corresponded to natural cycles; others responded to accidental occurrences.

Due especially to the presence of invading Europeans, the Creek world became terribly imbalanced at the dawn of the nineteenth century. In 1811, the Shawnee leader Tecumseh and his prophets inspired a new vision among the Creeks. Nine thousand Creeks joined a massive religious movement that became a revolt against the United States. The visions and ecstasies of their prophets merged with Shawnee religious dances, Afro-Christian apocalypticism, European biblical notions, and traditional Creek purification ceremonies. Balance was defined in terms of restoring proper boundaries between Indians and whites. This was an important religious duty that inspired political revolt. Militias from Georgia, Tennessee, and the Mississippi territory, in particular, put down the Creek revolt, under the leadership of Andrew Jackson in March 1814, at the battle of Horseshoe Bend. After that, Protestant missionaries settled in Creek villages, though the Creeks resisted conversion.

In the 1830s Creeks were removed under force of arms from Alabama to the Arkansas territory. On their journey of Removal, they carried sacred coals from their council fires in special containers and used them to rekindle a new fire to produce fresh coals for the next day's travel. Ancient copper plates, which were traditionally displayed only during special ceremonies, were carried by six warriors called Tuckabatchees. Each warrior had a plate, wrapped in buckskin, on his back. The warriors walked, in total silence and with ritual tread, a mile ahead of the main party of several thousand refugees. Before the rest of the party reached the night's destination, the Tuckabatchees buried the plates to create the center for a new ground and then set the coals in a new hearth there. Eventually, long after Removal, and after the formation of dozens of Baptist and Methodist churches within the Creek communities, the churches themselves came to incorporate much of the traditional religious symbolism of the Creek tradition. They became substitute *i:talwa*, ceremonial stomping grounds, or, as they were called, "square grounds," with which the fires and copper plates had been associated. Since, in their traditional view, Creeks viewed the world as a convergence of contraries with no final synthesis, the interaction of two separate categories — the traditional and the Christian — fell into the traditional process and logic. The notion that a full life depends upon contraries that are brought into dynamic relationship without losing their distinctiveness undergirds the entire system of Creek ceremony and practice, from marriage patterns to religious architecture, social division, ritual categories, and even special foods. Today there are some thirty thousand Creeks and nine thousand Seminoles in Oklahoma who keep the Creek religious traditions. Other groups exist in Florida and Texas as well. Poignantly, each summer Creek / Muskogee people gather to perform *póskita*, the green corn ceremony, which stresses forgiveness and renewal, two prized virtues kept central to Creek religious life.

Crying for a Vision

William K. Powers describes the religious life of the Lakota, the western division of the *Oceti Sakowin*, or Seven Fireplaces, now located in the states of North and South Dakota, parts of Montana, Wyoming, Nebraska, and Colorado. While the Lakota themselves underwent great change over the last centuries, shifting from being a Great Lakes culture to a Plains hunting society, their lifeways have had a great influence on the religion of other tribes and on that of many non-Indian peoples as well. The Lakota have managed the meaning of their own religious life not only by retaining their traditional spiritual focus on ceremonial life, but also by incorporating religious ideas from outside of their culture. But within their religious system the Lakota recognize that the continuity of their religious life has come at a great cost. They have been visited with suffering and destruction, reflected in the religious life itself. A regular part of contemporary Lakota ritual is *Istamniyan Pakin Tapi*, the "Wiping the Tears" ceremony, which memorializes those who have suffered and died. It addresses the profound grief associated with the loss of innocent life. The ceremony is an overt commemoration of the fateful ride of Big Foot and his followers from the Cheyenne River Reservation to Wounded Knee Creek, a massacre suffered at the hands of the U.S. government.

In order to understand present-day Lakota religious experience, one must understand the world inhabited by supernatural beings before humans came to exist. This world and these supernatural beings were made available through the myths of creation. Powers introduces us to *Takuskanskan* ("Something That Moves," the primordial creative force) and the supernatural beings who existed before time. Some of these beings found the Seven Fireplaces.

White Buffalo Calf Woman becomes essential to the relationship between the Creator and the people. She reveals a Sacred Pipe that they can smoke when they require help from the Creator. She teaches them the Seven Sacred Ceremonies, which become the foundation of Lakota religion. She instructs them carefully on how to perform every gesture. Today a special group, men and women endowed with supernatural powers, conducts rituals. Powers helps us understand their vocation and training, especially their relationship to visions, a source of their powers. In addition to healers, there are sacred impersonators (*Wakan Kaga*) who publicly enact their special visions. Powers portrays the inner life of these Holy Men and Women, beginning with the mystical experiences of their childhood. Visions, songs, dances and sacred language all play their special roles. Although the U.S. government attempted to curtail them at the end of the nineteenth century, the Seven Sacred Ceremonies are performed to this day and undergird Lakota religious life. Powers walks us through these ceremonies, giving us a feeling not only for their choreographies but for their inner intentions and experience. He points out which elements are longstanding and which have been adapted over time. The Ghost Dance, associated with the 1890 Wounded Knee massacre, has not been reinstated except for a couple of small-scale attempts. But the traditional religion has perse-vered. Powers takes note of the Native American Church as well as the thirteen Christian denominations currently active on the reservations.

The Lakota find their sacred history important, especially because they themselves have been a part of this prehistory. Each Lakota person is born with four aspects to his or her "soul." Some of these spiritual aspects are recycled anew in each generation. Life is, therefore, cyclical, just as is the movement in ritual. Over time and through space, the human being circles the Center of the Universe in a ritual pattern that allows one to light the Pipe that activates the spiritual powers of the Universe. The Lakotas look forward to the twenty-first century as a time to fulfill the prophecy of Red Cloud, called the Prophecy of the Seventh Generation, when their religious and spiritual hopes and practices will flourish without constraint and without end.

The Emergent Process of Moving About Ceremonially on the Path of Beauty

In "The Continuous Renewal of Sacred Relations: Navajo Religion," Trudy Griffin-Pierce presents the central features of the religious life of the *Diné*, "The People," as the Navajo call themselves. The Navajo are estimated to number a quarter of a million people, occupying the Four Corners area of the southwestern United States.

Griffin-Pierce is a creative visual artist of Native American descent. She uses her intellectual and artistic talents to convey the dynamic nature of the sacred in Navajo thought and practice. The Navajo worldview is based on movement, change, and flow. All of nature is filled with *Nílchi*, Holy Wind. Wind embodies the energy of change and creation. Ceremony recreates and restores the dynamic order that is in constant flux. Ceremonial life extends the creative process of or-dering, the process the Holy People used to set out the world in the beginning. Holiness is their process of ongoing, open-ended ordering of the world and its relations in beautiful form. Ideally, one is always moving, journeying on toward old age via the cultivation of spiritual beauty within and all around. This constant journey, which is a spiritual condition that joins living and dead in an ongoing process, is named with the highly valued phrase *są'a naagháii bik'e hózhǫ́*.

Griffin-Pierce explains the contexts in which spiritual life optimally unfolds: the *hogan* ("place home") belonging to a family, where ceremonies are held; the Four Corners area spread among the four sacred mountains; and the wider universe, wherein unfolds the vitalizing relations that exist among all beings in these contexts. It is the responsibility of humans to remain aware of proper relations with all aspects of the universe and to work to maintain them. Ritual is the exercise of this awareness and maintenance process. By acknowledging all parts of the universe as alive and interdependent, traditional Navajo thought and practice extend beauty and *hózhó*, harmonious conditions. Navajo religious thinking calls for a close coordination between inner understanding and outward expression. Every entity in the Navajo universe has an inner and outer form. Physical existence, seen in its outer form, has an existence independent of indwelling awareness. The inner forms were placed within all things after the Emergence. This indwelling endowed them with consciousness, life, movement, speech, and feeling. The same is true of the four sacred mountains that define the Navajo world. They were brought up from the previous worlds, at the time of Emergence, in the form of soil. Then each soil-mountain was placed in one of the four directions. Subsequently, an inner form of life was chanted into them. It is, therefore, a Holy Wind which vitalizes all forms of the universe and links them together in a distinctive way. One finds the signs of Holy Wind on the distinctive whorls that pattern one's finger tips and hair, for example. The act of breathing is, therefore, a sacred act, animated by the force that unites all beings and phenomena. The Navajo individual is connected at a profound level with all life. That connection is brought alive in a powerful way in ceremonial chant.

Griffin-Pierce introduces us to the *diyin dine'é*, the Holy People who existed in the first times and who are responsible for the way things are. In particular, Changing Woman, who embodies the powers of renewal inherent in the earth, is described. The actions of these Holy People, whom Griffin-Pierce calls "superbeing," are not always exemplary. They account for the conditions of existence, but they are in many ways inimitable. Nevertheless, the boundary between the *diyin dine'é* and human beings is fluid and permeable, like the wind, because the transformation of consciousness and the action brought about in ritual leads to the acquisition of knowledge which can, in turn, lead to personal holiness. The acquisition of knowledge about religious matters is essential to power, as exercised in ritual. Each myth chanted in ritual recounts the adventures of a hero who passes through supernatural domains and, over the course of this primordial journey, acquires ritual knowledge. So too does the chanter and ritual participant. The power of the Holy People is accessible to human beings through knowledge and ritual, properly performed outwardly and inwardly. Since so much of Navajo ritual is performed in response to individual misfortune or illness, Griffin-Pierce explores why this should be so. What are the causes of illness that link it so directly to religious life?

Since the world by its very nature is an every-changing place, the relationships that constitute it need constantly to be adjusted and removed. Griffin-Pierce outlines the kinds of relations that are established and restored in the various ceremonial practices. Many World War II and Vietnam War veterans, for example, were brought into right relationship with the ghosts of slain enemies through the healing actions of Enemyway. Other rites, such as Mountainway, deal with the arthritis and mental disorders healed by properly relating to certain animals and aspects of nature.

Male and female pairing is ubiquitous at every level in the world and is modeled on the complementary relation between Mother Earth and Father Sky. Griffin-Pierce explains exactly how male and female qualities are understood and united in Navajo religious thought and practice. Griffin-Pierce is a talented artist. I am pleased that her creative artwork is included in this volume. It is of special value in dealing with Navajo religious life and offers a different medium of interpretation that draws its inspiration from the extraordinary visual art of the Navajo.

Becoming Our Mother, the Source of All Life

The contribution of Inés Talamantez, "In the Space between Earth and Sky: Contemporary Mescalero Apache Ceremonialism," centers on 'Isánáklésh, one of the five deities present at the time of creation. In her compassion, 'Isánáklésh has provided knowledge and creative wisdom to healers about the beginning of time and about the animals, plants, and people so that those who suffer can find relief from their distress. Talamantez presents a myth given to the Apache people by 'Isánáklésh herself. It serves as the framework for a young woman's initiation ceremony as it is practiced today. Through the ceremony, grounded on the myth, Apache girls become charged with power, which is then used by the community to grow crops, prosper in good health, and live a long life. Talamantez shows how Mescalero Apache culture makes a link between female fertility and creative thinking. The link is forged in sound, spoken prayers, some chants, and ceremonial use of esoteric language. The renewable cycles of nature are studied by ritual specialists as the physical pattern on which to model other powerful patterns, both those of the ceremony and those of the life-cycle of the initiate. Each initiate is transformed into 'Isánáklésh, Our Mother, from whom all life comes. In the course of the girl's initiation the world itself is again created, as described in the efficacious words of the enchanted myth.

Talamantez draws our attention to this central theme: after creation, knowledge was the thing that was still missing to bring ongoing vitality. At the request of her son, the culture hero Child of Water, 'Isánáklésh appears and, with tender mercy for all her children, provides the knowledge necessary to maintain balanced relations among all things and heal those relations when they go awry. During the ceremony the *nadek-leshen*, the initiate's sponsor, acts in imitation of 'Isánáklésh to provide instruction on the use of herbs, plants, and other items. As described in the myth, in this way 'Isánáklésh gives her womanhood and knowledge to the initiate. The girl obtains the deity's power, which enables her to grow to maturity. In turn, through unification with the girl, the deity is made young again. The girl's body becomes like soft clay that is molded and modeled into the body of the female deity. Thus the cycle that links divine power to human form is reenacted through the girl's ceremony, as orchestrated by the myth.

Talamantez provides us a version of the myth recited by the chanter Willetto Antonio. Myth has a wholeness and integrity which must be maintained. In the symbolism of its performance it becomes evident that the myth must be told in its entirety. Willetto Antonio always started at the beginning of the story even after he was interrupted. Furthermore, when he was asked questions about specific elements from the last part of the story, he would always begin his explanation by reciting the story again from the beginning. This practice is widespread and has been witnessed by visitors to different cultures. The conveyance of the myth has a ritual structure all its own. Through Talamantez's translation work we are treated to the very words and explanations of Willetto Antonio, the powerful Apache healer and chanter. He explained to Talamantez precisely how various singers chant about specific body parts and characteristics of 'Isánáklésh and why this is so. This myth blueprints in an efficacious way the Mescalero Apache creative processes, both the fertility of women and the creative imagination at work in all concrete domains of Mescalero Apache culture. "They sang songs for her as this being came out of the water. Songs are sung on the last night of the ceremony today because that is when the girl *is* 'Isánáklésh coming out of the water. The girl is going through what 'Isánáklésh went through. The girl is becoming 'Isánáklésh, and on the last morning they paint half of her face white like 'Isánáklésh's face when they found her in the primordial waters, her face stained white from the minerals in the water."

During each of the stages of the ritual transition, the actions are accompanied with sacred songs that generate *diye,* special power. The songs alter the present condition and return the ritual actors and spectators to the time of myth, when the deities lived on the earth. The myth and the song transform the girl into a deity and then eventually into a new Apache woman. Talamantez notes that for the past decades there has been a strong effort by feminist writers to struggle for female identity. She believes that knowledge of the Mescalero Apache puberty rite can also provide meaningful paradigms for young women of mainstream America who are moving into the new millennium. The myth and the ceremony are, in one sense, already open and receptive to all of these women, for at the ceremony prayers are offered for all women, for the earth, and for all entities, including men. Through the instruction of 'Isánáklésh, all on the earth have been prayed over already.

Religious Reciprocities

Richard Dauenhauer writes about the Tlingit Indians in his contribution, "Synchretism, Revival, and Reinvention: Tlingit Religion, Pre- and Postcontact." The Tlingit live in southeast Alaska and in northwest British Columbia, dwelling in and on the edge of the most extensive temperate rain forest in the world, stretching from Puget Sound to Kodiak Island. Dauenhauer begins with a description of traditional Tlinglit religious life, starting with myths that describe the ancient covenants established between human beings and all other kinds of beings. Ritual life is the ongoing imitation, remembrance, or representation of those relations established during the period described in myth. Personal and private observances extend ritual practice into individual and daily life. In this way, religious thought, framed in myth, is linked with ritual action at the individual and community level. Before contact with outsiders, Tlingit religion emphasized that the moral order of the universe was maintained through proper thought, word, and behavior toward nonhuman inhabitants of the world, which included powerful spirits as well as tiny creatures. This concept of moral order and respect for all beings continues even into forms of practice and belief that have been heavily influenced by Christianity.

Tlingit society is divided into two moieties, or ritual halves, the Raven and the Eagle. Within each moiety are many clans, whose influence, in some cases, has been weakened in the past century. Each clan had its own leader and property, which included special stories, songs, chants, dances, art, and spirits. The spirits are made present and depicted in the art, dance, song, and performances particular to the clans. The art and performances are vehicles for bringing the spirits to mind and to life as they descend through time. Since no single clan owns the totality of spirits, reciprocity becomes extremely important for health and well-being. The popular Tlingit image for maintaining right relations with spirits and beings is *balance*. The spirits of clans from opposite moieties balance one another, for example, as do other significant relationships.

Dauenhauer details the beginning of Tlingit contact with outsiders, beginning in 1741 in the contacts with the Russian Orthodox Church. He explains the role of Ioann Veniaminov (1797–1879), a Russian Orthodox priest and bishop who lived many years in Alaska. Later he was elected patriarch of Moscow, the head of the Russian Orthodox Church. He was canonized in 1977. The Russian Orthodox contact is, therefore, the longest-lived immigrant influence on Tlingit religion. Dauenhauer points to positive attitudes he finds exemplified in Veniaminov, one of the architects of Russian Orthodox policy in Alaska. He chose to examine the spirits, following the advice given in 1 John 4:1. This opened Russian Orthodoxy to the use of Tlingit language in church services as well as to bilingual education and scripture translations. Through personal example and pastoral directive Veniaminov taught openness toward traditional language and culture and minimal dismantling of traditional Tlingit practices.

Dauenhauer also emphasizes the influence of Sheldon Jackson (1834–1909), who helped to design the missionary program of the Presbyterian Church in Alaska. In uncanny parallel to Veniaminov, Jackson, after serving as general agent of education in Alaska for twenty-one years, became moderator of the General Assembly of the Presbyterian Church in the United States, the highest ranking office in the Church. Though begun much later than the Russian Orthodox mission, the Presbyterian presence had the most far-reaching impact on traditional Tlingit religion, culture, and language. The attitude toward culture and language was much different in the Presbyterian influence. During the period of its influence, shamanism and traditional lifeways came under heavy criticism. Since the end of World War II Tlingit religion has been influenced most heavily by various Pentecostal and fundamentalist churches.

Dauenhauer is most interested in the ways in which Tlingit religious practice has creatively absorbed ideas and customs from the outside. For instance, contemporary Tlingit funerals (such as the Alaska Native Brotherhood Memorial), potlatch, and forty-day party are modeled on Orthodox Church brotherhoods and Presbyterian sodalities. Following Robert's Rules of Order, a business meeting is called to order and the roll is taken. When the departed fails to respond, his or her name is expunged from the membership book and is moved to the Book of Memory. This reflects the Protestant concern for polity and protocol. The Tlingit traditions also find a place in the transfer of ceremonial regalia from the deceased to a younger family member.

Similarly, Dauenhauer details the elements of syncretism found in the potlatch ceremonies, which are experiencing a revival today, as well as in the healing ceremonies and memorials. He also makes important observations of new ceremonies associated with the restoration and return of patrimony under the Native American Graves Protection and Repatriation Act of 1990 (NAGPRA). The ceremony is called the "Healing Blanket," "Healing Drum," or "Healing Totem" and forms part of a larger religious movement addressing contemporary spiritual needs such as drug and alcohol abuse, AIDS, teen suicide, family violence, and problems on a personal level.

Dauenhauer points to a new synthesis of religious practice which is still in a state of formation. He points to an irony at work in the attitudes of most scholars, seekers, and Native practitioners alike. Return to traditional spiritual contexts is often characterized by revival, invention, and reinvention. The language surrounding repatriation is typically that of ancestral pre-Christian or non-Christian religion. But the patterns and categories of thought often seem to involve a great deal of Christian religiosity and Western thinking. The irony is that the influence of pre-Christian indigenous thought and practice on the Christian thought and practice is easily accepted and expected, whereas it is less desirable to take note of the considerable influence of two centuries of Christian thought and practice on revitalized traditional spirituality. What exactly are the sources of the contemporary shaman's (*ixt'*) practice today? They range from long-lived fonts of traditional culture, to practices derived from other First Nations, to New Age handbooks and anthropological texts. Both the shamans and the context of his clients are in ever-changing contexts. Like the debates and dialogues mentioned in other essays, the internal and external discussions surrounding Tlingit practice are exciting and invigorating. The Tlingit remain intensely focused on their religious life.

Openings and Access for the Cycling Soul

In "Eye of the Dance: Spiritual Life of the Central Yup'ik Eskimos," Ann Fienup-Riordan presents the system of symbols and meanings that continue to guide the daily lives and ritual acts of the contemporary Yup'ik of southwestern Alaska. Central to the Yup'ik worldview is the knowledge that humans and nonhumans share important characteristics, especially the immortality of their souls, which return endlessly in cycles of birth and rebirth. The soul, for both humans and animals, is the principle that sustains life. Successful rebirth of the soul is contingent on appropriate thought and proper action, affected not only by one's own thought and acts, but by those of others. The essential aspect of a person is reborn in a new generation, received with the name of a recently deceased relative in the preceding generation. Soul and mind form the common ground on which the interaction between animals and humans is carried out, in hunting, ritual, eating, and so on. Although humans and animals may have been much closer to one another in the past, they are differentiated now by the diverse ways in which they perceive conventional reality.

Fienup-Riordan suggests that the differences between men and women may be thought of as similar to the differences between humans and animals. Men and women have different responsibilities, a division of labor replicated in the gendered division of residence space. Men live communally in a large central dwelling (*qasgiq*). Into the 1940s men worked in the *qasgiq* and also ate, slept, and instructed young boys there. There they entertained their guests, took sweat baths, and held complex ceremonies.

Women and children, by contrast, lived and worked in *enet*, small houses made of sod. The separate residential systems of the sexes had implications for the performance of ritual life and social responsibilities. The women's house was compared to the womb where production was carried out on a biological and also on a spiritual level. In their female houses, women transformed raw materials supplied by men into food and clothing. A pregnant woman was a model of her house; her body within her house was equivalent to the fetus within her own womb. The woman's house, then, was an instrument for intense reflection and even the power to reflect critically on the capacity to be reflective. One thinks of Inés Talamantez's claim that fertility and critical thought are yoked together. The woman's house and her womb were associated with the moon, which is home to spirit keepers and land animals. Shamans journey to the moon to induce land animals to come and visit the earth, presenting themselves to hunters. The activity and inactivity of women bore directly on a man's success in the hunt. Women's houses, utensils, actions, air, and eye contact all had a serious impact on the life of men and on the well-being of the community in general.

Vision and eye contact play an important role in Yup'ik life. The circle-dot motif found so often in Eskimo iconography is called *ellam iinga*, literally "the eye of awareness." The same design is used to mark tattoos on the joints of young people at puberty. It concentrates the spiritual activity and marks the presence of a "little soul" with special powers of perception and awareness. These locations marked by the circle-dot are associated with the power to pass from one world to another, to see another world and thereby obtain powerful knowledge about it. In that sense, they recall the smoke hole of the house, which opens access to the celestial realm, as well as the ice hole that offers access to the water world below. The shaman travels out through the smoke hole or down through a hole in the ice to visit "persons" of fish and game and invite them to return in the coming year. Special narratives and rituals help maintain a critical link between socially guarded sight and powerful supernatural vision.

In the men's house, young boys enter the social and ceremonial circle of the Yup'ik world. They receive technical training for economic responsibilities as well as behavioral and moral rules they must follow to be successful hunters. They learn that the water hole is a window on the world below and should be kept open. It is their responsibility. They are taught exercises that heighten their vision and acuity. Like the hole, they should keep their eyes open, but guarded. Young men seek clairvoyance, especially a clear vision of the underworld house of seals or the realm of the dead. The ice hole and smoke hole are both passageways between the human and nonhuman world. The circle-dot motif is echoed in the choreography of the ceremonial dances and also in the movements performed during formal greetings of strangers. One sees the circle-dot theme restated in large, hooped masks which function as eyes into a world beyond this one. The motif is restated also in the rounded lamp and in the ringed bowl, as well as in the hole of the kayak floatboard, the geometric decorations of ivory earrings, and rings suspended from the ceiling of the men's house during dance performances.

In fact, in the religious view that was learned by young Yup'ik, "the world was bound, the circle closed, yet within it was the passageway leading from the human to the spirit world." Peering like a dot through the round eye hole of the mask, the eye of the masker looked beyond this world into another.

Winter is the major ceremonial season for the Yup'ik. Fienup-Riordan details the five major ceremonies during this period, three of which aim to repair or adjust the relations between the human community and the spirit world on which the human community relies. The Bladder Festival reverses the separation of body and soul which takes place when a seal is killed. The Feast for the Dead invites the spirits of human dead into the community for food and clothing. The Gift Festival is an exchange between men and women of the same village. The Messenger Feast sees one village visit another to receive gifts. Each village composes special songs describing the objects of desire and the individuals from whom the objects are sought. The last major annual ceremony of the winter is the *Aguyuyaraq* ("Way of Requesting"). It is a complicated ritual event in which the *yuit* ("persons") of the animals are entreated in song and masquerade to appear again. The shaman guides the construction of masks, which have the power to evoke beings into the future. As a cycle, the ceremonies bring about in an effective way the cyclical view of the universe that they signify: proper ritual and moral action from the past reproduce themselves in the present to call forth abundance in the future.

The Struggle for Sacred Words
in Creative Literature

Franco Meli's elegant article is an appreciation of the religious contemplations and spiritual struggles emplotted in the creative writing of Native Americans today. Meli traces the persistence and the importance of the sacred in some of the most significant voices of Native American literature today. The very genre of the written novel as a primary means of expression for Native American ideas represents the dilemma of adapting to two cultures. The theme remains a leitmotiv in the literature.

Meli begins with Charles A. Eastman's *The Soul of the Indian* published in 1911. Eastman writes of the sacredness of oral tradition, an ironic exercise in itself, passed on from generation to generation. In this ironic condition, the sacred is inseparable from the ordinary; occult depth is embedded in the apparent surface of things. The tasks imposed by daily life are infused with the reality of the sacred.

Naturally enough Native American writers are captivated by the immense power of the word, which they often see as an enchanting expression that is part of its own narrative force. In Eastman's case, he was fascinated by two features of the oral tradition: a perception of space and an attitude toward language. Space and language were woven together into the story plot of a journey, which literally gave direction both to space and language. The direction is that of a return to the ancestral land. Space, language, journey, and return to the ancestral land become the guideposts to Eastman's literature and to much of the writing of Native Americans in the twentieth century. The return to the land of the ancestors structures much Native American literature around a circularity that is not vacuous but enriching. Meli takes the testimony of creative writers in this regard. The individual exists in a complex system of relationships. In Leslie Marmon Silko's *Ceremony*, the system is described as a spider-web, replete with a perfectly balanced network of reciprocal tensions. In preserving the balance of relations, it is a therapeutic necessity to return home, to balance the recognition of threat and near extinction from the outside by affirming continuity with home place and its deepest soul within. The "return home," though reluctant and ambivalent in much of Native American literature, is not seen as a defeat or failure. Rather, like ritual it establishes right relations and restores balance. Relationship with the life-giving earth launches the ancestors on their life-generating adventures in the first place and makes storytelling possible, for the land gives rise to characters in scenes that are set in tension and in struggle. Therefore, the return to home and land lends life an appropriate symmetry and balance as well as a sense of completeness. One does not turn to the past but to the permanent, the inexhaustible origins of creativity and well-being. It is not a return to what has been but what always is.

Sensitive to these special themes, Meli examines the work of D'Arcy McNickle, N. Scott Momaday, Leslie Marmon Silko, Sherman Alexie, Louise Erdrich, and John Joseph Mathews. For instance, in *House Made of Dawn,* Momaday, a master wordsmith, shows how his protagonist Abel is estranged from the powerful *word* of his people in ceremony. But at his trial he is overwhelmed by the deluge of words poured on him by the dominant society. The power of the word is recognized in both cases, but in neither is it mobilized on his behalf. Momaday does not close on a note of certain hope, but, in a world where words fail, his powerful writing ironically opens the possibility of hope in the symbols that erupt in the ceremonies surrounding the death of Abel's grandfather. In the constant rhythmic movements of the ceremonial dance, which move beyond thoughts of pain, Abel can take in the space that surrounds him and place himself at the ceremonial center where life began and where it is renewed. Over him rain the soft words of the ceremony, "House made of pollen, House made of dawn." In this mythical center of mythic origins one hears ritual words wrapped in a work of fiction — a mystery wrapped in an enigma — there lies the possibility of regeneration, of dawn, of spring shining anew on the ashes washing off Abel's torso in the spring rain.

Leslie Marmon Silko's *Ceremony* recounts the journey of the protagonist Tayo, a World War II veteran who returns to the Pueblo Laguna after military service on a Philippine island and period of time recuperating in a Los Angeles hospital, suffering from the traumatic stress of the war. That is, the story ends with Tayo's return to the beginning. The first pages of the novel introduce the creation myth of the pueblo in which Tayo stands. The opening poetry underlines the religious value of thought about the magical powers of language. The transmutation of ordinary words into mythic recitation and of ordinary gesture into the significant action of ritual becomes the goal of life and of the novel. The aim of *Ceremony* is to give life to the conditions that existed at the moment of creation, at the very beginning. A ceremony calls that spiritual world to life and holds it in symbolic suspension until healing harmonies sound forth. As Silko's story makes clear, things are always changing. Banished realities return in new form, undestroyed after all. As the character Betonie explains, "But don't be so quick to call something good or bad. There are balances and harmonies, always shifting, always necessary to maintain."[18] Betonie himself is a shifting balance in need of maintenance, being of mixed blood. Relocated at the spiritual center of the community at Laguna, Tayo's personal story becomes a collective experience, an act of transformation that is considered indispensable for completion of the ceremony and his own cycle of life. The creativity of the community is guaranteed by the flexibility and capacity for adaptation in the face of challenges imposed by the flux of shifting circumstance.

Themes in Common

Each of these essays emphasizes the particular way in which a specific community practices its religious life. Each essay examines the special historical circumstances and social context of religious practice and belief. Nevertheless, it is possible and helpful to point out some themes common to all of them. The special power of sacred knowledge, crystallized in mythic narratives and the symbolic action of rites, is central to religious life. The loss of this knowledge is felt sharply by many Native witnesses, but the struggle to remain true to what is known and to regenerate what is lost is powerfully present at the same time. I do not believe that readers in North America, and elsewhere for that matter, can learn about Native American religious life without incurring a sense of debt, both for what is present in the form of a gift and for what is lost in the form of destruction. Some of this may be inherent in a teaching relationship. But here there is something more: as one learns about Native American history and religion, there emerges a growing realization that relations between Native and non-Native peoples need to be righted.

This leads to another major theme common to the essays in this book. In the religious traditions depicted here, the establishment and maintenance of right relationships lie at the heart of the religious response to existence. Particularly important relationships in these essays

---

18. Leslie Marmon Silko, *Ceremony*, 137, as cited in Meli below.

include the ones between: individual and society; knowledge and action; humans and nonhuman beings in the natural and divine worlds; continuity and change; men and women; the living and the dead; myth and everyday reality; this world and other worlds. The right relationship among these terms is cultivated and the right balance among them is calibrated through special knowledge, a knowledge made known in myth and tradition, embodied and enacted in ritual performance. That is to say, right relations are established and maintained through critical experience and self-conscious reflection, together with a commitment to personal and communal action based on what is understood to be proper and called for. There is an intimate relationship between aesthetics and ethics, the two being combined in the fine art of "cutting a good figure," in every sense of the word.

Other common themes emerge as well. Let me state each one tersely in a sentence, without further development here. Individual achievements and the fruits of personal change ought to be conveyed to the community. Conversely, the collective ceremonies provide the moments, structures, and benchmarks that aid an individual in his or her advancement into spiritual knowledge. The journey motif, or odyssey, serves as an ordering concept of the "course" or "curriculum" of knowledge which one "runs" throughout life. Largeness of heart and generous action in service of general well-being are highly prized. Humans are born to share and to help one another. Humans are a complex of elements, powers, and features in constant flux, due in large part to their mortal nature. Death causes humans to undergo change and so is an integral part of religious experience at all points in life. For instance, death can be anticipated (as "symbolic death," "initiatory death," or "ordeals") in the moments of transition during the life-cycle rites.

The land is of singular importance. Knowledge of it arises from the land itself, linked as it is to the primordial beings who fashioned or found it in the first place. The resources of the land are part of the economy of ritual and of spiritual change.

Knowledge is a mode of existence that should be cultivated and is a distinct religious responsibility of human beings in the world. Thoughts and words have power that must be acquired in order to transform and renew realities, but it must be applied wisely, generously, and properly lest there be serious negative consequences for all involved. Let a word to the wise be sufficient.

☖ O N E ☖

Renewal as Discourse
and Discourse as Renewal
in Native Northwestern California

Thomas Buckley

In northwestern California in the lower Klamath River canyon at the Yurok Indian village of Pecwan in the ten days following September's full moon, every other year, men dance with beautiful regalia from morning to evening in the pit of a dismantled semisubterranean plank house. The dancers represent two complementary and competing "sides," taking turns in the pit, and as each side dances the deeply felt songs of the two lead singers who dance on either side of a "center man" interweave each other, bound together by a rock-steady chorus of men ranged symmetrically beside the singers, forming a line. Through the final days the beauty and antiquity of the regalia and the numbers of dancers and spectators deepen and grow. On the last day, young women join the men in the pit at either end of the dance line, but do not sing. Finally, all of the dancers, male and female, from both sides join together, momentarily resolving all differences and achieving wholeness and balance: "Fixing the World." This long process is called the "Jump Dance." It is intended to cure the world's ills, and to stave off evil.

During the dance the two sides (which represent two ancient village alliances) and their guests camp on either side of the small road that runs down to Pecwan from the junction of the Klamath with the Trinity River at Weitchpec, each equidistant from the pit and the sacred fire at its center. These camps are run by the senior women in the groups, who haul water and chop wood and prepare thousands of servings of acorn soup, salmon, venison, and smoked eels, as well as more modern fare. These women oversee the feasting and enjoyment that they share

with many visitors, keeping the camp "clean" — ritually pure and harmonious. The women in the opposing camps also compete with each
other, in an understated way, in hospitality and correctness. It is hard
work and this hard work is the women's prayer. The men from the two
sides dance and sing all day, by turns, in considerable heat and dust
and the smoke that rises from the sacred fire and the angelica root
burning in it. Many younger men fast and thirst for the full ten days,
and stay up most of the night singing ancient men's songs in the Jump
Dance Sweathouse, which has existed at Pecwan seemingly forever.
The cumulative experience that these men attain is not easily gained.

Julian Lang, a Karuk Indian scholar, author (e.g., 1994), and performance artist said, after the 1988 dance at Pecwan, "As Indians we
don't have many responsibilities, but one of them is to fix the world."
And later, "it's hard to be an Indian."

In light of this hard work and the deep experience earned by it, writing about "fixing the world," as many have come to call it, is awkward.
"World renewal," as most anthropologists refer to it, is something that
people *do*, and its meaning is not separable from experience and the
ways in which this experience transforms people, in their hearts. This
much becomes clear through participation, even as a spectator, but it
is also apparent in some written Native accounts of the dances as well
as in people's oral testimony today.

The first book published by a Yurok Indian, *To the American Indian*,
by Lucy Thompson, appeared in 1916 (it has recently been reissued
[Thompson 1991]). Thompson centers her book on the great dances
that she took part in as a young woman, in the 1870s, stressing transformative experience at both personal and communal levels. She recalls
the beauty of the "flints, white deerskins, fisher skins, otter skins, silver
grey fox skins and fine dresses made of dressed deerskins, with fringes
of shells knotted and worked in the most beautiful styles, that clink
and jingle as they walk and make one have a feeling of respect and
admiration." Thompson writes ecstatically about the pleasure of going
from camp to camp, enjoying the good food and company while "up-
wards of three thousand Indians" speaking "five different languages"
called each other "brother" and "sister"; of how the songs were "most
perfect in time and tune and [make] one feel the love of the great Creator of all things" and how "the eyes will strain to look on this most
pleasant sight, which can never leave one's memory that has seen it."

The witness of spectators seeing the dances is itself a form of prayer, a contribution to fixing the world as important as any.

Like Mrs. Thompson, Kathy Heffner-McClellan, a contemporary Wailaki Indian researcher, recognizes the significance of the spectator's experience as well as that of the more active participants (1988:10): "Attending these ceremonies and directing their prayers to the spiritual world held the people together at the base of their belief system; for they were attending and participating for the same reasons — lifting their prayers for continued proper existence."

Spectators and participants, men and women, the two sides in the dance, humans and the spiritual beings — I'll call them "Immortals" — who "cry to see the feathers dance," invisible on the edge of the dance ground reserved for them ("Give them what they cry for!" a Hupa Indian participant exulted), even numbers of dancers arranged on each side of the "center man" in the pit (dressed in regalia that "cries to dance"): everything and everyone seems to come in pairs. These pairs complement and oppose each other, and pairs complement and oppose other pairs. In one sense, the purpose of the dance is to bring all of these oppositions together in wholeness, always present as a possibility — in the pit, the fire, the center men; *that* is "fixing the world." The competition between sides and camps, usually constrained by common purpose, is transcendent, itself becoming an expression of wholeness during the course of the dance.

During the final round of dancing at Pecwan in 1990, on the tenth day, the heat finally broke as both sides danced together, raising in unison the medicine baskets that each male dancer held in his right hand. As they did so, spectators said later, a great spiritual force rose from the pit to hang in the sky above. People were happy (and perhaps relieved) as they went off to feast and talk in the two camps. "If we can get through the dance we can get through the next two years," they said.

Fixing the world manifests primary communal concerns with and commitments to balance. While most Native people today call this balance or wholeness "unity," world renewal is negotiated in terms dictated by the tensions between people rather than by an abstract "unity" that remains largely a yearning: "the joy of man's desiring," as Katherine Clarke nicely translated the novelist Jean Giono's "Que ma foie demeure" (1940).

The Ethnology of "World Renewal"

There is another opposition to be remarked upon here, that between myself and my esteemed anthropological predecessor, A. L. Kroeber, the premier "salvage" ethnographer of Native northwestern California's traditional cultures. Together with his student and colleague, Edward W. Gifford, Kroeber wrote the standard work on these dances, "World Renewal: A Cult System of Native Northwest California" (Kroeber and Gifford 1949). The Jump Dance at Pecwan, Kroeber wrote, is part of a "closed system" that he dubbed a "world renewal cult." In the following, I take issue with Kroeber's nomenclature and with the theoretical approach that led him to it.

Kroeber included the Pecwan Jump Dance along with dances and rituals once held at twelve other ceremonial centers in Native northwestern California in the world renewal "cult system." While acknowledging that this system was not a Native construct, he held that it was indeed a reality, an ethnographic "pattern" established through the trained ethnologist's "apperception" and by "natural analysis" (Kroeber and Gifford 1949:1). The Yurok, Hupa, and Karuk Indians who once participated in the "cult," Kroeber said, recognized only "dances," although the Karuk language has a single term designating "world-making" or "world-fixing" dances. Kroeber (and presumably Gifford) viewed the cult as "one of the closed systems of native American religion," comparable with the Plains Sun Dance, the Kachina Cult of the Southwest, or the Hamatsa Cult of the Northwest Coast (Kroeber and Gifford 1949:1).

For Kroeber the world renewal cult in northwestern California once comprised an organized variety of diagnostic elements. Each of the thirteen events manifested different combinations of these elements, which may be briefly summarized following Kroeber and Gifford (1949:1–3):

1. The rituals that accompanied the dances themselves focused on the reestablishment or firming of the earth, and thus

2. the prevention of disease and calamity for another cycle.

3. Rituals might include first fruits rites or

4. building a new fire, and often

5. rebuilding a sacred structure.

6. The entire scenario for each dance was introduced by the pre-human Immortals, whose words, preserved in narratives, provided the bases for

7. formulas recited by priests who

8. followed set itineraries for visits to specific places near the dance site, manifesting the

9. intense localization typical of the cult.

10. All events associated with a given dance had to be completed within one lunation.

In the midst of this esoterica, one of two dances — called, in English, the Jump Dance and the Deerskin Dance — was given for a period that varied from ten to sixteen days with up to forty-eight repetitions of the dance per day. In these dances, teams displaying elaborate regalia belonging to families who owned rights to outfit the dancers with what amounted to items of wealth (again, the regalia / wealth is sentient) danced to the accompaniment of trained singers. Camps were set up by the two sponsoring villages at each dance and all visitors were freely fed. (Kroeber estimated that the entire cult comprised approximately ten thousand adherents before massive contact, in 1850, with crowds of three to five thousand sometimes gathering for a single dance in the late summers and early autumns of the nineteenth century.)

Kroeber and Gifford's accounts were for the most part reconstructions of dances apparently long extinct when they published their monograph in 1949. In that monograph, as in all of Kroeber's comparable work, "the present tense must be construed as a narrative one, referring to a century or more ago," when "the undisturbed, pre-1850 native culture seems to have been largely in static balance" (Kroeber 1959:236), before this "primitive culture . . . went all to pieces" (Kroeber 1948:427). Kroeber and Gifford valued the "native opinion" of their informants in establishing what "does and does not belong together in the native culture, as to organization or systematization" (1949:1). However, Kroeber's ethnology stressed the "deliberate suppression of individuals as individuals" (1952:7–8). While individual variation and idiosyncrasy undeniably existed in societies, a valid cultural anthropology, for Kroeber, had to be based in the abstraction of the concrete "products" of human thought and behavior from the

matrix of individuality. This Kroeber called "realism" and found necessary in the — ideally, statistical — effort to establish the elements and
traits comprising a cultural pattern as a "closed system" in a culture
held in "static balance," as an integrated and unified "organization."
"Apperception" of such a systems thus demanded that the ethnologist disregard any disagreements among individuals and the creation of
a normative, putatively consensual, homogeneous cultural whole (cf.
Buckley 1996).

For example, in the "World Renewal" monograph, Kroeber cites
Lucy Thompson's *To the American Indian* (1991 [1916]) because of its
detailed, catalogue-like descriptions of the Yurok renewal rites at Kep'el
and at Pecwan. However, he does not directly quote Thompson, finding
her writing "sometimes prolix or ethnographically irrelevant." None-
theless, Thompson's book "contains some new items," writes Kroeber,
and "[t]herefore I put it on record here in condensed and reworded
form"/(Kroeber and Gifford 1949:82).

By way of historical comparison, we might note that Kroeber's position in "apperceiving" world renewal as a closed system is comparable
with Durkheim's method for perceiving "social facts," discernible only
by trained, scientific observers (Durkheim 1938 [1895]), especially as
this method was developed into the theory of the "total social phenomenon" by Durkheim's student, Marcel Mauss (1954). For Mauss, such
phenomena (the Northwest Coast Indian "potlatch" provided an ideal
example) simultaneously included religious, mythological, economic,
jural, and social-structural elements in a normative unity apparent
only to the objective social scientist observing from without. Today,
two problems with these totalizing approaches are apparent.

First, this order of objectification must exclude individuality and
history alike as important analytic concerns. The erasure of both individuality and time in ethnology, which various postmodernists have
more recently sought to rectify, in fact was challenged far earlier by
the importance placed by fieldworkers like Dorsey on the notable
lack of consensus among Native American informants regarding social organization (Barnes 1984). It was an objection largely disregarded
by Kroeber, the "Dean" of American anthropologists during his life-
time (Steward 1961) — as were the contributions of both Durkheim
and Mauss.

Second, in creating systems closed to individual and subgroup creativity and conflict, focused on the "millennial sweep and grand

contours" of a virtually metaphysical history (Kroeber 1918), trans-
muting time into place, in the form of "culture areas" (Kroeber 1939;
cf. Buckley 1989), Kroeber omitted from the ethnographic record the
"pitiful history of little events" (1918) that recounts the daily lives of
individuals like Lucy Thompson and Dorsey's Omaha informant, Two
Crows. By doing so, he created essentialized cultures and closed systems
of spiritual renewal alike that "could not move easily through time,"
as Julian Steward noted (1973).

In this chapter I enter into complementary opposition with Kroeber,
much as dance sides and camps do with each other, hoping that the
tensions between our work, separated by almost a century now (from
the beginning of his to the end of mine), might tend toward some
broader, holistic understanding.

For Kroeber, the world renewal cult was a thing of the past. Both
in view of the fact that the Jump Dance at Pecwan did survive, and
to make room for individuals like Lucy Thompson, we need a different understanding of culture, of specific cultural productions, and of
contextualized spirituality than those that Kroeber maintained. This
is necessary because only through admitting individuality and history
into interpretation can we move closer toward comprehending how
the Jump Dance works to fix the world (that is, comprehending what
people *do*).

Renewal as Discourse

The dances continue to contain the elements that Kroeber and Gifford identified and to which he reduced Lucy Thompson's testimony,
and there could be no great dances without them. But fixing the world
cannot be reduced purely to these elements or to the structures that
they form. Rather, renewal, fixing the world, is also the goal of a discourse into which these elements enter as central motifs or themes and
is thus a process, something emergent, rather than a reduced "system,"
"pattern," or "organization."

Kroeber sought to reconstruct a static system on the basis of a
consensus that he imposed, an imagined normative "native opinion."
But no culture, or analytic domain like "religion," or specific religious
production like the Jump Dance, can be comprehended (rather than
explained) as a closed and static system. Stasis, finally, is antitheti-
cal to life, and human lives are what we are trying to comprehend.

Rather than an abstract assemblage of structural elements, social life
as lived is the ever-emergent result of the "running back and forth"
(the etymological meaning of "discourse") through a community (however defined) of the thoughts and feelings and words and actions of a
plenitude of individuals, both in agreement and in conflict. It is also
a running back and forth between a broadly shared cultural ideology
of authenticity — a received, ideal structure of yearning — and the in-
escapable facts of difference and change. This, of course, is what the
two sides are engaged in at Pecwan. While discourse *theory* may provide
an interpretative mode for understanding what these people do, what
they do *is* a mode of discourse, of oppositions simultaneously yearning
toward wholeness

Mikhail Bakhtin's understanding of discourse as "dialogue" may
be particularly helpful here (1981). In this understanding, dialogue
is discourse on differences that leads to further ramified differences,
not to synthesis or any other order of lasting resolution. It differs, in
this, from classic dialectics. Dialogue is discourse on the irresolvable,
and a phenomenon like the Jump Dance emerges through time from
the differences among people and those between people's experience
and their ideals: their yearning. Paradoxically, the transformation toward unity that Thompson and Heffner-McClellan write about, "fixing
the world," can only occur through the dynamics of difference between individuals and between those individuals' experiences and their
shared ideals. And it can only lead to reengaging these dynamics with
renewed vigor.

After the dances, for instance, participants often go off with their
friends to relax. Talk is usually about the dances and their side's suc-
cesses in being better than the other side, and about dances to come,
when they'll have even more dancers, more and older regalia, and their
side's dance maker (chief regalia manager and choreographer, by inheritance) will again outdo the other's. Difference reasserts itself almost
immediately, though gently at first. Fixing the world has indeed suc-
ceeded, but only momentarily, as an acrobat on the high bar swings to
the top and comes momentarily to rest, feet straight up in the air in
a beautiful but extraordinary posture, before swinging down again to
hang by his hands and swing again. By a year and a half or so after a
dance, people have lost the joy and relief of the last dance's final moments. There is trouble, anger, illness, perhaps floods, pollution in the
world. It is time to start working toward the next dance, through care-

ful negotiations with regalia owners and elders and participants until people can come together again, putting aside bad thoughts, "lifting their prayers for continued proper existence."

Kroeber held that there was a closed system unknown, or at best dimly perceived by the social actors themselves. But I am revising his statement by saying that there is no fixed system. Rather, systematicity constantly emerges through dialogic discourse on what does and does not belong in an ideal system that Indian people engaged in fixing the world are fully capable of — indeed, dedicated to — imagining. In this, the progress of a single year's dance instantiates the immemorial, general process.

Dialogues

As was every aspect of indigenous life, the world renewal dances were grievously affected by massive contact with whites, fomented by the California gold rush of 1849. One by one the dances were curtailed or extinguished throughout the region, although the Yurok Jump Dance at Pecwan was made more or less continuously until the Second World War. The Hupa Deerskin Dance at Takmilding was never entirely lost and reemerged strongly in the 1960s. In the 1970s, the Karuk "world fixing" at Katamin was fully restored. In 1984, the Pecwan dance was once again put up, to be repeated biennially through the present. The Tolowa "Feather Dance," comparable to Kroeber's "world renewal" dances, also has been given regularly again since the 1970s, on the Smith River, north of the Klamath.

All of these dances are, to a greater or lesser degree, interdependent, each depending to some extent on the participation of regalia owners, singers, and dancers from the other tribal groups, and they are also among the strongest expressions of autonomous group identities. Thus Heffner-McClellan writes that the dances "[reinforce] the bonds of Indian heritage, tribal identity, inter-tribal relations, and most important of all ... [people's] bond to the spiritual world" (1988:28). To participate in the dances in any way is to both express one's Indianness and to become more Indian. The longer one dances, Hupa Indian participants say, the closer to restoring world balance the dance comes, the more *xoche* each person becomes, the more "right," "clean," "real" — the more Indian. For these reasons, the discourse on fixing the world in northwestern California today at once includes dialogues on being

Yurok (or Hupa or Karuk), on being within the small world of Native northwestern California correctly, and on being Indian. Indeed, all of these dialogues implicate all of the others, simultaneously. Very often, specific dialogues occur as debates.

Kroeber's ethnological question was, what really belongs in the closed system of world renewal and what does not, whether or not Native people recognize it? This, for instance, was the basis of his interest in Mrs. Thompson's book. It is of note that world renewal discourse in northwestern California today is much concerned with the same question, as might be expected in the midst of ongoing efforts to restore traditional ways correctly. Let me give a sampling of debates that were in the air at the time of the Pecwan Jump Dance in 1990:

• Should dances be given up entirely, rather than doing them incorrectly and possibly causing the world harm?

• Do changes in materials and techniques for making regalia change its meaning and efficacy?

• Should male dancers appear nude under their deerskin wraps, as they did before the 1870s, or should they wear shorts as is currently the custom?

• What is the proper relationship between Christian believers and the dances? Should Christians be invited to pray at the non-Christian dances, in light of the high regard in which some Christians are held as spiritual leaders?

• What is the proper timing of dances? Should unscheduled Jump Dances be held in the high mountain spiritual precincts as they once were, in world emergencies, or has the knowledge of these "calamity dances" been so completely lost that efforts to put them up now can only be destructive?

• What is the relationship between death and world renewal? Is a death during a dance a sign that mistakes are being made, or is it in fact a good time to die?

• And what is the appropriate role, if any, of non-Indians? Should they be permitted to dance? To be there at all?

These are not trivial questions. Rather, they are the organizing topics of some of the most intense spiritual, intellectual, and political dialogues in the region, and "Fix-the-World People" take them very seriously. In part, this is because dialogues on world renewal have far broader cultural relevance and purpose. World renewal discourse is a means of manifesting and enhancing regional Native culture, and also for exploring its proper nature. The primary locus for these dialogues during the dances themselves is at the camps' tables, and there is a dialogue going on, including these verbal dialogues, between the (women's) camps and the (men's) dance pit. The fruits of discussions in the camps, in a sense, dance along with the regalia. At times, discussions within and between the camps grow heated, indeed. Not too long ago this dialogical process included terrible arguments between the two camps at a major dance, whose respective leaders were, at the time, vying for wider influence in the community they shared. The sacred fire was put out, regalia owners withdrew their "stuff" from both sides, the county sheriff was called in, and the dance ended with bad feelings all around, one leader going into seclusion in its aftermath. Things didn't settle down for months, and when they did, people returned to a changed life.

It might seem that confrontations like this have nothing to do with "fixing the world" per se, but that they are basically political, rather than spiritual, arguments. Such distinctions have to be made carefully. It may be that "religion" and "politics" are usefully distinguished as analytic domains, but on the ground, so to speak, each is in dialogue with the other and all are subsumed in an overarching social discourse. This has been most easily recognized, by anthropologists, in small, face-to-face, traditional societies. It is what Arnold Pilling meant when he wrote that, among Yurok Indians on the Klamath, "law, health, and religion are all one topic" (1969). "Jump Dance *is* politics," said an Indian friend. This is nothing new on the Klamath: "Sandy Bar Bob (ca. 1900) was considered a wealthy man because he was a responsible religious person whereas Sawmill Jack had little respect because he was not considered to be a religious person who was concerned for the community" (Heffner-McClellan 1988:12).

Again, one might think (as do, in fact, many of the more skeptical Native people) that these religio-political-cultural disputes are clear signs that it *is* too late to restore the dances, whose true spirit has been lost. It is interesting then, to find that acrimonious disputes over the correct way to do the dances seemingly go back to earliest mythological times among the Immortals and to have been quite common at human dances in the nineteenth century as well. Contention would seem to be in the very nature of the dances.

A Yurok myth, for example, tells of the efforts of the Creator Wohpekumeu and nameless Immortals to begin a new Deerskin Dance on the Pacific coast, south of the Klamath:

> At Melekwa, by the trail, on a big rock, they saw two men sitting. He said: "I come because I want to see you also have the [Deerskin] dance." But they said to him, "No, I saw you, you tried it. You saw for yourself that you lost the song, because that sort is not good about here. It will be best not to have it." He said, "I thought it would be well." But they said, "No, we do not want it." . . . He looked across [the lagoon] and saw they were beginning at Hoslok. Those about to begin the dance were with Wohpekumeu. Now he who had come was angry. As they were commencing, "That dance they shall not have here," he said, and blew out [made a bad wish] toward them. Thus he did. Then they all remained standing on the hill. One can see them now, those firs, standing like a Deerskin Dance. (Kroeber 1976:197–98)

Such myths of the origins of the various dances, upon which the formal dance prayers are based, are accounts of trial and error, of failed attempts made by the Immortals to do the dance correctly, for all time, and of their ultimate success. The Yurok Deerskin and Jump Dances at Weitchpec began this way:

> Then that one went to get his deerskin. When he brought it, he said, "This dance will be so. They will not begin in the morning. As long as this world lasts, if my dance is straight, they will begin toward evening. That is how it will be." Then toward evening they began. They began to make the dance from that place. They started down the sand beach. "How will they stand?" his friend asked him. "One will stand in the middle. He will face in the direction which I grew. Some will turn to Hupa. Some will face upriver. So we shall reach all those places with the dance." "Yes," he said. And then they began to dance there.
>
> In the morning his friend came over (from Pekwtuł) again and said, "That (also) did not go right. I think something bad will happen. Let us try to dance in another place." "Yes. Let us wait until evening." Then they went to where the dance was to start.

He said to them, "Try it (facing) downstream." Then they tried it. When they swayed their deerskins once the sticks broke off where they held them. "I think it will be best if we bring it up to where my house is," he said. Then they went uphill. When they came to where the dance place is (now), one of them said, "Let us try it here. Let the people go uphill; no one is to stand below. We shall stand in a row facing them, and hold the deerskins pointing uphill." Then they tried it so. When they saw it, they were happy. All felt good. Looking about, they saw everyone in the crowd smiling; some were laughing. The Weitspus young man said, "Well, how do you feel about it now?" "This is a good place. When I look away, I think that I see nearly the whole world, the day is so fine." (Kroeber 1976:30–31)

Note how the Immortals, too, set the dances for all time, instantiating an ideal structure, but then had to revise again, through dialogue. Like the founding Immortals, human beings today ultimately find that doing it right when they do it, seeing that "all feel good" at the end of a specific dance, may be the best that they can do.

Thus these myths suggest that the constant effort *to* get it right is of equal importance and interest to *getting* it right. If so, then what is going on in the constant debates over what is and what is not appropriate to fixing the world is not a historical aberration encountered in a culture "going all to pieces"; it is central to the process of world fixing, and always has been.

And note that while Kroeber, too, sought a fixed system, valid for all times, he found as well that historical experience has always been at variance with the ideal. For example, while the origins of the Weitchpec dances were attributed to the Immortals of the mythical beforetime, Kroeber's Yurok informants knew that the dance had been inaugurated when the town had become wealthy and influential enough to do so and held it to be to their political advantage (Kroeber and Gifford 1949:66). Arnold Pilling (1978), another anthropologist with a deep command of Yurok data, speculated that a dance came and went on the upper reaches of Blue Creek, above Pecwan, during relatively recent times. Again, the aboriginal details of scheduling that Kroeber reconstructed suggest that he and Gifford, despite their insistence on a closed system, were quite aware that the dances comprise processes within other, wider processes, rather than being static, ahistorical epistemic objects:

Throughout our data, and in fact in earlier ones since Goddard [1902–3], there runs a wavering of native statements as
to whether dances were made every year or every other year....
Many Indians seem to believe that in the good old days rituals
were annual, and that the every-second-year schedule is a result
of modern breakdown. Kroeber encountered this belief not only
recently but more than forty years ago; and Goddard suggested
it in 1903. It would therefore seem that indecisiveness in this
matter is an old feature of the system, rather than a symptom of
its decay.... In prosperous periods, there might be year-after-year
dancing in a town for a while. But let the acorns or salmon be
low, or sickness or death invade the strength of the leading household or two, and respites would be taken. (Kroeber and Gifford
1949:129)

By the same token, Kroeber and Gifford knew that, despite the sys-
temic ideal of settling or laying aside all outstanding litigation, quarrels
and sorcery attempts — all "bad thoughts" — before putting up or
attending a dance (1949:82), quarreling broke out at the dances themselves with some regularity, occasionally resulting in the truncation of
the event (1949:66, 68, 69–70, 78, 81–82). Heated arguments also
resulted in changes in the planned transmission of esoterica for certain
dances (1949:97). Like the Immortal who turned his enemies into fir
trees at Hoslok in the beforetime, the elder who ostentatiously cursed
("deviled") a Dance Maker during a dance a few years ago was acting in a manner as old as the putatively ideal dance forms that many
Native people believe once existed, and seek today. Yet we notice that
Native people have in the past, as today, declared that witchcraft and
sorcery are not permitted at the dances (Robert Spott, in Spott and
Kroeber 1942).

Cultural Politics

People do not easily agree upon what the ideal forms once were, on
how to seek them out today, or on appropriate ways to communicate
about them. Efforts to resolve such issues are as significant and intense
as the effort to renew the dances themselves today and as intense as the
Immortals' efforts long ago to discover the correct forms at Weitchpec.

For example, some people today claim that the appropriate epistemology is purely spiritual; that knowledge of the ideal dances can best be rediscovered through asceticism, solitary vision seeking, and inspiration by the Spirit. Others hold that this charismatic approach is fraudulent and that claims to spiritual inspiration comprise political moves rather than religious inspiration (separating the two as do most members of the dominant society and unlike the man who said that "Jump Dance is politics" and whose statement may itself embody an ideal rather than a conceptual reality fully operable in modern times). These people argue that the most reliable route to safe and efficacious restoration of the dances is careful scholarship — largely, out of necessity, in the writings of A. L. Kroeber who, while "he didn't know what things meant," at least "got his facts right." The matters being debated here, of course, are not limited to the dances, but concern the sources of authentic culture and appropriate modes of leadership in Native communities as well.

In this debate, or dialogue, language plays a central role. The original dance prayers, or "formulas" as Kroeber and Gifford had it, were once couched in a special, high register of ritual Yurok, an Algonquian language largely moribund today. This speech register identified the priests (now, "medicine men") with the Immortals, to whom it was attributed, and it gained some of its ritual power through the contrast it formed with ordinary, human speech. Use of this variety of speech also identified any speaker as a member of the elite, the aristocracy whose superiority was evident in economic, intellectual, political and spiritual ascendancy alike (Buckley 1984; cf. Sandy Bar Bob, cited earlier). As English became the first language along the lower Klamath, "high language" Yurok, as a coherent register, disappeared. By the 1970s, ordinary Yurok, now commanded fully only by a few elders, replaced the high register in ritual contexts as English replaced ordinary speech. In the mid-1980s these elders began to succumb to old age, virtually en masse, and the younger generation of ritually active men and women, who spoke little or no Yurok, were faced with a dilemma. What was the appropriate register of English to use in religious contexts? High-register English, "the way lawyers [and preachers] talk," might be suitable, but it was identified with whites and with the Christian churches from which the younger Fix-the-World People sought to distance themselves. One solution has been sought in ordinariness itself.

An alternate or accompaniment to both modes of dance leadership (charismatic and intellectual) has all along been to "just do it" — to act with heart and head together, without too much show or talk. This, if anything, is seen as the "real" Indian way and itself comprises a sort of ideal (as authenticity often does, in the world at large). It is difficult to achieve, resting on complete confidence — hard to acquire as one feels one's way along in the risky task of dance restoration — and perhaps especially so for those who are, like their old-time predecessors, among an educated and cosmopolitan minority. The most active people in restoring the dances, naturally enough, are often intellectuals and artists and other creative people with some experience in the sophisticated world beyond the lower Klamath.

One solution to the problem of speech that has been tried by some in this group is "broken English," called "Indian English" by many whites. This regional dialect connotes membership in a group of Indian people who "just do it," surrounded, as they say, by "inlaws and outlaws," maintaining the low profile, independence, and, often, the isolation and poverty that are parts of the price of "living like a real Indian" in the United States today. But the irony of invoking this speech in a group of people most of whom have at least graduated from high school and many of whom have college and graduate degrees is lost on no one. (The hot reading among Yurok dancers at Pecwan in 1988 was Stephen W. Hawking's *A Brief History of Time* [1988].) Again, of course, the issues are simultaneously political, spiritual, and cultural but here political in the acutely modern terms of class conflict. There are other terms as well.

While ideally the dances "reinforce the bonds of inter-tribal relations," as Kathy Heffner-McClellan wrote and Lucy Thompson witnessed, they are also used as forums for manifesting the fissures in those regional relationships. This may be especially true as regards Yurok and Hupa Indian relations at the end of the twentieth century, mightily strained as these are by decades of conflict over reservation lands and resources. The 1988 Pecwan Jump Dance, for instance, was avoided by most Hupa tribal activists because at the time of the dance, in Yurok territory, the Yuroks and Hupas were embroiled in a particularly bitter altercation over the formal splitting of the reservation that they still shared then. It would have been bad manners indeed for Hupas to bring those bitter feelings into the sacred space of the dance, so they stayed away. The alternative would have been to settle the dispute before the dance — as the old-time law required — and that was out of the question. The issue was an especially painful one for the many people who have deep affiliations with both, somewhat artificially constructed, modern tribal groups.

Fixing the World

"I wish the rains would come and wash all the bugs and ticks and spiders and Yuroks down the river," said a man at the Hoopa Valley shopping center in the late summer of 1988. "Don't say that," said a second man, active in the dances. "You'd wipe out half of your relatives."

I have presented some of the more heated dialogues on the lower Klamath in 1988 in binary terms: Christian versus non-Christian, Indian versus non-Indian, Yurok versus Hupa, ordinary versus elite, life versus death, religion versus politics — like the two sides with their separate camps at Pecwan. These dialogues go on, not only between individuals and groups, but, perhaps most important, within the minds of single individuals and in their hearts, where alone the world may finally be fixed. What goes on in these dialogues is not a zero-sum effort to establish one side as the winner, enduringly and isolatedly superior. Such victories could only be pyrrhic, when half of one's friends and relatives are Hupa or white or Christian or women or lawyers or dance on the other side or whatever. The real, realistic victory comes in emulation of the two lead singers in a dance whose voices, when they are equally good, harmonize rather than strike a single note.

Nor I think is the effort in these dialogues directed to *dialectically* resolving differences in synthetic consensus: "unity." Rather, it seems to me that the point — so entirely lost on those outsiders who have held "factionalism" to be the downfall of Native American communities, rather than a creative means of social survival — is simply to keep talking and even arguing. In this creative discourse, albeit occasionally disguised as creation's necessary complement, destruction, is the very renewal of the world that is fervently desired. As the old myths tell us, this discourse on the dances itself realizes the objective of the dances, fixing the world. "Jump Dance *is* politics," yes, but politics is Jump Dance, too — a point that, like Kroeber's closed system, is perhaps most accessible to disengaged outsiders. Like many outsiders, most Native people tend to see these disagreements as destructive "factionalism," far from the idealized unity that they seek through fixing the

world. But I disagree with *them* as well as with Kroeber. I see differences and distances from the ideal as crucial to creative action and
expression and survival, as the loci of what is most vibrant and vital in
the dances, as the very means through which the dances *work*. And so
I enter the discourse on world renewal, as on anthropology, hoping to
offer encouragement, rather than a further, authoritarian inscription of
meaning or proper method.

Of course, what I am representing as creative cultural life, the process through which an ancient regional culture constantly emerges in a
tumult and dissonance of dialogues, renewing itself, approximates what
Kroeber saw as that culture's "going all to pieces." Yet it is what he himself witnessed regarding the dances, and what the oldest myths speak
of, too. We have no basis on which to believe that the dances ever
manifested for more than a moment an ideal and fixed, or closed, system — and then only when the yearned for "real, Indian way" had been
earned, by *doing*. The "real" dances attributed by old-time people to the
Immortals and by contemporary people, as by Kroeber and Gifford, to
the "real, old-time Indians," comprise an ideal that people engage in
dialogue with their own dissatisfactions, as a form of yearning: this immemorial dialogue is the very essence of spiritual practice rather than
evidence of decline.

The discourse on fixing the world, then, includes dialogues on most
of the largest-order questions of the day: life and death, language,
gender, politics, identity, spirituality, survival, freedom. The marvel of
Kroeber's "world renewal cult" is not its standing among the great
closed systems of Native America, but its flourishing anew among the
great open processes to be found there. It is a master discourse that
encourages dialogues on all of culture and all of life for those who
enter into it. The questions that arise within individuals but manifest
most clearly as differences between groups have no answers, immediate or otherwise. They might better be understood as longing than as
argument. They will not be resolved through discussion or feud, either.
Their function is to foment negotiation, even in violent forms — creating and re-creating, renewing a discourse that is endless and timeless.
It has gone on, been done, in northwestern California, ever since the
Immortals took it up in the beforetime.

Finally, I intend that what we have grown used to calling "the world
renewal cult" — or, for that matter, "Yurok Indian culture" — are not
things, epistemic objects, to be explained as systems only; they are open

processes that, as long as they survive, defy all totalizing statements. The totality of fixing the world is ever-emergent, a product of sub-discourses, or dialogues. When this discourse stops, world renewal will *become* a closed system, and fail.

References

Bahktin, Mikhail M. 1981. *The Dialogic Imagination: Four Essays*. Trans. C. Emerson and M. Holquist; ed. C. Emerson. Austin: University of Texas Press.

Barnes, R. H. 1984. *Two Crows Denies It: A History of Controversy in Omaha Sociology*. Lincoln: University of Nebraska Press.

Buckley, Thomas. 1984. "Yurok Speech Registers and Ontology." *Language in Society* 13:467–88.

———. 1989. "Kroeber's Theory of Culture Areas and the Ethnology of Northwest California." *Anthropology Quarterly* 61, no. 2:15–26.

———. " 'The Pitiful History of Little Events': The Epistemological and Moral Contexts of Kroeber's Californian Ethnology, 1900–1915." In George W. Stocking, Jr., ed., *History of Anthropology*, vol. 8: *Volkengeist as Method and Ethics: Essays on Boasian Ethnography and the German Anthropological Tradition*. Madison: University of Wisconsin Press.

Durkheim, Émile. 1938. *Rules of the Sociological Method*, 8th ed. Trans. S. A. Solovay and J. H. Mueller; ed. G. E. G. Catlin. Chicago: University of Chicago Press [1895].

Giono, Jean. 1940. *The Joy of Man's Desiring*. Trans. K. A. Clarke. New York: Viking Press.

Goddard, P. 1903–4. "Life and Culture of the Hupa." *University of California Publications in American Archaeology and Ethnology* 1:1–88.

Hawking, Stephen W. 1988. *A Brief History of Time: From the Big Bang to Black Holes*. New York: Bantam Books.

Heffner-McClellan, Kathy. 1988. " 'People of Substance': Communication Networks of the Indians of Northwestern California." USDA Forest Service, Six Rivers National Forest, Eureka, Calif. Duplicated.

Kroeber, A. L. 1925. *Handbook of California Indians*. Bulletin of the Bureau of American Ethnology 78.

———. 1939. "Cultural and Natural Areas of Native North America." *University of California Publications of American Archaeology and Ethnology* 38:i–242.

———. 1948 (1923). *Anthropology*. Rev. ed. New York: Harcourt, Brace and Co.

———. 1959. "Yurok National Character, in Ethnographic Interpretations, 7–11." *University of California Publications in American Archaeology and Ethnology* 47, no. 3:236–40.

———. 1976. *Yurok Myths*. Berkeley: University of California Press.

———, and E. Gifford. 1949. "World Renewal: A Cult System of Native Northwest California." *Anthropology Records* 13:1–155.

Lang, Julian, ed. and trans. 1994. *Ararapikva: Creation Stories of the People*. Berkeley, Calif.: Heyday Books.

Mauss, Marcel. 1954. *The Gift: Forms and Functions of Exchange in Archaic Societies.* Trans. I. Cunnison. Glencoe, Ill.: Free Press.

Pilling, Arnold R. 1969. "Yurok Law — Ways and the Role of Yurok Medicine Men." NIMH Grant GMS-11 Final Summary Report. Duplicated.

————. 1978. "Yurok." In *Handbook of North American Indians,* vol. 8: *California.* Ed. R. Heizer. Washington, D.C.: Smithsonian Institution. Pp. 137–54.

Spott, Robert, and A. L. Kroeber. "Yurok Narratives." *University of California Publications in American Archaeology and Ethnology* 35, no. 9:143–256.

Steward, Julian. 1961. "Alfred Louis Kroeber 1876–1960." *American Anthropologist* 63:1038–59.

————. 1973. *Alfred Kroeber.* New York: Columbia University Press.

Thompson, L. 1991 (1916). *To the American Indian.* Berkeley, Calif.: Heyday Books.

ᛤ T W O ᛤ

Traditional Ways and Contemporary Vitality: Absaroke/Crow

John A. Grim

The Absaroke/Crow are a Siouan-speaking people located on the northern Missouri River drift plains of the North American continent and in the nearby Wolf, Big Horn, and Pryor mountains in the states of Montana and Wyoming. Originally one people with the Hidatsa, a settled agricultural people, the ancestors of the Crow, led by their visionary ancestor, No-Vitals, broke from the Hidatsa. After a lengthy migration this group became the formative core of the Absaroke in the early seventeenth century. This people's name for themselves, Absaroke, means "large beaked bird" and refers to a mythical creature.[1] French traders, such as Jean Baptiste Trudeau in 1795 and François Larocque in 1805, continued a Native sign language reference in which the Crow were identified by two hands flapping like birds wings. This sign gave rise to the term *gens des corbeau* among the French.[2] Americans have continued the mistaken reference by calling this nation the Crow.[3]

---

1. Various spellings have been used for this tribal name, such as Apsaalooke, Absaalooka, Absaroka, Absarokee, and Absaroko.

2. See Jean Baptiste Trudeau, "Journal of Jean Baptiste Trudeau among the Arikara Indians in 1795," ed. Mrs. H. T. Beauregard, Missouri Historical Society *Collections*, vol. 4 (1912): 22; and "Trudeau's Description of the Upper Missouri," ed. Annie Heloise Abel, *Mississippi Valley Historical Review* 8, nos. 1–2 (1948): 175. For Larocque, see François Larocque, *Journal of Larocque from the Assiniboine to the Yellowstone 1805*, Canadian Archives Publication no. 3 (Ottawa, 1910): 68–69.

3. The Crow tribal historian, Joseph Medicine Crow, writes in his work *From the Heart of Crow Country: The Crow Indians' Own Stories* (New York: Orion, 1992), 2, that "[i]n the Hidatsa language, Absarokee means 'Children of the Large-beaked Bird' (*absa* meaning 'large-beaked bird' and *rokee* meaning 'children' or 'offspring'). Other Indian tribes called these people the 'Sharp People,' implying that they were as crafty and alert as the bird *absa* (probably the raven) for which they were named. In referring to them in the hand-sign language, they would simulate the

While "Crow" is the more familiar term in English, both terms, Crow
and Absaroke, will be used here. This dual reference accentuates the
recovery in the late twentieth century of both the indigenous voice in
these discussions as well as the limitation, in Absaroke understanding,
of any one person fully explaining Crow ways. Use of these two socially
constructed terms, Crow and Absaroke, also draws attention to the
simultaneously humorous and serious interplay of caricature and ideology in both Absaroke thought about themselves and outsider thinking
about Crow anthropology of the sacred.

The Absaroke often say, "It's up to you!" This simple phrase suggests
the decidedly personal exchange believed to occur between *maxpe*, the
sacred, and an individual.[4] The spiritual beings who transmit these
efficacious blessings are associated with aspects of the Crow universe.
The Creator, *Acbadadea,* is believed to have set the world in motion.
He is known by such names as First Maker, Starter or Maker of All
Things, the One Above, the Old White Man Above, the Above Person
with Yellow Eyes, He That Hears Always, and He That Sees All Things.
Every Crow person who experiences the sacred has "to bring it [*maxpe*]
out" in their own way and, in expressing this gratuitous and sacred
gift, the traditional Crow of the buffalo hunting days acquired both
personal status and spiritual identity as well as positions of leadership
in warrior societies. Crow perspectives on the sacred have changed both
in the period before contact with Europeans and during interactions
with mainstream America; yet, a vibrant cultural sense of the sacred
continues among these people.

A fundamental tenet of traditional Absaroke religious anthropology
accentuates individual experience of the sacred during solitary visions
in isolated places. "Castle Rocks" in the Pryor Mountains are renowned
for spiritual blessings from the "spirit dwarfs." The *maxpe* spirits more
typically manifest themselves in animal forms to a solitary faster. An
unusual or intense visionary experience might cause a Crow individual
to become an *akbaalia* ("one who makes things") or healer. An appropriate response to an encounter with the sacred would be to assemble
physical objects in medicine bundles. These complex assemblages of
personal power symbolized in physical objects, songs, and ritual gestures enabled a visionary to demonstrate spiritual abilities in private

---

flapping of bird wings in flight. White men interpreted this sign to mean the bird *crow* and thus
called the tribe the 'Crow Indians.' "

4. Some writers express this term as *baaxpe, baxbe,* or *makpay.*

openings of these bundles after the first thunder sounds or during the full moons of fall and spring.

In the buffalo-hunting days, this "bundle way" was at the center of Crow anthropology of the sacred. Often large bundles were taken out of their special repository location in the tipi and placed on tripods, where they were exposed to the renewing energies of the sun. These *xapaalia* ("medicine bundles") legitimated healing acts in family settings and stood as silent witness to such public events as narrations of war honors. These traditional practices have been transformed by the Crow in response to historical situations, but they do continue into the present when, for example, medicine bundles are opened in the spring, healers "doctor" in their communities on the Crow Reservation, and military veterans narrate war exploits during public rituals. The fuller meaning of such experiences is not simply subjective and idiosyncratic, however, because every experience of *maxpe* is set in the context of the tribe or social dimension. Personal religious experiences are brought back from their liminal setting into the context of the community where they find their deepest meaning.

This community concern is not simply a relationship between the human and the sacred supernatural beings of the Absaroke worldview; rather, Crow anthropology is a complex expression of spiritual knowledge which flows from personal experience but which also embraces ethical concerns for the larger community. One perspective on Crow life in the late twentieth century comes from Thomas Yellowtail. He was a respected Sun Dance chief and healer of the Absaroke/Crow. Thomas Yellowtail collaborated in the publication of a book about his life and Absaroke religion before his death in 1993 at the age of ninety-seven.[5] He was one of the last Absaroke elders who knew the "old-timers" of prereservation days, that is, before 1884, when the Absaroke moved to Crow Agency on the reservation in Montana. His opening concerns and views in his autobiography provide us with an orientation in this discussion of Absaroke anthropology of the sacred. He began his book by saying:

> *Acbadadea,* Maker of All Things Above, hear my prayer. Now we have filled our pipe and offered our smoke to the Heavens Above,

---

5. See *Yellowtail, Crow Medicine Man and Sun Dance Chief: An Autobiography* as told to Michael O. Fitzgerald (Norman: University of Oklahoma Press, 1991).

to Mother Earth, and to the directions of the Four Winds. Before
we start our work, we must send this prayer....
    I think it is necessary that the younger ones know something
about their religion. Their minds are confused, not knowing what
they should do. They should know that there are religions, that
their people have a religion that is different from other religions,
and our religion was given to us Indian people long before our
time.[6]

Praying in the context of his cultural beliefs, this Absaroke elder
opens by using the traditional pipe and tobacco to establish right relationship with cosmological powers, namely, the Creator, *Acbadadea*
("Maker of All Things Above"), as well as "the Heavens Above,"
"Mother Earth," and "the Four Winds." His traditional prayer of relationship frames for him the focus of his concern, namely, the youth
of his people. Yellowtail's prayer and the subsequent narration of his life
are the means by which he rethinks the knowledge that the youthful
members of his nation need to live in the confusion of contemporary
American life. In his prayer he emphasizes knowledge of Absaroke religion and awareness that the Absaroke ways are unique and different
from other religions. He ends by saying that Crow religion is ancient,
given by the spiritual beings long before the present.
    The following remarks explore Absaroke anthropology of the sa-
cred by building on and expanding the structures suggested by Thomas
Yellowtail. Three aspects will be presented — namely, social-historical-
mythical interactions, cultural religious expressions, and contemporary
vitality of Crow lifeway — in an effort to understand how individual experiences of the sacred continue to pervade Crow community life and
to evoke commitment to traditional ways in the midst of economic
and social crises. The term *lifeway* is used here to suggest the close
interaction of worldview and economy in this small-scale society (a
cosmology-cum-economy society). The contemporary reservation life
of the Crow, while inextricably tied to the American and global mar-
ketplace, still preserves core experiences of the traditional lifeway in
such ceremonial acts as "giveaways" and in such social structures as
clan reciprocity. These core experiences of the Absaroke, rather than
having been lost or completely subverted by dominant American val-

---

6. *Yellowtail*, 1.

ues, have been transmitted in changed settings and reinterpreted by creative individuals.

Social-Historical-Mythical Interactions

Central to this section is the underlying proposition that Crow anthropology is synthetic, or a binding together of distinct experiential and cognitive realms. In Western analytical thought, these realms are often understood as separate conceptual categories, namely, as social, historical, and mythical dimensions. Thus, the following discussions of the Crow social system, historical events, and mythical stories of the formation of the Absaroke are presented as mutually implicating forces in the identity of a Crow communal "self." In this sense, Thomas Yellowtail talked of his own recollections as a child: "As children we listened to warriors telling legends of all kinds, and just hearing old warriors tell their stories helped us to learn about the quality of their lives. They would even sing songs to accompany the story they were telling."[7]

Yellowtail's reflections constitute a Crow psychology in which one's individual persona is understood as embedded in the memory and flowing out of the narratives of the people. Moreover, the tribal narrative memory is both oral and musical; that is, the sonic character of the narrative may carry the very *maxpe* of the speaker. The intuitive, spontaneous, and intimate nature of the communication makes Absaroke "tradition" both responsive to creative individuals and vulnerable to ideological subversion. Distortions and new developments occurred when disconnections fragmented community life from the feedback systems of ritual knowledge and ecological ethics which nurtured that lifeway. Historical revisionings of Absaroke identity occurred, for example, with the formation of the Crow people (seventeenth century), with the conflictual movement onto the northern plains previously held by Shoshone peoples (eighteenth century), with the movement onto the plains of Lakota Teton peoples (nineteenth century), and with the demographic, military, and ideological invasions of the North American continent by Euro-American peoples (nineteenth / twentieth centuries).

Binding these distinct social-historical-and mythical realms are core experiences of the sacred which, in Crow thought, are mutually en-

---

7. *Yellowtail*, 180.

hancing. That is, the pathways of experience lead directly to cognitive, affective, and connative reflection on personal levels and flow back into social realms by means of ritual and mythic narratives. In addition to the "synthetic" interpretative position underlying this section is a reading of Crow tropes for the sacred as synecdoche. This figure of speech highlights a cardinal character of the Absaroke worldview in which the forms of discourse identify the part within the whole, or synecdoche. Traditional Crow speakers do not distinguish a religious self apart from the whole community. Thus, in the preceding quotes from Thomas Yellowtail, the "I," the "children," the "younger ones," the "old warriors," and the "Indian people long before our time" should not be understood as separable autonomous individuals or groups. Rather, these references as a form of speech, or synecdoche, link moments in the experience of the sacred which identify the people as Absaroke. Foremost among these synecdochic forms of speech are kinship terms arising out of, and giving rise to, the clan system.[8]

Social Structures and the Transfer of Power

Absaroke people still treasure their clan system, *ashammaleaxia*, in which every individual is embedded in an intricate web of kinship. Crow anthropology of the sacred, associated here with the term *maxpe*, is subtly woven into the "Crow kinship system." At Little Big Horn College, the Crow tribal college on the reservation at Crow Agency, Montana, contemporary cultural studies courses explore in an academic setting this kinship system, which is considered exemplary among America's indigenous peoples.[9] In addition, participants in these classes themselves experience a lived social structure in which distinct individuals are related and an efficacious sacred power is transferred between maternal and paternal lineages of these individuals. The Crow clan system establishes order in this society as well as simultaneously chal-

---

8. The synecdoche perspective can be found in Arnold Krupat, *Ethnocriticism: Ethnography, History, Literature* (Berkeley: University of California Press, 1992), 86. On Crow kinship and clan system see Rodney Frey, *The World of the Crow Indians: As Driftwood Lodges* (Norman: University of Oklahoma Press, 1987), 40–57. Interestingly, Joseph Medicine Crow, the Absaroke tribal historian, disagreed with Frey's translation of *ashammaleaxia* as driftwood lodging in a river torrent, saying instead that it referred to the gathering of lodges in the spring-summer annual buffalo hunts. Communication during June 13–18, 1994, summer Newberry Library-National Endowment for the Humanities seminar on the Crow Reservation.

9. See Robert Lowie, "The Omaha and Crow Kinship Terminologies," *International Congress of Americanists* 24 (1930): 102–8.

lenging individuals, by means of narrations of mythical and historical ancestors, to live more creatively within that society.

In Absaroke mythic understanding, from the period after creation the spirit beings called "Two Men" identified the clan system and set an internal flow pattern for the evocation, transfer, and return of sacred power through the paternal and maternal lineages.[10] An individual takes his clan identification from his mother's lineage. Maternal clan members traditionally give assistance during need and, in the buffalo-hunting days, joined revenge raids. Clan members address one another as brother and sister, and, as an ideal which is now much weakened, they marry outside their own clan. One's maternal relatives respond to physical and emotional needs by giving material assistance and emotional support as well as by mourning at death. That same individual becomes a "child" of his father's clan. The paternal relatives transfer spiritual power which brings good health, wealth, and social status. Paternal relatives promote a "child's" status through announcing achievements and dream blessings as well as testing the individual as her "teasing clan." Maternal relatives feast and celebrate their paternal relatives for their gift of efficacious power given through prayers and public narrations of praise.

In the buffalo-hunting days the Crow also divided themselves into subdivisions, or phratries, which cut across clan divisions in drawing together larger numbers of people for cooperative work efforts.[11] The eleven clans of the Crow arranged themselves in five phratries. The first phratry joined the Greasy Mouth (Uutuwasshe) and Sore Lips (Ashiiooshe) clans. The second brought the Whistling Waters (Bilikooshe) together with the Bad War Deeds (Ashkapkawiia). The third consisted of the Ties-in-a-Bundle (Xukaalaxche), the Filth Eaters (Ashpeennusshe), and Brings Home the Game Without Shooting (Uussaawaachiia). The fourth united the Treacherous Lodge (Ashbatsua) and Blood Indian Lodge (Ashkaamne). The fifth phratry was composed of Big Lodges (Ashitchite) and the Newly Made Lodges (Ashhilaalioo).[12] Remnants of the phratry system persist, and six of the current eight

10. Fred W. Voget, They Call Me Agnes: A Crow Narrative Based on the Life of Agnes Yellowtail Deernose (Norman: University of Oklahoma Press, 1995), 21–26.

11. Timothy Barnyards, Baleeisbaalichiwee: Crow Social Studies Teacher's Guide (Crow Agency, Mont.: Bilingual Materials Development Center, 1986).

12. Robert Lowie, "Social Life of the Crow Indians," Anthropological Papers of the American Museum of Natural History 9, 2 (1912): 189–90; and Lowie, The Crow Indians (1935; New York: Farrar and Rinehart, 1956), 15–16; Frey, World of the Crow Indians, 40; and Timothy P. McCleary,

clans have paired relations in distinct regions of the Crow Reservation in Montana.[13] These relations between allied clans function in Crow ceremonial life when, for example, financial and material support is provided at "giveaways." So also, labor and trees are volunteered through the clan system for the building of *Ashkisshe* (Sun Dance) lodges. This tenacious family-clan-phratry social arrangement embodies a creative tension between a fierce individualism and an equally strong communalism. This creative tension is an abiding religious characteristic of the Absaroke lifeway in which relationships are established so that sacred power can be transferred between individuals and groups.

Absaroke communal order and individual creative life are in dialogic tension in the Crow worldview. A cosmology emphasizing trickster modes, in which Coyote Old Man made an ambiguous world, serves to affirm the teasing relations of one's paternal cousins. Yet the cosmology also speaks of the powerful spirits giving blessings by way of adoption to selected individuals. Often the path for ceremonial participation is through adoption by a tribesperson who already holds the privilege of participation, or by a spiritual power who sanctions an individual's claim to the privilege. Thus, adoption, as a core experience of the cosmological powers, pervades traditional Crow symbolic life, uniting subsistence practices, social structure, and ceremonial activity.[14] Absaroke rituals and ethics continue to augment cosmological thought by bringing ideal values into daily life. The values and ideals are still sung and this singing itself constitutes a unique Crow critical reflection upon individuals and upon the tradition itself. Crow rituals provide the means for individuals and groups, up to the level of the society itself, to search for generative *maxpe* which enables this creative critical reflection. Absaroke ethics simultaneously ground their religious anthropology in the sacred land. It is in this synthetic sense that the terms *cosmological ritual* and *environmental ethics* are used in this treatise.

"*Akbaatashee:* The Oilers, Pentecostalism among the Crow Indians" (master's thesis, University of Montana, 1993), 39–40.

13. The eight clans that continue into the present are Newly Made Lodges, Big Lodges, Greasy Mouth, Sore Lips, Bad War Deeds, Whistling Waters, Ties-in-a-Bundle, and Blood Indian Lodge / Piegan. See Frey, *World of the Crow Indian,* 40.

14. This understanding of "adoption" in Crow religious life is explored in Peter Nabokov, "Cultivating Themselves: The Inter-play of Crow Indian Religion and History" (Ph.D. diss., University of California at Berkeley, 1988).

Historical Conflicts and Crow Lifeway

Creative life has not always been easy for the Crow, but their "tradition" has always been capable of change and has accommodated many influences from other cultures, both indigenous and Euro-American. The last 150 years of contact with mainstream U.S. society have brought acute challenges and changes to Crow lifeway. Still, the Absaroke acknowledge that dramatic transformations occurred well before this contact period, even as early as their mythic-historical beginnings as a people. As will be discussed in the section on the Crow mythic dimension, the mythic-historical journey of the Crow to find their homeland is set in the visionary context of the ancient progenitor, No-Vitals. This founding ancestor received his revelation in the form of a particular tobacco species and subsequently led his people toward a promised homeland where this sacred tobacco grew. It was in the Missouri plains country of the current state of Montana that the Crow first settled and encountered white Euro-Americans.

In 1805, the French trader François Larocque recorded the first written account of the Crow and of their religious concepts and practices:

I don't know what they believe as to their origin or their opinions, more than that they believe in Good and Bad Spirits, and in a Supreme Master of life.... What they call spirits are quadrupeds or fowls which they think acts [sic] as guardian angels. They have no notion of spirits in the sense we have it is certain, but they believe these are invisible beings who have the power to do them Ill or Good and to them they make their offerings. One thinks that it is the Moon that watches over him and another thinks that it is a Bee or a Mouse and so on. It is their dreams that cause them to worship one thing rather than another, but the sun, moon, stars, heaven and earth are of General worship and an Oath on one of them is reckoned inviolable. There is not an animal, fowl, reptile or insect that is not worshipped by some of these Indians who think that the object of his worship can save his life and render him invulnerable, whether it be a bee or a mouse. Inanimate things such as a ball and stone, etc., are likewise thought to be able to do good or harm.[15]

15. François Antoine Larocque, *Journal of Larocque from the Assiniboine to the Yellowstone*, publication no. 3 (Ottawa: Canadian Archives, 1911).

Larocque's account, while not insensitive to Absaroke lifeways, suggests some of the difficulties inherent in religious anthropology, namely, a readiness to attach the more familiar to that which is strange and unknown and the tendency to draw on one's own worldview terminology to explain the world of the "other." Thus, Larocque imposes on Crow religious life, especially on the category of "spirits," the ethical distinctions of "good" and "bad." He attaches "guardian angels" to the concept of spirits. He also describes balls and stones as "inanimate," although the Absaroke attribute will and intention to the *maxpe* spirit manifested by the object. Larocque seems to have no sense of the relational process established between Absaroke visionaries and these objects, though he is aware of propitious offerings. It seems that he gained no understanding of either the synthetic perspective or the origin story of the Crow, despite the importance of that type of logic and of the sacred migration in their identity as a people. Yet, Larocque did recognize several key characteristics of Absaroke religious life which are confirmed in the later writings of Crow thinkers and non-Crow observers.

Larocque observed, for example, a plurality of sacred manifestations to individuals, especially in dreams, as well as an overarching concept of absolute reality which manifested itself in the world. The sacred relationship established between individuals and animals, celestial bodies, and objects in the terrain was embodied in medicine bundle (*xapaalia*) gatherings, which were sanctioned by the individual's numinous experiences. This anthropology of the sacred which Larocque attempted to describe was probably already developed by the Absaroke before their migration from the agricultural-hunting and gathering lifeways in what is now North Dakota. According to that early memory, the Crow lived with their Hidatsa tribal relatives until they undertook their sacred journey westward. Later, in their Montana homeland, the Crow took to the horse-and-buffalo culture which characterized northern Plains tribes.

A similar skepticism of non-Crow historical accounts can be brought to an early description of an encounter with Crow peoples by Father Pierre-Jean De Smet:

But what appeared to interest them more than aught else, was prayer (religion); to this subject they listened with the strictest, undivided attention. They told me that they had already heard of it, and they knew that this prayer made men good and wise on earth, and insured their happiness in the future life. They begged me to permit the whole camp to assemble, that they might hear for themselves the words of the Great Spirit, of whom they had been told such wonders.[16]

The intention of this letter appears to be an attempt to persuade the romantic European audience who funded mission work in the New World, rather than an ethnographic statement describing Crow religion. De Smet displayed his outsider naïveté as well as an awareness of the seriousness with which the Absaroke considered oral prayer. Missionary contact followed communication with fur trappers and preceded the collision with settlers, miners, and ranchers. The Absaroke still survive in the northern Plains country, having lived with the historical pressures and transformations brought to them by dominant American culture.

The geographic boundaries of Crow country are currently limited by their reservation in south-central Montana. Of the 2.25 million acres on the reservation, approximately 55 percent is owned by the Absaroke. Loss of land by the Absaroke over the past one hundred years is a complex historical issue interwoven with the civilizational and Christianizing drives of dominant America. The Crow believe that their elders predicted the arrival of whites and that they welcomed the whites as allies against their enemies on the Plains. The Lakota, Cheyenne, Blackfoot, Piegan, Shoshone and other tribal groups contested the claim of the Absaroke to hunting and grazing lands. By the 1830s, the movements of tribespeople onto the northern Plains, especially the Lakota and the Blackfoot, threatened to overwhelm the Crow. In this military setting, the Absaroke allied themselves with the westward-moving Americans in an effort to preserve their way of life. Toward that end the Crow were willing to grant concessions of land. Thus, the Absaroke, though they scouted for numerous United States military expeditions against their mutual enemies, accommodated demands for land by American settlers, miners, ranchers, and politicians by selling 30 million acres in 1880 after the "Indian Wars" of the 1860s and 1870s.

---

16. Pierre-Jean De Smet, *Letters and Sketches*, quoted from Reuben Gold Thetis, ed., *The Jesuit Relations and Allied Documents: Early Western Travels (1748–1846)*, vol. 27 (Cleveland: Arthur H. Clark, 1906), 394f. Also, in George E. Tinker, *Missionary Conquest: The Gospel and Native American Genocide* (Minneapolis: Fortress Press, 1993), 68. Tinker presents a full critique of De Smet's missionary agenda.

During the 1880s Catholic missionaries and other Christian sec-
tarian evangelists established themselves on the Crow Reservation
in accordance with President Grant's "Peace Policy," which turned
over the governance of Indian agencies to missionaries from different
Christian denominations. Catholic and Baptist missionaries established
boarding schools for Crow children, and by 1887 they were prohibit-
ing these children from speaking Absaroke while the schools were
in session.

In 1882, the Absaroke were coerced to sell another 1.5 million acres.
Lack of buffalo as a food resource led the Crow in 1883 to follow the
suggestion of their agent to move from the mountains onto the plains
around Crow Agency and accept treaty rations. Prohibitions against
Crow religious practices and the termination of intertribal warfare
both contributed to a spiritual malaise among the Absaroke. In 1887,
a group of young warriors under Wraps-Up-His-Tail, a twenty-four-
year-old visionary who subsequently received the name Sword Bearer
after participating in an illegal Sun Dance with the Cheyenne, led a
successful revenge raid against the Piegan. Following this raid, Sword
Bearer attempted to foment a "rebellion" against the U.S. agent at Crow
Agency.[17] During these events, Sword Bearer, a Crow woman, and one
soldier were killed. After it ended, eight Absaroke were imprisoned.
While the "rebellion" did not develop into a major military incident,
this episode indicates the individual and national crises through which
the Crow passed at this time. More important, this "rebellion" signals
the reaction against the ideological subversion of a former ally's lifeway by dominant America. The Sword Bearer event marks the loss
of two major religious paths for expressing sacred power among Crow
warriors, namely, the military societies and intertribal warfare.[18] Moreover, political pressures were being brought to bear in this period which
fragmented the special character of social cohesion between the Crow
people and their communally held land.

---

17. See Colin G. Galloway, "Sword Bearer and the 'Crow Outbreak,' 1887," *Montana: The
Magazine of Western History* (Autumn 1986). Galloway gives the differing versions of this event
based on the Billings *Daily Gazette*, military reports, and Lowie's reconstructions from accounts
of Crow eyewitnesses (Lowie, *The Crow Indians*).

18. For Crow military societies see Robert Lowie, "Military Societies of the Crow Indians,"
in *Anthropological Papers* of the American Museum of Natural History (1913) 11:143–217; and
Thomas E. Mails, *The Mystic Warriors of the Plains* (New York: Doubleday, 1972). For the extinction of intertribal warfare see Anthony McGinnis, *Counting Coup and Cutting Horses: Intertribal
Warfare on the Northern Plains* (Evergreen, Colo.: Cordillera Press, 1990).

In the Dawes Allotment Act of 1887, provisions were made for the Crow Reservation, as well as all other Indian lands set aside as reservations under specific treaties, to be arbitrarily divided into parcels and allotted to Native individuals with all unallotted land being opened to non-Native settlement. Such legislation as the act of 1887 gives some sense of how treaties with Native peoples were manipulated by dominant American interest groups. As with all indigenous peoples in the United States, the Crow were subject to unilateral congressional reinterpretation of these treaties. Moreover, the implementation of imposed treaty stipulations was undertaken by bureaucratic federal government agencies such as the Bureau of Indian Affairs. These ideological, economic, religious, and political pressures further fragmented Crow understanding of communally held land which was central to their lifeway. These "civilizing" measures were forced on the Crow in the name of "progress." The Absaroke fought this and other legislation, but the military, technological, and ideological strength of the United States subverted the integral religious life of their former Crow allies. Absaroke population fell below two thousand at the turn of the twentieth century and only recently has recovered to precontact numbers of more than eight thousand.[19]

Mythical Narration as Sacred Reflection

The prereservation "homeland" of the Absaroke, in the states of Montana and Wyoming, was described at a council meeting in 1873 by Sits-in-the-Middle-of-the-Land (or Blackfoot), who used the metaphor of four tipi poles: "When we set up our lodge poles, one reaches to the Yellowstone; the other on the White River [Milk River]; another one goes to Wind River; the other lodges on the Bridger Mountains. This is our land."[20] The image of the tipi is not simply an indication of boundary. Rather, this synecdochic figure of speech distinguishes each tipi pole as a mythic marker describing the larger tribe in relation to the land. In Crow understanding, the tipi is a spiritual habitat which symbolically embraces her occupants as a mother.[21] Thus, the tipi as

---

19. For demographic figures on the Crow Reservation period into the nineteenth century, as well as a discussion of Absaroke adjustment to reservation life, see Frederick E. Hoxie, "Searching for Structure: Reconstructing Crow Family Life during the Reservation Era," *American Indian Quarterly* 15, no. 3 (Summer 1991).

20. Joseph Medicine Crow, *From the Heart of Crow Country*, 37. Joseph Medicine Crow has been the Tribal Historian of the Apsaalooke since 1948.

21. Personal communication from Harry Moccasin during Crow Fair 1994.

sacred metaphor for Absaroke land carries an image of a nourishing and nurturing country. Moreover, the habitat symbol accords with the Crow matrilineal clan system in which succor and aid are sought from one's maternal relatives.

The opening paragraph of the contemporary Crow Studies "Curriculum Rationale" at Little Big Horn College at Crow Agency on the Crow Reservation announces:

> When the Crow Indian people moved to this land, it was with divine guidance. 'No-Vitals' received a vision from the spirit world which showed him that the life of the Crows was to find its future at the place where the sacred tobacco seeds grew. After a search through many places, spanning many generations, the Crow people found the sacred tobacco here where the Crow people now live.[22]

This statement, prepared both as "rationale" in a college accreditation context and as the official story of tribal formation from the Crow Cultural Commission, is interesting for what it reveals and for what it conceals. It lays open characteristic symbols of Crow identity, but it covers over the diverse narrations of this very story. It tells us of a people who reflect upon their emergence as a divine revelation to a warrior leader, No-Vitals, in a visionary manner which is well known in the oral narrative traditions. Absaroke tribal identity, according to this brief migration story, is linked to a sacred tobacco plant.

The official origin version, used in bilingual instructional materials, refers to the great spiritual journey of the ancestors which is known to have taken the Absaroke through diverse geographical settings from Canada through Utah to Oklahoma and up the Missouri River to Montana. After the arduous migration the tobacco plant was found in the mountainous Plains region of south-central Montana where the Crow now reside. The ancient leaders transmitted the vision of No-Vitals during their search for the right place, namely, the place of the sacred tobacco. Contemporary Absaroke continue to tell this story as a means of reflection upon their search for the right place in current American life.

What this official text does not tell us is that there are many versions of the original separation and migration of the peoples who became the

---

22. *Little Big Horn College Catalog* (1986).

Absaroke. There are many stories of the wanderings of the band led by No-Vitals who separated in the early seventeenth century from the Hidatsa groups led by their visionary leader, Red Scout. These related Hidatsa peoples have continued to live in what is now North Dakota. Diverse origin narratives are transmitted by many families among both the Hidatsa and the Absaroke. These stories reflect the memories of different bands who joined the Crow at later times in their history.[23] Thus, the Absaroke and their Hidatsa cousins affirm a synthetic and pluralistic perspective in which a vision experience integrates a person into self and society identity and in which multiple versions of their historical origin are acceptable.

The tribal affirmation of independent thought is well known on the high Plains of North America as well as the right of individuals to speak for themselves and their lineages. Seasonal spring gatherings of the traditional Absaroke promoted tribal unity and shared narratives just as much as late summer buffalo hunts prepared for the division of the tribe into separate band winter quarters. Four bands are known: the Mountain Crow, River Crow, Kicked in the Bellies, and a group, the Beaver Dries Its Fur (*Bilapiiuutche*), who are remembered in both the historical record and the oral narrative tradition as having been lost. The original eleven clans, organized into five phratries, have narrowed to eight clans which continue into the present. So also the fours bands of old, of which three are still active references in Crow memory, have been effectively replaced by the division of the Crow Reservation into seven districts: Black Lodge, Reno, Lodge Grass, Wyola, St. Xavier, Fort Smith, and Pryor.

The official version of the Absaroke migration story, given in the curriculum statement quoted earlier, does not dwell on the religious dimension activated in the ethnic relationship with sacred tobacco. On the northern Plains tobacco was used to communicate across diverse social and supernatural boundaries. For example, tobacco mediated intertribal relations which had been severely disrupted by warfare. Trade was conducted in the context of tobacco smoking in which breath, rhetoric, and ritual enabled the possibility of exchange in a

---

23. See Alfred Bowers, *Hidatsa Social and Ceremonial Organization*, Smithsonian Institution, Bureau of American Ethnology, bulletin 194 (Washington, D.C.: Government Printing Office, 1965); Frey, *The World of the Crow Indians;* Robert Lowie, "Social Life of the Crow Indians," *Anthropological Papers* of the American Museum of Natural History 9, no. 2 (1912): 179–248; and Lowie, "The Separation of the Crow and Hisdatsa," in "Myths and Traditions of the Crow," *Anthropological Papers* of the American Museum of Natural History 25 (1918): 272–75.

potentially hostile setting. Tobacco rituals communicated the authenticity of one's economic transaction. Most important, tobacco enabled
the reciprocal exchange with those other-than-human powers (*baaxpe*)
who pervaded the cosmos, empowered individuals, and legitimated the
very presence of a people in their bioregion.[24]

A unique ritual practice of the Absaroke is the Tobacco Society
(*Baasshussheelaakbisuua*, "tobacco dance adoption").[25] Believed to have
been given to No-Vitals by the stars, especially Morning Star, the
chapters or divisions of this religious society had special ritual prerogatives such as the Beaver dance (*Baasshussuua*). No other Native
North American peoples have such a ceremony in which the planting and harvesting of tobacco, as well as associated ritual practices,
transmitted the identity of the nation. As one researcher put it, "In
the case of the Crow and their Tobacco Society . . . investigating ritual
is investigating history; their 'historical consciousness' results from a
dialectic with their religious consciousness: their rituals are validated
by their history, their history is legitimized by their rituals. As tobacco
seeds are carried to the sacred lodge during the adoption ritual, so were
the original tobacco seeds borne by the legendary No-Vitals to the Big
Horn Mountains."[26] Interestingly, the unique tobacco plant grown by
the Crow in this ceremonial context is no longer actually smoked by
the people.

Recently, this singular religious ceremonial of the Tobacco Society
has diminished among the Absaroke. Some of the Tobacco Society ritual paraphernalia has begun to be sold to non-Native traders. The lore
of the society, transmitted by ritual adoption into specific lodges of the
society, is weakened by lack of participation. This seeming fragmen-
tation of the Tobacco Society in the late twentieth century, however,
is paralleled by earlier prohibitions beginning in 1882 against American Indian lifeway rituals generally and in 1915 against the Tobacco
Society specifically.[27]

Between 1884, when the Indian Department instituted its "New
Rules and Regulations," and 1934, when the policies of Indian Com-

---

24. For a discussion of a similar legitimating ritual expression among the Tsistsistas / Cheyenne
see Karl Schlesier, *Wolves of Heaven* (Norman: University of Oklahoma Press, 1987).

25. See Robert Lowie, "The Tobacco Society of the Crow Indians," *Anthropological Papers* of
the American Museum of Natural History 21 (1919): 103–200.

26. See Nabokov, "Cultivating Themselves: The Inter-play of Crow Indian Religion and
History."

27. Ibid., 370–89.

missioner John Collier allowed Indian cultures to resurface, the U.S. government prohibited many Indian ceremonials. Indian agents and missionaries on the reservation actively discouraged Crow religious anthropology. The Christianizing and civilizing ideologies of missionaries and "friends of the Indians," namely, white Americans who extended philanthropic assistance to Indians, held that assimilation to dominant American cultural practices was the only way to ensure survival of these indigenous peoples.[28]

The endurance of Absaroke lifeways has often depended upon the creative capacity of individual religious practitioners to rethink traditional ways so as to respond to the needs of new generations as well as to maintain and to renew the spiritual lineages with the past. Such a revisioning of the sacred is not an abstract, cognitive act but a search for integrity which is prompted by historical realities, legitimated in experiential encounters with the sacred, and grounded in an abiding interaction with sacred sites on the land. This brings us to consider diverse cultural activities among the Crow.

Cultural Religious Expressions

Among the Absaroke each person seeks with sincerity and purpose (*diakaashe*) his or her own experiences of sacred power (*maxpe*). It is in this sense that the Crow speak of "one's own religion," *alachiwakiia*. In the buffalo-hunting days, one's devotion to the Medicine Father (*Iilapxe*), or spirit being, who gave a blessing was primary, but that relationship did not preclude belonging to other ritual organizations or participating in other ritual activities. He or she may be assisted by an older shaman (*akbaalia*, "one who makes things") through fasting ordeals (*baawalishtakooshtechiiluua*, "fasting in hopes of acquiring a dream") and with the interpretation of extraordinary dreams and visions. While the sacred opens the possibility of any individual acting as a healer or diviner for herself or her family, an *akbaalia* is believed to be able to evoke power consistently and to heal the sick upon request.

---

28. See Frederick Hoxie, "The Crow," in *Indians of North America* (New York: Chelsea House, 1989); Robert F. Berkhofer, Jr., *Salvation and the Savage: An Analysis of Protestant Missions and American Indian Response, 1787–1862* (New York: Athenaeum, 1972); Henry Warner Bowden, *American Indians and the Christian Missions: Studies in Cultural Conflict* (Chicago: University of Chicago Press, 1981); Francis Paul Prewash, *The Churches and the Indian Schools, 1888–1912* (Lincoln: University of Nebraska Press, 1979); and Prewash, ed., *Documents of United States Indian Policy* (Lincoln: University of Nebraska Press, 1990).

Through the conjunction of these time-honored patterns of older mentor, personal effort, and spirit blessing, a traditional Absaroke sought a spiritual helper, or Medicine Father (*Iilapxe*), from the super-natural clans. Those spiritual beings, who have no need for fire and the cultural comforts it supplies, are called "Those Who Have No Bodies" or "Other Side Camp." The animal and chthonic beings who mani-fested *maxpe* power within the Absaroke world are called the "Without Fires."[29] These invisible beings respond to the sincere efforts of fasting humans. Considering these fasters in their liminal state as "orphaned" (*akeeleete*, "one who taken on the pathetic state of being abandoned"), the spirits may "adopt" a human and become his or her helper and guide. The spiritual beings may also give to an adopted human their revelatory direction through dreams or waking visions to gather a sacred medicine bundle (*xapaalia*).

The specific religious exchange between an individual and his or her Medicine Father (*Iilapxe*), which might result in a medicine bun-dle, takes place in the context of the larger Absaroke worldview. This world picture opens an individual to all aspects of the local bioregion as having the potential for hierophanous irruption of the sacred into the world. These relationships are framed for Absaroke individuals by such religious experiences as sacred dreams, vision fasts, and rit-ual participation. So also, a large body of myth narratives transmits ancient thought about the mysterious world of powerful beings. The Absaroke oral myths describe trickster beings like Old Man Coyote, heroes like "Lodge Boy," "Thrown Away," and "Old Woman's Grand-child" (*Karicbapituac*, Morning Star) as well as dangerous beings like "Red Woman."[30] These mythic narratives are termed *baitsitsiwa* and other variants which all reduplicate the verb *to tell*. Doubling is a recur-ring Crow practice for amplifying the sacred. The double, or intense, narrations tell of an interconnected world in which *maxpe* power is

---

29. This particular Crow understanding is an excellent example of the latitude of understanding in Crow anthropology of the sacred. This position is largely consistent with these sources: Voget, *They Call Me Agnes*, 6; Lowie, "Myths and Traditions of the Crow Indians," 315–43; Edward S. Curtis, "The Absaroke, or Crows," in *The North American Indian* (1909; New York: Johnson Reprint Corp., 1970), vol. 4, 52–54; and Frey, *World of the Crow Indians*, 88ff. William Wildschut describes these spiritual clans differently. He writes that the "Without Fires" are the spiritual clan of the sun, moon, stars, thunder, and all the animals; whereas the "Other Side Camp" clan is the earth and all that springs from earth's life, such as plants, flowers, trees, and rocks. See his *Crow Indian Medicine Bundles*, ed. John C. Ewes. Contributions from the Museum of the American Indian Heye Foundation, vol. 17 (New York: Museum of the American Indian, 1975), 2–3.

30. See Robert Lowie, "Myths and Traditions of the Crow," *Anthropological Papers* of the American Museum of Natural History 25 (1922).

neither "good" nor "bad" but efficacious. Contacting *maxpe* does not elevate a person into an autonomous self but rather establishes a person into a set of obligations and privileges. Often these ethical precepts are established in relation both to the animal *maxpe* of the vision as well as the place where that vision occurred. Contemporary Crow individuals continue these patterns, expressing regard for the sacred, in quest of renewing power.

One anthropologist observed:

The Apsaalooke [*sic*] view a world in which all entities and all phenomena are interconnected, animal with plant with land with human with spirit. The human being is intrinsically linked to and part of the assemblage of human and spiritual personages that surrounds him or her. The world and the individual are necessarily not separate and autonomous. The focus of the individual's identity and activities is not on the self as a self-reliant entity but rather on the network of human and spiritual beings of which he or she is a part. The world does not exist in a void, meaningless and inanimate, but rather it has a dynamic and a vitality upon which all entities interdepend. It is animated with meaningful patterns and a life-force. A human being does not so much assert control over the world as attend to the guidance and transformative power offered in it. In exchange for what is offered, and to maintain participation in this world, the individual reciprocates unselfishly. Gift exchange characterizes human and spiritual relationships. Consequently the individual's immediate world is neither one of abandonment nor one inhabited by adversaries. It is a home to human and spiritual kinfolk, and it is endowed with significance and life. While participating in this world, a human being is assured of support, adopted by that which is greater than the self.[31]

Such a worldview of reciprocity, adoption, and exchange carries both obligations and privileges. The numinous exchanges sought in vision fast and gratuitously given in medicine dreams are also fraught with responsibility. Just as social connections can problematize individual ego drives, so also power experiences demand self-discipline, sincerity, and cooperation. Such a path was not undertaken casually, for both

---

31. Frey, *World of the Crow Indians*, 5–6.

maturity and understanding of the commitments were evident even to ordinary Crow.

Two Leggings, one of the last of the Crow warriors to know and practice the traditional Absaroke sacred ways, described sacrificial practices often undertaken by Crow men and women in fasting for a vision or in mourning:

> As I walked among the barking and staring prairie dogs I thought that maybe these earth creatures who live underground as the birds live in the sky could help me receive a powerful medicine.
>
> I found the biggest hill in the dog town and dug away some earth with my knife to make a more comfortable resting place. Then, I lay down facing the east. The next morning...as I walked around I found a root-digger's stick. I turned toward the sun and drew out my long knife. On the ground I crossed the knife and the stick and then raised my left index finger.
>
> I called the sun my grandfather and said that I was about to sacrifice my finger end to him. I prayed that some bird of the sky or animal of the earth would eat it and give me good medicine because I wanted to be a great chief some day and have many horses. I said that I did not want to stay poor.[32]

Leggings's comments picture the walking style of the Crow individual fast as well as the underlying cosmological regard for place of the animal spirits. That is, where a person finally received a vision and from which animal were all significant considerations interpreted by *akbaalia* for a faster so that he or she might properly discharge their obligations to their Medicine Father. Two Leggings placed himself on a hill closer to the powerful aviary spirits, as well as digging into the ground to open the possibility of a deep earth spirit blessing. He faced east when he lay down, which opened him to the powerful rays of the all-seeing sun and Morning Star. He called upon the sun with an endearing kinship term and cut off the final joint of a finger as an offering given to the sun, just as the sun might lead a powerful spirit to him with a blessing. Two Leggings hoped that such a vision would have lifeway efficacy and enable him to become a competent leader and successful provider. On this vision fast Two Leggings did receive medicine songs which he

---

32. Peter Nabokov, *Two Leggings: The Making of a Crow Warrior.* Based on a field manuscript by William Wildschut (New York: Thomas Y. Crowell, 1967), 50.

remembered and sang into his old age, but he did not receive the most powerful of Crow visions, namely, the visionary sanction to assemble a medicine bundle.

Medicine bundles (*xapaalia*), which typically resulted from encounters with spiritual beings, are composite liturgies of material objects which have been revealed to an individual by a Medicine Father spirit (*Iilapxe*). By "composite liturgy" is meant the synthesis of various material items with chants, ritual manipulations, and mental attitudes, all of which constitute the medicine bundle. The actual physical gathering of such objects as individual feathers and whole wings of selected birds, colored clays, animal skins and horns, fossil-bearing rocks, dream objects crafted from wood or leather, and multiple wrapping cloths do not in themselves constitute a medicine bundle. Rather, the performative character of the chants and manipulations as well as restrictions regarding seasonal openings, attending guests, storage of the bundle, and offerings to the bundle spirits are all instrumental for evoking the sacred. Thus, the medicine bundle brings together ritual, experiential, social, and ethical dimensions of religion.

One classification of traditional Crow medicine bundles lists the following types: Sun Dance bundles or war medicines that were used to seek revenge but that were not taken on raids; war medicine bundles, containing the material representations of visions and dreams, such as symbolic hoops and arrows, used for success in war and horse raiding; shields, which were painted and decorated often with covers; skull medicine bundles, considered especially powerful in obtaining personal desires and healings; rock medicine bundles, often centered on an ammonite fossil as a personal sacred medicine frequently handed on in a family; medicine pipe bundles, associated with the medicine pipe ceremony and believed to have come from other tribes to the Crow; love medicine bundles with the power to influence the sexual behavior of others; witchcraft bundles used to harm, control, and influence others; healing bundles for assisting the wounded and sick; and, finally, hunting bundles for success in bringing home game.[33] Medicine bundles are considered ancient ways of encountering the sacred among the Crow, and they continue to have a central role in Absaroke lifeway.

---

33. Wildschut, *Crow Indian Medicine Bundles*, 16–17.

The ethical dimension of owning a medicine bundle echoes the pervading Crow religious anthropology. These ethical injunctions are evident in Thomas Yellowtail's observations:

The way in which medicine bundles are kept by their owners shows the way in which an individual must treat his spiritual possessions. The medicine bundle contains the things that a person has been directed to collect as a result of his vision or dream. The medicine he has been given links him to all of the medicine powers of the universe. He will probably be told how he should prepare his medicine bundle in order to protect his medicine. The instructions can come directly from the Medicine Father, whether he be a bird, an animal, or whatever, or the medicine man of the tribe can explain to the person what he should do. After a man takes these steps, he has new responsibilities, and he must follow new, difficult rules to protect and keep his gift. These responsibilities are both outward and inward.[34]

The centripetal forces that coalesce in the medicine bundle are in continuity with the historical and cosmological forces that the Crow believe drew them into a long tribal migration and their eventual formation as a people. The origin stories, the Tobacco Society ritual, and medicine bundles express the cosmological dimension of Absaroke identity. Each practice forms a unique branch in the tree of Crow religion.

Another ancient Crow religious practice, which interweaves experiential, social, ritual, and cosmological dimensions, is the sweat lodge. The purifying sweat bath, or sweat lodge (*awushua*), enables intimate contact with the spiritual world. The ritual is conducted in a specially prepared lodge built of saplings bent over and tied so as to form a dome with a radius of three to five feet. The privilege of building a sweat lodge is carefully monitored among the Crow, as is the right to pour water during the ritual. These privileges are transmitted by spiritual injunction often passed down by religious purchase. This type of acquisition of sacred power accentuates both the process of transfer as well as the content. In such a ritual transfer a part or a replica of an individual's medicine would be given to another, after a payment of goods or money, so that that person might begin to assemble his own bundle.

---

34. *Yellowtail*, 17.

Among the Absaroke this is an accepted means for individuals to gain access to the sacred because it is presumed that the individual seeking the sacred object is also motivated by *diakaashe* or sincerity of effort. The sweat lodge is the most appropriate place for evoking sincerity of purpose; thus, the sweat lodge ceremony is often a daily occurrence as well as a ritual performed prior to all ceremonial activity.

An account by Three-Wolves, given earlier this century, accords with current Crow practices of this ritual. He described the procedure of the ritual saying:

The first four stones [which have been heated on an external fire] are put into the [sweat lodge], one by one, by means of a forked stick. When the fourth has been deposited, the stone-bearer voices some wish [and those attending say Aho! in gratitude], whereupon he may throw in as many rocks as he pleases, two by two. Water is set down by the stones. The bathers enter one by one, never walking in front of the stone-tender. The lodge is covered, then one man dips his hand into the water and sprinkles four handfuls on the rocks, whereupon four wishes are expressed. The man nearest the entrance tells of a dream, such as, "I have seen snow on the ground," or, "I have seen horsetracks." The rest cry, "Thanks!" and pray aloud: "May I get there!" (if a season has been mentioned.) The door is flung open and the inmates cool off. The dreamer recounts a second dream, then the cover is put on again. Now seven handfuls are poured on the rocks to symbolize the Dipper. After the period of sweating the second man from the door tells of his dreams, and the lodge is uncovered for a while. Next ten cupfuls are poured on the rocks and the third man tells his dreams. The fourth time they throw on an uncounted (*tsimusua,* the "infinity" round) number of handfuls. The fourth man tells only one dream, then cries, "Throw the door wide open!" All now jump up and run into the river. While inside the bathers scourge themselves with horsetail [buffalotail] or sagebrush whips in order to perspire still more. In the smaller lodges five or six sweat themselves at a time; in the larger ones from ten to twelve.[35]

---

35. Robert Lowie, "Religion of the Crow," *Anthropological Papers* of the American Museum of Natural History 25, pt. 2 (1922): 430.

While current practices derived from individual spiritual sanctions and contemporary needs may differ slightly, this description conveys the general structure of the ritual according to the Crow. The sense of rebirth and purification engendered by the heated rocks and steam in the domed lodge joins with the prayers of the participants. To cry in prayer (*chiwakiia*) and to ask repeatedly for one's wishes is juxtaposed with narrations of sacred dreams and the steam-breath of the heated stones. This ritual continues to be widely practiced on the Crow reservation and is one indication of the endurance and resurgence of traditional religion.

Contemporary Vitality
in Absaroke Religious Anthropology

Four issues are discussed in this final section. First, there is the enduring Crow relationship with their land. While a nineteenth-century statement opens this section, a contemporary expression of that relationship is described to emphasize the significance of place in contemporary Crow anthropology of the sacred. Second, the introduction of the Peyote Way constitutes a major ritual complex now widely practiced by the Crow. Third, the ceremony of *Ashkisshe,* or "Sun Dance," has moved to the center of traditional Crow life in the late twentieth century. The story of the transmission of that ceremonial and a brief description suggest the capacity of Absaroke anthropology of the sacred to adapt to changed situations. Finally, the emergence of Absaroke Pentecostal Christianity is described, and the political importance of this religious development is briefly outlined.

Central for understanding Absaroke survival as a people is their continuity with the land. The sacred relationship of the Crow with their mountainous homeland is not articulated in a vague manner but in robust statements of life lived in proximity to the natural world. The nineteenth-century Absaroke chief, Arapooish, expressed his understanding of the sacred movement on the land in this manner:

> The Crow country is exactly in the right place. It has snowy mountains and sunny plains; all kinds of climates and good things for every season. When the summer heat scorches the prairies, you can draw up under the mountains, where the air is sweet and cool, and grass fresh and the bright streams come tumbling out

of the snowbanks. There you can hunt the elk, the deer and the antelope, when their skins are fit for dressing; there you will find plenty of white bears and mountain sheep. In the autumn, when your horses are fat and strong from the mountain pastures, you can go down on the plains and hunt the buffalo, or trap beaver in the streams. And when winter comes on, you can take shelter in the woody bottoms along the rivers; there you will find buffalo meat for yourselves, and cottonwood bark for your horses; or you may winter in the Wind River Valley where there is salt weed in abundance. The Crow country is exactly in the right place. Everything good is to be found there. There is no country like the Crow country.[36]

Arapooish's lyrical statement carries a moral subtext that one should move in this country in a manner so as to cultivate all the goodness which can come from this land. An aesthetic charge in this statement flows from its powerful ethic, which understands the appropriate use of the resources in the land. What is apparent, however, is that Arapooish is speaking to his own people and in his own time. The sacred goodness of Crow country in that day was in its ability to provide a lifeway and livelihood for the people. We would not expect this worldview value to be expressed by contemporary traditional Absaroke people in the same words and in the same manner as when Arapooish spoke so eloquently. This is the case because much of the Absaroke homeland described in this statement was taken from the Crow through treaties, land purchases, or land thefts. Yet, the Absaroke still speak about their land as sacred despite years of pressure to abandon traditional values and give up their land.

"The sky is my Father and these Mountains are my Mother." This prayer is often heard at Crow ceremonies. It summarizes the endurance of traditional relations between these horse-loving Native peoples and their northern Plains homeland. The expansive clear skies of the state of Montana, in which the Absaroke have their reservation, contrast sharply with the wooded horizon cut by the surrounding Wolf, Big Horn, and Pryor Mountains. In the Absaroke worldview the relation-

---

36. Published in "The Crow," *Sheridan Post*, July 10, 1902. It is a reprint of Robert Campbell's account of Crow Country. Robert Campbell worked with the Rocky Mountain Fur Company in 1832 and negotiated with Arapooish as the major Crow chief. This quote is also found in J. Donald Hughes, *American Indian Ecology* (El Paso: Texas Western Press, 1983), 142; and Stewart L. Udall, *The Quiet Crisis* (New York: Holt, Rinehart and Winston, 1963), 17–18.

ship established between the human and the presence of the sacred is especially focused on the mountains as the sources of fecundity and material blessings.

This relationship between the Crow and mountains is especially evident in the "New Year" dance on the last day of Crow Fair, the major reunion, powwow, and rodeo event in late summer. This dance, with its four stops (symbolizing autumn, winter, spring, and summer), is led by a pipe carrier across whose path no human or animal should pass. This honored leader prays that everyone will be healthy for the year and will return again to Crow Fair. People dance behind him in traditional garb; others participate by gathering alongside the dance route. During this dance all the participants gesture in unison toward the mountains as a sign of loving respect for their Mother, the mountains. This is a striking transmission of an ancient worldview value and ritual evocation of human-earth relations in the modern setting of the Crow Fair.

Peyote Way came to the Crow in 1910.[37] While this ceremonial was not a traditional bundle way, it did involve like-minded Crow men and women in a ritual evocation of sacred power, in giveaways, and in traditional repetitive, emotional prayer. Peyote Way arrived at a time in Crow history when the people suffered from both dominant American pressures to abandon the Absaroke lifeway as well as internal challenges to self-confidence regarding appropriate modes of adaptation to changing economic and social circumstances. Both the Christian cross altar and the more traditional half-moon altar forms of Peyote Way developed on the Crow Reservation. However, the traditional half-moon form of this ceremony has become dominant among the Crow.

In this ceremony a tipi is set up in which a clay-ridge altar in the form of a half-moon is built in the center of the tipi. A peyote cactus button is placed on the altar. Participants sit around the edge of the tipi while the officiants, led by the Road Man, Cedar Man, and Drummer, have prearranged positions at the west side of the tipi opposite the entrance. The Fire Man and Door Man take their positions on the north side of the eastern entrance. Participants sing highly structured peyote songs, which are often transmitted from other tribal groups, as they consume peyote. The peyote cactus is cleaned and mashed and

---

37. See Omer Stewart, *Peyote Religion: A History* (Norman: University of Oklahoma Press, 1987), 184–89; and R. C. Kista, "Preservations of Aboriginal Values as Evidenced by Crow Peyote Leaders," paper delivered at the Northwestern Anthropological Conference, April 26–27, 1963, Eugene, Oregon.

eaten in small round balls or drunk as a tea. The peyote is considered a sacrament in the sense that the participants believe that they are eating a sacred substance which may reveal its will and intention to them during the ceremony.

The aesthetics of the Peyote Way ceremonial are an integral component of individual ritual acts and prayers. Each individual, accompanied by the Drummer, may sing holding the Road Man's fan, staff, and rattle. Other participants join in with individual singers in the four rounds of each song. Simultaneously, the Fire Man builds and refurbishes the central fire in the tipi as the overnight ceremony proceeds. As the cottonwood limbs burn into ash, the Fire Man "paints" with the coals, forming glowing images of animals, especially a great eagle, eventually filling the space between the horns of the half-moon altar. Prayers filled with emotion echo traditional concerns for sincerity (*diakaashe*) and alternate with the singing in the regulated movement of the ritual. The trajectory of the ritual reaches a significant catharsis moment when, at early dawn, the Water Woman brings water and prays for all the participants' needs. The deeply moving and personal narratives, the finely controlled fire, the skillful manipulation of the smoke flaps of the tipi, the beaded patterns decorating the various fans, all work in concert with the singing to create a profound aesthetic experience of the sacred for the Crow participant.

While Crow Fair continues to be celebrated each year on the third weekend of August and Peyote Meetings occur frequently, the *Ashkisshe* or Sun Dances of the Crow are held earlier in June and the beginning of July. The *Ashkisshe* is held in a specially prepared lodge called the "Big Lodge." The lodge has a central forked cottonwood tree ringed by twelve smaller forked trees which are joined by rafter poles often made of lodgepole pine. Three points provide an overview of this contemporary revitalization of a traditional ceremonial which was lost in 1875, namely, historical developments, ritual process, and symbol systems.

The current ceremony, referred to as a "Sun Dance," came to the Crow from the Shoshone people of Wyoming in 1941.[38] The older traditional Crow Sun Dance (*Baaiichkiisapiliolissua*, "fringed ankle dance")

---

38. In light of the historical changes in the Crow *Ashkisshe* as well as the random use of one term to describe different ceremonies of many northern Plains Native peoples, there is some question of the appropriateness of the English term Sun Dance. See Karl Schlesier, "Rethinking the Midewiwin and the Plains Ceremonial Called the Sun Dance," *Plains Anthropologist* 35, no. 127 (February 1990): 1–27.

was a different ceremonial. The older ceremonial was oriented toward the clan revenge ideal of the Crow. In that ritual, an individual, supportive clan members, and friends undertook self-torture and fasting so as to acquire a vision of the success or failure of a raid to revenge the death of a clan member. This older Sun Dance was last sponsored in 1875.

In 1941, the current Crow-Shoshone Sun Dance, or *Ashkisshilissuua* ("temporary lodge dance") was brought back to the Crow by the Crow-Shoshone Sun Dance Chief, John Trujillo, at the invitation of William Big Day.[39] This dance is a community renewal ceremonial with only subtle connections to the earlier revenge ritual. Since 1941, however, the *Ashkisshe* has changed in terms of the motivations of the dancers, in the structure of the ceremony as determined by Sun Dance chiefs and sponsors over the years, and in the role of the ceremony in Crow religious life.[40] For example, the original impulse for many Crow to join in the new *Ashkisshe* ceremony was spiritually to support sons and relatives who were fighting in World War II. The structure of the *Ashkisshe* was changed in the early 1950s when women entered the lodge and began to dance with the men. The role of the *Ashkisshe* in Absaroke religious life has significantly increased from 1941, when it was marginal to the more central "bundle way." Now, many Crow see it as at the center of traditional Absaroke religion.

Second, the description of the "Big Lodge" and a participant's perspective on the dance itself do not give the reader a full sense of the larger ritual process prior to the dance.[41] For example, beginning a year before the actual dance, there are conversations by the sponsor of the dance and the Sun Dance chief who has been selected to lead the *Ashkisshe*. On the four full moons before the dance there are also four "Medicine Bundle Openings" and four "Outside Dances." The later "Outside Dances" are like dress rehearsals in which only the sponsor and a relative dance at the site where the *Ashkisshe* lodge will be built. Finally, there may possibly be a buffalo hunt among the Crow tribal

---

39. That historical transmission and the role of other individuals and families in the 1941 Sun Dance is explored in Fred Voget's book, *The Crow-Shoshone Sun Dance* (Norman: University of Oklahoma Press, 1984).

40. For a straightforward description of the fiftieth-anniversary *Ashkisshe* sponsored by Heywood Big Day, the son of William Big Day, see Michael Crummett, *Sun Dance* (Billings, Mont.: Falcon Press, 1993).

41. The most important source on this issue is *Yellowtail*, especially the sections discussing the Sun Dance religion, 99–183.

buffalo herd for the giveaway feast following the ceremonial. These activities, which unfold in the time before and after the actual dance itself, are integral to understanding the significance of the ritual process. This process holds meaning and purpose both for individuals and for the community because it both transmits ancient concerns for intimate, oral transactions and also allows for adaptation of older ways to new conditions.[42]

Third, the symbol system of the Crow *Ashkisshe* is neither static (fixed) nor relative (subjective). At each dance a number of men and women dancers enter the "Big Lodge" and fast for three, four, or five days, as determined by the sponsor and Sun Dance Chief in deliberation. The intention of the dancers is to assist individuals other than themselves as well as to renew the sacred vitality of the Absaroke community of land, animals, and humans. While the structure of the ritual activities may appear to be fixed, it can actually vary a great deal. For example, sponsors may or may not allow non-Crow or non-Native participants. The Sun Dance Chief may choose to conduct the ceremony for three, four, or five days. Individuals dance to the central tree according to their own motivation and in their own way; yet, they are urged to dance in unison with the drummers and singers to augment spiritual blessings for the whole community. The prayerful mood of the days-long dance opens individual participants to unique religious experiences; yet, there is a strong sense of shared spiritual exchange as all participants work for the good of the community. The individual experiences and group ritual activities are more significant than any "orthodox" interpretations. While interweaving symbol systems might be labeled "traditional," there is no one Crow interpretation, no one symbolic understanding, or one exclusive Absaroke practice of any religious experience or ritual. Rather, the Crow understand that interpretations will vary a great deal but that ritual practice will be somewhat standardized. Changes in standardized rituals by a recognized visionary are accepted, with a typical response being, "It's up to you!"

Three traditional Crow symbolic acts which evoke the sacred are fasting, self-effacement during prayer, and personal exchange with a spiritual helper. Fasting as a religious act among the Crow appears to have devel-

---

42. Crummett's photographic and editorial work, *Sun Dance,* is helpful for understanding this ritual process.

oped in the precontact period.[43] In the *Ashkisshe* the women and men dancers go without food and water for the duration of the dance, which is set in terms of the number of nights. This bodily deprivation is believed to put the dancer in a spiritual state most appropriate for prayer. The sincerity and determination (*diakaashe*) of a dancer are not simply interior, experiential states. This Crow virtue of *diakaashe* also has ethical dimensions. For example, Thomas Yellowtail spoke of learning the Crow language and entering into Crow spiritual songs as part of this sincerity.[44] In that cultivated state of sincerity, then, the dancer is humbled as if she or he were "orphaned."[45] To be "orphaned" is to be aware of one's limits, to know that one's pathetic state opens oneself to the possibility of spiritual blessing by a Medicine Father (*Iilapxe*). This personal exchange with a sacred helper is not simply a subjective and individualistic salvation experience. Rather, the experience is more correctly understood as communal and cosmic. "Communal" refers to the positive effect of personal prayer for the vitality of Crow humans as well as for the community of beings in the bioregion. "Cosmic" refers to the holistic ethic that underlies the *Ashkisshe*, namely, the dance and deprivation arise from out of the larger cosmos, and their effects reach into the unity of the Absaroke world.[46]

The final expression of Crow cultivation of the sacred is the contemporary Christian Pentecostal movement. The arrival of Christian missionaries among the Absaroke led to the development of various denominations on the reservation. Both Baptist and Catholic churches have been active on the Crow Reservation since the 1880s. However, the evangelical Christian sect identified with "holiness gifts" and "Pentecostal manifestations of the Holy Spirit" is an early-twentieth-century religious movement which arrived on the Crow Reservation through the Four Square Gospel Mission of Aimee Semple McPherson. In 1923 a Crow, Nellie Stewart, with five other Absaroke attended a revival held

---

43. The example of Crow women from Edwin Thompson Denig, *Five Indian Tribes of the Upper Missouri* (Norman: University of Oklahoma Press, 1961), 155–56, is instructive. The elder Barney Old Coyote has often critiqued this description in Denig's writings. Denig derides the moral character and physical appearance of Crow women based on one example he describes. Barney Old Coyote points out, however, that this description in Denig is typical of a fasting widow who has cut herself and undertaken a miserable life as an act of mourning.

44. See *Yellowtail*, 179–80.

45. The term *akeeleete* is sometimes used to mean "orphan," "one with no possessions," "one who has nothing." See Frey, *World of the Crow Indians*, 182.

46. For stories of that understanding in the Crow tradition see Joseph Medicine Crow, *From the Heart of Crow Country*.

by McPherson at Miles City, Montana.[47] Following a training period in Los Angeles, California, Stewart returned to the Crow Reservation and gathered a core of followers in the Black Lodge district. Stewart blended traditional Crow beliefs and practices with her Christian Pentecostalism. For example, she often fasted in the hills for visions and songs, which she taught to her community. She also claimed to "own" these songs as well as leadership of the Pentecostal Church, just as older Crow owned medicine materials, songs, and ritual prerogatives.

The Holiness Pentecostal movement among the Crow came at a time of accelerated social, political, and economic change for these people. Traditional tribal lifeways, such as intertribal warfare, status based on military exploits, and community activity based on band needs, had all ended through a complex historical process involving the emergence of new socialization patterns in the reservation districts, as well as government prohibition of the intertribal warfare system, and the promotion of settled agricultural life. The settlement established around Crow Agency became, during the 1920s and 1930s, the locus of intense debates among the Crow regarding acceptance of the Crow Allotment Act of 1920 and the Indian Reorganization Act of 1934. Both of these political acts struck Crow social and political life like a maelstrom, disrupting traditional lifeway patterns of subsistence, governance, and ritual expression. Horses were at the center of these changes. The Crow used horses as a marker of value in many ritual transactions, and the U.S. government sought stock reductions, ostensibly to save pasture land but the Absaroke experienced this policy as a direct attack on their traditional lifeway. Many adult Crow men completely lost hope in any recovery of their former meaningful life when their horses were taken from them.

The Holiness Pentecostal Church alleviated the pressures of these times, to some extent, by drawing older Absaroke views of the sacred into Christian syncretic rituals. For example, holiness gifts associated with oral modes such as speaking in tongues and interpreting tongues and prophecy all paralleled Crow narrative traditions. In the traditional ways, a visionary injunction was required to speak of sacred matters, to validate ownership of specific modes of spoken and sung prayer, and to deliver public rhetoric as a signal of leadership. So also, the holiness gifts associated with power, such as personal faith, miracles,

---

47. For this development and Crow Pentecostalism, see McCleary, "*Akbaatashee:* The Oilers, Pentecostalism among the Crow Indians."

and healing, were acculturated by Crow Pentecostals as replacing older belief systems, healers (*akbaalia*), and traditional rituals. These gifts of power mimicked the older "bundle way" minus the physical objects gathered in a *xapaalia* bundle, the animal *maxpe* exchange, and the specific symbol system of the older Absaroke worldview.

Gradually the Holiness Pentecostal Church among the Crow became a major religious and political force on the Crow Reservation when they voted as a block. Since the 1970s, Absaroke Pentecostal sects have been a significant factor in every tribal election, providing tribal chairpersons in all but one election since the 1980s. Ironically, the Crow Pentecostal churches became much more politically involved earlier on than their mainstream Christian counterparts in American fundamentalism. Moreover, the Pentecostal movement, while drawing on Absaroke traditional beliefs and practices early in its formation, has become increasingly hostile to many traditional Crow lifeway practices, including the prayers of clan aunts and uncles after special events, kinship transactions (especially giveaways), and rituals such as the sweat lodge, Tobacco Society, *xapaalia* bundles, Peyote Way, and *Ashkisshe.*

A Concluding Comment

Absaroke language continues to be spoken, with approximately 30 percent of the people being fluent. Language courses are taught in the tribal college. This capacity of the Crow language to creatively renew traditional ways of expressing the sacred is inextricably tied to other vocabularies of sacred expression such as song and dance. A contemporary resurgence in the numbers of Crow individuals practicing traditional Absaroke rituals such as the sweat lodge and Sun Dance suggests that these paths for self-expression and community reflection can coexist with ritual paths introduced to the Crow, such as Peyote Way and Christian Holiness Pentecostalism. Some religious groups such as the Catholic Kateri Tekakwitha Societies on the reservation have actively explored the question of a unique Absaroke Catholicism. It is their hope that an indigenous language liturgy and traditional symbol systems can be used to rethink the theological beliefs associated with Euro-American Catholicism. Ecumenical and interreligious dialogues and liturgies on the Crow Reservation suggest that *maxpe*, the sacred, is still a medium for conversation and communication among the people.

ᗺ THREE ᗺ

Rebalancing the World in the Contradictions of History: Creek/Muskogee

Joel W. Martin

Each summer at ceremonial grounds in Oklahoma, Creek (Muskogee) people gather to perform the *póskita* or green corn ceremony, "a rite of resonant renewal, of forgiveness."[1] Two hundred years ago, when most Creeks lived in what is now Georgia and Alabama, the ceremony focused on the ignition of a holy fire and the symbolic sacrifice of the Creeks' most important foods and medicines. Then, every Creek was affiliated with an *i:tálwa* (square-ground town) and was obligated to attend the *póskita* (fast).[2] As a visitor wrote in 1791, "After the fire is sufficiently kindled, four other young men come forward in the same [formal] manner, each having a fair ear of new corn, which the priest takes from them, and places with great solemnity in the fire, where it is consumed."[3] Also "given to the new fire" were portions of black-drink tea leaves, bear oil, freshly killed deer meat, and button snakeroot medicine.[4] By ritually removing corn and other important foods and medicines from ordinary patterns of human consumption, and giving them instead to the new and powerful sacred fire, eighteenth-century Creeks ritually resanctified the sources of life. Today, similar actions continue to constitute an important part of the ceremony. Creeks

---

1. Joy Harjo, "Family Album," *Progressive* March 1992, 22.

2. Creek terms are represented in this essay according to the orthography established by Mary R. Haas. See William C. Sturtevant, "The Mikasuki Seminole: Medical Beliefs and Practices" (Ph.D. diss., Yale University, 1955), 20.

3. Caleb Swan, "Position and State of Manners and Arts in the Creek Nation, in 1791," in Henry Rowe Schoolcraft, ed., *Information Respecting the History Condition and Prospects of the Indian Tribes of the United States* (Philadelphia: 1855), 267.

4. Ibid., 267.

gather for a four-day ceremony focused on the rekindling of a sacred fire. They carefully regulate the interaction of men and women. They invoke the symbolism of the number four, arranging four logs and four ears of corn around the fire. They celebrate the completion of the ceremony with a feast.[5]

Yet, if similarities abound, much has changed as well. Red root is used today instead of yaupon holly (*Ilex vomitoria*) to make a ritual infusion. New dances have been added. Moreover, in modern times, not all Creeks participate in the green corn ceremony. Thus, continued participation in the green corn ceremony connotes a more "traditional" identity. By performing the green corn ceremony, Creeks link their ancestors and their progeny, demonstrate the resilience of their own religion, and bear witness to a signal truth: they have survived against all odds. As the Creek poet Joy Harjo explains, "We dance together in this place of knowing beyond the physical dimensions of space, much denser than the chemicals and paper of photographs. It is larger than mere human memory, than any destruction we have walked through to come to this ground of memory."[6]

It is appropriate to begin a survey of Creek religion with a discussion of the green corn ceremony, not only because it has long been the Creeks' most important ritual, and not only because it involves symbols that are millennia old, but also because it has changed over time, assuming new meanings and value as the historical context changes. This points to a dialectical truth about Creek religion: on the one hand, it demonstrates remarkable continuity with the ancestral past; on the other, it is dynamic, truly historical, and continually innovative. In this survey, I wish to emphasize the latter point, without losing sight of the former one. Creek religion is deeply dependent upon the past,

---

5. On the meaning of sacrifice in religion, see Georges Bataille, *Theory of Religion*, trans. Robert Hurley (New York: Zone Books, 1989), 50–54. On the modern Creek green corn ceremony, see Amelia R. Bell, "Creek Ritual: The Path to Peace" (Ph.D. diss., University of Chicago, 1984), 157–90.

6. Joy Harjo, "Family Album," 25. Creeks have faced many threats to their existence. These include Soto's gold-crazed, horse-mounted, armor-wearing army (1540); catastrophic smallpox, influenza, and yellow fever plagues (sixteenth and seventeenth centuries); Andrew Jackson's land-crazed, massacring Tennessee militia (1814); the United States' policy of Indian removal, which ripped Muskogees from their ancestral homelands in Alabama and compelled them to move to "external colonies" in Oklahoma (1832–38); the American Civil War, which divided them internally and forced them to give large land cessions; the Curtis Act of 1898, which stripped Creeks of their sovereignty as a nation, placed them under the Dawes Allotment Act of 1887, and thereby pulverized and reduced Indian land holdings; and Oklahoma statehood (1906), which began a period of economic subjugation and further land loss.

but always moving forward toward something novel. In sum, the story of Creek religion is the story of something alive.

In surveying the history of the last ten thousand years of Creek religion, it is fair to say that at least four major religious transformations have occurred. The first transformation took place three thousand years ago when hunter-gatherers in the Southeast began cultivating domesticated crops and adopted a settled way of existence. The second transformation occurred a little more than a thousand years ago as Creek ancestors involved themselves in the "Mississippian" cultural complex. The third occurred when that complex civilization collapsed and the Creeks became participants in a new colonial order of transatlantic, multinational trade (1540–1812). The fourth took place when the Creeks were displaced from their ancestral homelands by settler occupations and an American military invasion, and then forced by U.S. army to "remove" west to Oklahoma (1813–38). With each major transformation, Creeks altered their religious formation, making it distinct from what had preceded it, yet clearly dependent upon the past for key symbols, rites, and values. In what follows, I will refer to these as the Woodland, Mississippian, the classic Creek, and the modern Creek religious formations, respectively. Before proceeding, however, an important methodological point must be made. By relating religious change to changes in subsistence, politics, economics, and landscape, I do not mean to imply that changes in Creek religion were caused by nonreligious forces or secular events. Nor do I mean to invoke a theory of religion that sees religion as a simple reflection of society. The actual point is that Creek religion was tightly integrated with subsistence, social life, politics, economics, and landscape. Creek religion affected multiple spheres of life, and these spheres affected Creek religious history. Changes in subsistence and politics influenced religion, but the reverse was true as well.

The ancestral homeland of the Creeks is in the southeastern region of what is now the United States, particularly in the piedmont region where rivers originate in the Appalachian foothills and flow south to the Gulf of Mexico (the Tallapoosa, Coosa, Chattahoochee, and Flint rivers).[7] Initially, Creek religion was closely tied to hunting-

---

7. Muskogee migration legends, *if taken literally*, imply an origin considerably west of this area and suggest that the Muskogees gained possession of the region by conquering a prior population of inhabitants. Yet, to interpret these stories literally is reckless and distorts their purposes. Migration stories were not intended to be understood In the manner of objective historical texts, but as

gathering subsistence (the Paleo and Archaic periods, ten thousand to three thousand years ago).[8] The temptation for scholars is to assume that this form of Creek religion was "animistic," a worldview discerning spirits at work in all of nature. This oversimplifies. This orientation was far more complex and supple than we will ever fathom. It was a religion that glorified the drama of the hunt. It relied upon the interpretative skills of shamans and visionaries. It marked the passages of human life with significant ceremonies. It provided men and women with a complex set of stories and rites to symbolize, dramatize, and interpret their rich natural environment.

About three thousand years ago, Southeastern Indians began relying more on domesticated crops and garden horticulture, cultivating a wide variety of plants producing consumable seeds. These included sunflower, sumpweed, chenopodlum, knotweed, pigweed, giant ragweed, and maygrass.[9] To store these seeds and the nuts they gathered, they grew gourds, but they also began using pottery, including storage pots, on a much larger scale. This increased reliance on garden horticulture along with new storage technologies encouraged a more sedentary life. It was during this time, which archaeologists have named the "Woodland" period, that men and women constructed the first relatively permanent houses in the Southeast.

In many cultures across the globe, the shift toward horticulture and settled life is associated with new religious emphases and practices. This was true among Southeastern Indians as well, although it is difficult to be very specific. Archaic Indians had shown great concern for the treatment of their deceased kin, often including in the grave such things as "red ocher, weapons, tools, and the bodies of their dogs."[10] Woodland Indians shared this concern, but perhaps because they were more settled they were able to carry it to another level. They constructed burial mounds, some of immense size, throughout the region. They also built effigy mounds, shaped in the form of animals such as snakes or eagles.

---

narratives revealing sacred values and vital alliances. Modern archaeological research provides no evidence of any massive, pre-Columbian invasion of the southeastern interior. The Muskogees were and are the direct descendants of the original inhabitants of this region.

8. In the Southeast, Archaic Indians also made use of domesticated plants, although they did not practice garden horticulture. Gerald F. Schroedl, C. Clifford Boyd, Jr., and R. P. Stephen Davis, Jr., "Explaining Mississippian Origins in East Tennessee," in *The Mississippian Emergence,* ed. Bruce D. Smith (Washington, D.C.: Smithsonian Institution Press, 1990), 191.

9. Charles Hudson, *The Southeastern Indians* (Knoxville: University of Tennessee Press, 1976), 59; Schroedl et al., "Explaining Mississippian Origins," 191.

10. Charles Hudson, *The Southeastern Indians,* 55.

All of these mounds should be understood as religious objects. They were icons, the embodiment of mythological forces in matter artfully shaped and publicly presented. Perhaps more than any other thing, these mounds distinguished the religion of the Woodland people from that of their ancestors.

From around 700–1000 C.E. the next important transformation took place, culminating in the more complex form of society known as Mississippian. While archaeologists have yet to explain this change, they agree that an increase in reliance upon corn production was central.[11] Some Woodland Indians in the Mississippi Valley greatly intensified their production of a new type of corn, "eastern flint," which proved more suited to the region's climate than earlier varieties. A religious motivation may have been at work. Corn may have been considered "food for the gods." Increasing its culture may have been a ritual, moral act. In any case, the increased production of corn evoked a new range of iconographic and mythological meanings. For instance, it was probably at this time that stories concerning the Corn Mother first became central to the religious life of Southeastern Indians. The Corn Mother allowed herself to be cut to pieces and buried in the earth in order that she might return as maize to feed her human children. While specific to the Southeast, this type of narrative resembles those found in other cultures involved in cereal production.[12]

With increased production of corn came the need for "large-scale food storage" and protection for dispersed farmsteads. The solution came in the form of a fortified center where food could be stored and distributed. In part, this development was pragmatic. In part, it was religious, for when it came to locating and legitimating a communal center, the proto-Mississippians did not hesitate to associate it with archetypal symbolism tied to mortuary mounds. The mortuary mound, often of pyramidal shape with a flat top, became the administrative, physical, and religious center of Mississippian society. In some cases, however, the sequence of change was not so simple: culture, architecture, settlement patterns could change *before* maize agriculture was

---

11. John E. Kelly, "Range Site Community Patterns and the Mississippian Emergence," in *The Mississippian Emergence*, 144; James A. Brown, Richard A. Kerber, and Howard D. Winters, "Trade and the Evolution of Exchange Relations at the Beginning of the Mississippian Period," in *The Mississippian Emergence*, 257.

12. John H. Blitz, *Ancient Chiefdoms of the Tombigbee* (Tuscaloosa: University of Alabama Press, 1993), 18–19.

well entrenched. This points to the multidimensional aspect of the Mississippian emergence, its dependence upon cultural and religious innovation as well as material and practical change.[13]

Mississippian mounds were built by communal labor, in multiple stages, in periodic rites motivated by symbolic crises.[14] The community would add a new blanket of earth to the mound, symbolically bury-ing it and restoring its purity. Its purity was important, for the mound was the most important sacred icon created by Mississippian Indians. It functioned "as both a cenotaph and an icon, both an empty tomb, a monument honoring an important person or event, and a holy place, a contact point between the sacred and the secular."[15] A true *axis mundi*, the mound constituted a sacred center, a place where earth met sky. Not surprisingly, it was the place where the most important rites of the Mississippians were performed. Yet, if all Mississippian town dwellers participated in constructing, renewing, and protecting the mound, not all had equal access to it. Unlike Woodland society, Mississippian so-ciety was hierarchical. Access to the top of the mound was limited to an elite class of chiefs and priests.[16]

Chiefs belonged to "privileged unilineal descent groups or clans."[17] They possessed authority because they had special religious status. They controlled "esoteric knowledge" related to warfare and mythological beings such as the winged snake and enjoyed superior access to the supreme sky being. In life and death, the chiefs' clan wore, possessed, and manipulated specially crafted objects of rare materials that symbol-ized their influence in warfare and cosmogonic matters. These objects included embossed copper plates, engraved shell cups, and monolithic axes. Paramount chiefs — chiefs of mound centers that exercised au-thority over other mound centers — enjoyed a monopoly on prestige

---

13. Brown et al., "Trade and the Evolution of Exchange Relations," in *The Mississippian Emergence*, 257.
14. Vernon James Knight, Jr., "The Institutional Organization of Mississippian Religion," *American Antiquity* 51, no. 4 (1986): 675–87; Frank T. Schnell, Vernon J. Knight, Jr., and Gail S. Schnell, *Cemochechobee: Archaeology of a Mississippian Ceremonial Center on the Chattahoochee River* (Gainesville: University Press of Florida, 1981), 142–45.
15. Richard A. Krause, "The Death of the Sacred: Lessons from a Mississippian Mound in the Tennessee River Valley," *Journal of Alabama Archaeology* 36 (December 1990): 94.
16. John F. Scarry, "Mississippian Emergence in the Fort Walton Area: The Evolution of the Cayson and Lake Jackson Phases," in *The Mississippian Emergence*, 231, 235; John H. Blitz, "Big Pots for Big Shots: Feasting in a Mississippian Community," *American Antiquity* 58, no. 1 (1993): 80–96; Blitz, *Ancient Chiefdoms*, 17; Charles Hudson, *The Southeastern Indians*, 80–82.
17. Knight, "The Institutional Organization."

goods like these. In less complex polities, this may not have been true. In simple chiefdoms, laypeople may also have had access to prestige goods.[18]

Priests apparently administered a temple-based cult of ancestors. The Mississippian temple featured stone, wood, or ceramic statuary of human figures, often in the throes of birth or death. Not chiefs, but possessing unique access to the temple mound and the forces of life and death, priests may have served an important mediatory role between the elite religious institution centered on warfare and that communal one centered on fertility. On the one hand, they advised chiefs and protected the sanctity of the chiefly lineage. On the other, they supervised the ceremonies that celebrated the life cycle of corn and renewed the mound itself.

During the Mississippian period, the ancestors of the Creeks lived on isolated farmsteads, in villages, within simple chiefdoms, or among one of three or four paramount chiefdoms. The largest and politically most stratified chiefdom in Creek country was called Coosa, located on the upper and middle Coosa river. Other paramount chiefdoms existed on the lower Tallapoosa and lower Chattahoochee, and farther to the west, east, and south. These were dynamic polities, sometimes in conflict, and linked by a trade network to much of North America. Nearly everyone of them was severely impacted by the Soto *entrada.*

From 1539 to 1543, a Spanish military expedition led by Hernando de Soto traveled across the Southeast searching for gold. This encounter produced novel interpretations and mutual disaster. Southeastern Indians treated Soto as if he was a Mississippian leader, giving him the gifts befitting a visiting diplomat. Meanwhile, he compared the Native leaders to Spanish aristocrats, albeit "heathen" ones. As a Christian leader, he felt justified in exacting tribute and slaves from them, using violence often to gain his desires. His army devastated many towns and entire chiefdoms, enslaving hundreds of men, women, and children, and killing far more. Southeastern Indians, including some likely ancestors of the Creeks, attacked Soto's army at a site in what is now Alabama, but did not prevail. Soto escaped.[19]

---

18. John E. Kelly, "Range Site Community Patterns," 145; Brown et al., "Trade and the Evolution," 260; Paul D. Welch, "Mississippian Emergence in West-Central Alabama," in *The Mississippian Emergence,* 198; Blitz, *Ancient Chiefdoms,* 178.

19. Jerald T. Milanich, *Hernando de Soto and the Indians of Florida* (Tallahasee: University Press of Florida, Florida Museum of Natural History, 1993); Charles Hudson, *The Forgotten Centuries: Indians and Europeans in the American South, 1521–1704* (Athens: University of Georgia Press,

Soto and other Europeans brought devastating diseases in the six-teenth century. Smallpox, measles, and influenza killed the great majority of the region's population. The size of towns shrank in Coosa, and survivors spread themselves more thinly over the land. The col-lapse was even more dramatic in the lower Chattahoochee chiefdom. The chiefdom system of governance ended. In most places, mound building stopped.[20]

Given their central symbolic importance and sheer physical mag-nitude, it is understandable that Mississippian mounds have come to symbolize Mississippian religion. Nevertheless, we need to keep in mind that the mounds were merely part of the religious system of the period, and they represented only one particular phase of religious expression in a much longer history. Perhaps the best way to think of the Missis-sippian phase is as a Braudelian conjuncture between Creek religion and the chiefdom type of social formation. Temple mound construction signaled the onset of this conjuncture. When temple mounds stopped being built, it meant that the conjuncture had ended. It did not mean, however, that Creek religion stopped. Instead, Creek religion under-went a third transformation and blended with a new type of social organization.[21]

Communal religious forms came to the fore. What mattered most to postholocaust Creeks was not the prestige of the chief or the cult of the ancestors, but the wholeness of the village. Wholeness meant balance, between the spirit of war, symbolized by red, and the spirit of peace, symbolized by white. Wholeness meant equilibrium between the Upper World and its powers and the Lower World with its contrary powers. The Upper World was associated with power or order and regularity. It was symbolized by the light of the sun and associated with the god Maker of Breath. The Lower World was associated with its powers of creativity and fertility. It was incarnated in the prolific growth of plants in the moist, warm southern landscape. It was associated with the Corn Mother, who sacrificed her body to feed human beings. These

1994); George Sabo III, "Encounters and Images: European Contact and the Caddo Indians," *Historical Reflections / Réflexions Historiques* (Spring 1995): 1–26.

20. John W. Verano and Douglas H. Ubelaker, eds., *Disease and Demography in the America* (Washington, D.C.: Smithsonian Institution Press, 1992).

21. This religious system is described in Joel W. Martin, *Sacred Revolt: The Muskogees' Struggle for a New World* (Boston: Beacon, 1991), 17–45; William Bartram, *Travels through North and South Carolina, Georgia, East and West Florida, the Cherokee Country, the Extensive Territories of the Muscogulges, or Creek Confederacy, and the Country of the Choctaws* (New York: Penguin, 1988) [first published in the United States, 1791], 393–95.

two types of power were invoked in daily activities as well as in special ceremonies.

If they were concerned with ceremonial propriety, Creeks did not think of racial purity. Unlike Europeans in the Southeast who were busy outlawing intermarriage and writing Black Codes to regulate the activities of their African slaves, Creeks did not enforce ethnic exclusivity or draw tightly demarcated tribal boundaries. Throughout the seventeenth and eighteenth centuries, strangers came to live among the Creeks. Initially these included the remnant survivors of Native groups devastated by disease or European colonization: Yuchis, Tuasis, Taskigis, Napochies, Alabamas, Shawnees, Tamas, Guales, Apalachees, Timucuas, Stonos, and Natchez Indians. Later, they included many more Europeans and Africans, as the Spanish missionized Florida, the English founded Carolina (1670), and the French founded Louisiana (1699). In Creek country, diverse peoples brought their cultures into contact, created a southeastern "middle ground,"[22] and transformed one another as a result. As defined by Richard White, a "middle ground" consists of "an elaborate network of economic, political, cultural, and social ties" that enable two or more societies to engage in multiple forms of reciprocal exchange. Indians, European settlers, and African slaves traded deerskins, cloth, rum, corn, and horses, but they also intermarried, mixed genes, and produced new peoples; they also swapped ideas, songs, poems, stories, and symbols; they also exchanged and compared religious perspectives. By 1783, when the United States was founded, a great diversity of peoples lived among the Creeks, including Jews, Catholics, Anglicans, Lutherans, Methodists, Moravians, Baptists, Muslims, and practitioners of the religions of West Africa. One could argue that in terms of sheer diversity, cultural pluralism was stronger two hundred years ago than it is today. The difference is that two hundred years ago diverse peoples living in Creek towns were required to respect the dominant culture of the Creek (Muskogee)-speaking core population. They did so, to such an extent that some whites and blacks assimilated entirely and became Indians. The experience of cross-cultural contact, in other words, did not destroy Creek religion.

---

22. For the metaphor of "middle ground," see Richard White. *The Middle Ground: Indians, Empires, and Republics in the Great Lakes Region, 1650–1815* (New York: Cambridge University Press, 1991), 33. White applied the concept to one specific region. Here I do the same. In general, such "middle grounds" were rare. See my "From 'Middle Ground' to 'Underground': Southeastern Indians and the Early Republic," in David G. Hackess, ed., *Religion and American Culture* (New York: Routledge, 1995), 127–46.

Because contact brought literate people among the Creeks after 1540, we have far more records describing this phase of Creek religion than any prior phase. Using these documents and relying upon the Creeks' oral tradition, a rich portrait of this phase can be created. What follows is all too brief and hardly does justice to this phase, which I term "classic" Creek religion.

The ceremonial space at the center of classic Creek religion was not the Mississippian mound, but the town square: "A quadrangular space, enclosed by four open buildings, with rows of benches rising above one another." Every Creek was affiliated with a town square even if he lived in a village lacking one. Just as every Creek had a primary clan identity (that of his or her mother), each Creek was affiliated with a square-ground town, or *i:tálwa*. The most important political unit in the classic Creek world, it was governed by a council of clan elders, medicine people, and chiefs. This type of organization enabled Creeks to unite across clan lines, carry out collective projects such as clearing fields and performing the green corn ceremony, organize ball games against other towns, debate trade relations and political matters, and decide how to redistribute surplus corn.

Unlike the moundtop ceremonial platform, the square ground was accessible to all town dwellers, including non-Creeks. Like the mound, however, it was square in shape and decorated with art featuring cosmogonic beings associated with warfare. Like the mound, the square ground was the place where chiefs heard counsel and priests performed their rituals. Further, the square ground, like the mound, was renewed annually in a ceremony that sometimes involved symbolic "burial" under fresh, pure sand. Creek civic and ceremonial life centered on the square ground, and almost every village and individual was affiliated with a square-ground town, or *i:tálwa*. The square ground served not just as a place for social ranking, not just as sanctorium, but also as art gallery, armory and trophy room. In short, the square ground seems to have taken over and "communalized" much of the symbolism and practice associated with the mound.[23]

Richly imbued with social and symbolic meaning, the square ground inevitably served as the ceremonial center within which were performed many of the Creeks' most important ceremonies. During the warm

---

23. William Bartram, *Travels*, 360; Swan, "Position and State of Manners," 266–67; Knight, "The Institutional Organization," 683–84. The following analysis of classic Creek ceremonial life reproduces material from *Sacred Revolt*.

season, the square ground provided the place where men gathered to drink and then disgorge or spout *asi:*, "a strong decoction of the shrub well known in the Carolinas by the name of Cassina." Called the "black-drink" by European visitors because the liquid was dark as molasses, the beverage, rich in caffeine, was brewed daily from the leaves of *Ilex vomitoria* by ritual specialists in a small shed near the square ground. Shortly after dawn, young warriors warned "the people to assemble by beating a drum." All adult men within earshot were obligated to come and drink the decoction, for the beverage had a salutary social effect. A late eighteenth-century Anglo-American visitor reported that *asi:* "purifies" the Creeks "from all sin, and leaves them in a state of perfect innocence; ... it inspires them with an invincible prowess in war; ... it is the only solid cement of friendship, benevolence, and hospitality." The Creeks called the beverage the white-drink, despite its dark color, because it produced harmonious feelings that they associated with the color white.[24] By consuming the beverage regularly in the square ground during the warm season or the rotunda during the cold season, Creek men repeatedly reaffirmed their connection to the Maker of Breath.[25]

As important and ennobling as it was, the *asi:* ceremony had to be canceled if the world became spiritually imbalanced. This occurred when death stripped the square ground of one of its members. "If a man [or woman] dies in the town, the square is hung full of green boughs as tokens of mourning; and no black-drink is taken inside of it for four days." This interval provided sufficient time for the spirit of the dead person to depart the village. Unfortunately, no interval of time was sufficient, if the person had been murdered. "If a warrior or other Indian is killed from any town having a square, black-drink must be taken on the outside of the square; and every ceremony in its usual form is laid aside until satisfaction is had for the outrage." Until the dead person was avenged, the spirit of the deceased polluted the square ground and frustrated normal religious life.[26]

Whether it was a single murder or a large-scale war, bloodshed and conflict polluted and therefore canceled ceremonies devoted to peace and order. Just as the wrongful death of a single man prevented the

---

24. Swan, "Position and State of Manners," 266.
25. Bartram described the *asi:* and calumet ceremonies he witnessed in the rotunda of Autossee (*Travels*, 358–59), and Swan described the square ground version of the *asi:* rite he saw in Little Tallasee. ("Position and State of Manners" 266–67).
26. Swan, "Position and State of Manners," 265.

Creeks from performing their ordinary ceremonies, so war prevented them from performing their most important and serious communal rite, the *póskita* or Busk. Red, the color symbolizing war, temporarily supplanted white, the color symbolizing peace. Ceremonies of war supplanted the Busk. War chiefs sent messages to allied towns. Warriors sequestered themselves in the hot-house for four days and drank the purifying *miko hoyanidja* (willow bark tea). Shamans consulted auguries and prepared special protective medicines and talismans.[27]

In times of peace, however, the Busk could be performed. A ceremony requiring considerable preparation, involving the entire community, and carrying tremendous social and spiritual significance, the Busk was the Creeks' greatest rite. To match its meaning, one scholar has stated that Europeans or Anglo-Americans would have had to combine Thanksgiving, New Year's festivities, Yom Kippur, Lent, and Mardi Gras. An annual ceremony, the Busk ceremony lasted four days in smaller towns and eight days in important ones such as Cussetuh or Tuckabatchee. It almost always occurred in July or August. Linked to the ripening of the second or late crop of corn, the ceremony was the most important of twelve monthly feasts dedicated to the first fruits of horticulture and hunting. Other feasts celebrated the gathering of chestnuts, mulberries, and blackberries. In the Creeks' lunar calendar, the Busk took place at the time of "the big ripening moon," and its celebration marked the turning of the seasons from summer (primarily devoted to horticulture and harvest) to winter (primarily devoted to gathering and hunting).[28]

One of the crucial ritual acts of the Busk was the kindling of a new, pure fire. The fire was the people's link to their ancestors and to the power of the Upper World. Like the sun, it could illumine, but it could also burn. It was a powerful living presence that supported order and punished violations of the proper rules of behavior. In the Busk ceremony of Autossee, the making of new fire occurred on the fourth morning. In some square grounds, it was on the third morning. In Little Tallasee, the fire was ignited on the first day. "On the morning of the first day, the priest, dressed in white leather moccasins and stockings, with a white dressed deer-skin over his shoulders, repairs at break of day, unattended to the square. His first business is to create the new

---

27. Benjamin Hawkins, *Letters, Journals and Writings*, ed. C. L. Grant (Savannah, Ga.: Beehive Press, 1980), 1:324–25.
28. Hudson, *The Southeastern Indians*, 374–75; Hawkins, *Letters, Journals and Writings*, 1:322.

fire, which he accomplishes with much labor by the friction of two sticks. After the fire is produced, four young men enter at the openings of the four corners of the square, each having a stick of wood for the new fire; they approach the fire with much reverence, and place the ends of the wood they carry, in a very formal manner, to it." Specifically, the logs were placed so that they pointed "to the four cardinal points," invoking the symbolism of the entire world.

Once ignited and sufficiently kindled, the new fire, understood to be most pure, was an extraordinarily powerful embodiment of the sacred. It was used for cooking meat or warming hominy, but it also possessed the power to resanctify things, relationships and the entire community. During the Busk, the Creeks tapped this power in a series of carefully performed rites, the first and perhaps most important being the sacrifice of corn. By allowing the holy fire to burn and destroy the first ears of the new corn, the Creeks expressed their profound awareness that the corn had once belonged entirely to the sacred realm. In celebrating the primordial origins of maize, the Busk challenged the Creeks to remember that maize was rooted not just in little hills of earth, but in a mystery.[29]

The plant, as sacred myths related, was originally given to the Creeks by a woman. More precisely, corn came from the body of a primordial woman, an earth goddess. In one myth, "she washed her feet in water and rubbed them, whereupon what came from her feet was corn."[30] In another, she scratched "the front of one of her thighs, whereupon corn poured down into the riddle." In both of these stories, ungrateful males would rather not consume food thus produced. Always giving, the goddess ultimately sacrificed herself by telling these men to burn her body or drag her bloody corpse across the ground so that they might have future crops of corn. Thus, the story symbolized the way life came from death, the unlimited power of female fertility, and the important, but circumscribed, power of males to impose order upon that fertility. The myth reminded listeners that no matter how successfully they controlled the production of corn, maize was ultimately a gift given to the Creeks by a primordial mother.

---

29. Bartram, *Travels*, 399; Swan, "Position and State of Manners,"276–77; Hudson, *Southeastern Indians*, 365.

30. George E. Lankford, *Native American Legends: Southeastern Legends — Tales from the Natchez, Caddo, Biloxi, Chickasaw, and Other Nations* (Little Rock, Ark.: August House, 1987), 147, 155–56.

Just as Creek mythology affirmed the power of a corn goddess, Creeks esteemed the special powers of ordinary women. Women had access to sacred powers that men poorly understood. Because they knew the secrets of plants and fertility, women made better herbalists or medicine people and monopolized midwifery. Women's activities and experiences were also symbolized as sacred through ritual events. Among the Creeks, a woman's first menses signaled that she was moving from childhood to adulthood. This passage evoked an initiation ceremony. Pregnancy was a season also regulated by taboos, especially concerning food.[31]

Because men and women were considered to be "separate people" in touch with contrary types of cosmological power, Creek religion carefully regulated their relations. Men ventured out into the external forest world where violence was required. They could lose their humanity through encounters with formlessness. They could become possessed with the spirit of war or dehumanized by excessive anger and conflict. Women were not as exposed to these precise dangers. They controlled domestic compounds which were grouped according to matrilineal clans. Women reared children and fed men. However, if a menstruating woman fed a man or even came into contact with him, it would ruin his power to hunt. During their menses, women sequestered themselves. Their form was fluid during this period. Because they could not avoid menstruation and exposure to formlessness, women could not be counted on to regulate the affairs of the *i:tálwa*. Men had to do this work, to oversee the affairs of the square ground. Thus, while women fed men, men fed the sacred fire, the communal symbol and guardian of properly ordered life.[32]

Warfare, hunting, menstruation, and childbirth were but a few of the sacred times, seasons, events, and relationships that Creeks marked with ritual, signified through altered behaviors and sacralized through symbolic performances, exchanges, and punishments. The list could be extended indefinitely and would include sacred times that involved different subsets of Creek society — individuals, clans, men, women, villages, clusters of villages. It would include sacred times related to

31. Lyda Averill Taylor, "Alabama Field Notes," National Anthropological Archives, Smithsonian Institution, Washington D.C., MS, 1, 4; Hudson, *The Southeastern Indians*, 320. For a discussion of discourses and practices concerning menstruation among contemporary Muskogees, see Amelia R. Bell, "Separate People: Speaking of Creek Men and Women," *American Anthropologist* 92 (1990): 332–45.
32. Bell, "Creek Ritual," 81.

subsistence activities, others related to the human life cycle, and still others that were gender coded. Some ritual times corresponded to natural cycles, others responded to accidents, and still others occurred because of human initiative or historical events. Some rituals marked crises in social relations or responses to natural emergencies (famine, disease, drought).

Some rituals depended to a great extent upon specialists who possessed esoteric knowledge and practiced arcane magic, but many could be performed entirely without their participation. A survey of Creek rituals would show decisively that time for the Creeks was anything but homogeneous. It would also show that these times and rituals shared a common goal: to alter or restore the balance among contrary powers. Anything that altered or restored the balance was called *hiliswa* ("medicine"). When the medicine was good, and a proper balance was successfully achieved, things were said to be *sintackita* ("marked off").

As the nineteenth century dawned, the Creek world became terribly imbalanced. Traditional territorial boundaries had been transgressed by invading Europeans. Creeks faced a depleted supply of game and hunting grounds occupied by settlers. European Americans no longer gave generous gifts, and the rum trade brought debt and misery to villages throughout Creek country. Millions of acres of Creek land had already been ceded to European Americans, and the U.S. government systematically absorbed much of the land that remained in Creek hands. Government agents and Christian missionaries attempted to destroy Creek culture by teaching the virtues of commercial agriculture, a market economy, private property, and the patrilineal family. Simultaneously, wealthy cotton planters in Georgia, Tennessee, and Mississippi were calling for the extermination of the Creeks, and organizing militias to carry out this objective. This multidimensional crisis was deep, tore the people apart, and threatened their religious tradition to the core. To weather this crisis and preserve their sense of the sacred, the Creeks relied upon extensive intertribal syncretism, significant intercultural borrowing, and bold religious innovation.

In 1811, the Shawnee leader Tecumseh and his prophets visited the Creeks and promoted a new vision of pan-Indian solidarity. Inspired by this vision, nine thousand Creeks joined a massive religious movement that culminated in a revolt against the United States and the ongoing white invasion of their lands. The rebels blended elements present in the southeastern middle ground (the visions and ecstasies of Alabama prophets, Afro-Christian apocalypticism, a Shawnee dance, traditional Creek purification ceremonies, the European idea of the Book) and improvised new rituals, including attacks on cattle and chiefs. Restoring the symbolic boundaries between Indians and white became a religious duty; political revolt a sacred cause. Using the old and new, fusing the Native and non-Native, Creek rebels attempted to show that they were indeed still the masters of the land and all of its symbols. They sought to restore a lost balance. Similar anticolonial movements had occurred among other Native American groups, including the Guales (1576, 1597), the Tarahumaras (1616), the Powhatans (1622, 1644), the Apalaches (1647), the Timucuans (1656), the Pueblo peoples (1690), the Yamasees (1715), the Natchez (1729), the Delawares (1760), and the Shawnees (1805). Most of these revolts were decisively defeated by Europeans. The Creek revolt ended no differently. The Creeks were vastly outnumbered and outgunned by white militias from Georgia, Tennessee, and the Mississippi Territory.

After Andrew Jackson's army of Tennesseans and Cherokees crushed the Creek Redsticks' sacred revolt in March 1814 at the Battle of Horseshoe Bend, all Creeks confronted an unprecedented situation: they had become a dominated, increasingly colonized people. Not coincidentally, for the first time, Protestant missionaries settled in their villages. Associated with the invaders and all the pain they inflicted, missionaries received a hostile reception from Creek people. Creek officials forbade Christian preaching. When evangelicals insisted upon witnessing to Christ, townsmen pretended not to understand English. And, eager to guard their own religion, Creeks purposely kept aspects of it beyond the gaze of Christians. Tuckabatchee Creeks, for example, normally displayed their town's ancient copper plates during its *póskita* ceremony. During the 1820s, however, they banned whites from seeing these plates.

Creeks tried to hide other cherished ideas, beliefs, dances, and practices, but they also developed new stories and ceremonies to reinforce their sense of themselves as a separate, special people. Although Creek religion became that of a colonized people, it continued to express their determination to control their own interior lives, nurture their communities, and affirm their own Indianness.

In the 1830s, still not Christianized, the Creeks were removed forcibly from Alabama to the Arkansas Territory. They carried key symbols of their religion with them. For instance, Tuckabatchee people carried from Alabama to the west an ark containing sacred coals from their council fire. Each night of the journey the guardians of these coals used them to kindle a new fire and create fresh coals for the next day's travel. Additionally, six specially selected warriors carried Tuckabatchee's ancient copper plates, sacred items that traditionally were displayed only during that town's Busk ceremony. "Each one had a plate strapped behind his back, enveloped nicely in buckskin. They carried nothing else, but marched on, one before the other, the whole distance to Arkansas, neither communicating nor conversing with a soul but themselves, although several thousand were emigrating in company; and walking, with a solemn religious step one mile in advance of the others." Once they reached their destination, the Tuckabatchees carefully buried the plates at the center of a new square ground and set the coals in a new hearth. Other groups built additional ceremonial centers around "fires" transported from Alabama. Thus, the Creeks began a new life away from their ancestral homeland. As these significant gestures suggested, even as they embraced life in yet another new world, they remained oriented toward and sustained by their traditional sense of the sacred.[33]

After Removal, "warfare no longer structured Creek interaction as it had previously."[34] Creeks started using English names, settled in a more dispersed manner, and after initial resistance, eventually formed dozens of Baptist and Methodist churches. These churches' architecture, governance, and ritual calendar were distinctively, traditionally Creek. They offered an alternative to participation in the rituals and dances associated with ceremonial "stomp" grounds. Indeed, the churches eventually formed an alliance in opposition to stomp grounds. They became substitute *i:tálwa* in their own right. Thus, a Creek can be considered a Creek without being affiliated with a square ground. This division is the essential thing that defines the modern period of Creek religion. The division is so strong that "clan relations are not recognized by members of one division in interaction with members of the other."[35] (Creeks are divided into more than eight clans. An individual's primary clan affiliation is his or her mother's clan identity.) However, if the division between churches and stomp grounds is stable, individuals can move from one division to the other, depending upon their relationships, desires, and spiritual needs.

---

33. Albert James Pickett, History *of Alabama, and Incidentally of Georgia and Mississippi, from the Earliest Period* (Birmingham, Ala.: Birmingham Book and Magazine Company, 1962), 86–87.
34. Bell, "Creek Ritual," 67, 72.
35. Ibid., 129.

The fact that modern Creeks do not affiliate with a square ground may seem to be a significant departure from tradition, if not an actual decline. Some traditionalist Creeks see it this way. However, the departure may not be as radical as it seems. Creek churches incorporate much of the traditional Creek symbolism.[36] Moreover, most Creeks understand the division between square grounds and churches as yet another instance that proves the wisdom of deep Creek principles. Specifically, Creeks like to structure things as an interaction of two separate categories. They envisage the world as convergence of contraries, without a final synthesis. Other examples of this include the contrast between men and women, between "mixed-bloods" and "full-bloods," between the formless and the formed, between the powers of the Lower World and those of the Upper World. The division between churches and square grounds, then, is but another instance of a basic cultural imperative.

The contrast between churches and square grounds reinforces the basic Creek teaching: a full life depends upon contraries locked in a dynamic relation where neither loses its distinctiveness. In this religious system, for instance, marriage is called *sihokita*, "two standing up together." The emphasis is not on the union but on the relation. This principle is seen even in the preparation of quintessential Creek foods. In the spring, Creeks enjoy wild onion dinners. Onions represent the wild external realm. They are cooked in eggs, which symbolize female power and its ability to domesticate the external. The definitive Creek food, *sofki:*, is made in almost every Creek home. It consists largely of corn, which is closely associated with female power, cooked with wood ashes. The ashes are produced by men who have "killed" something from the external realm and brought it home (trees). *Sofki:* and the pots it is boiled in have iconic power. This food's preparation is tied to womanhood and can signal a readiness for matrimony. Its consumption seals friendship. As in so many other areas of their lives, so it is in the preparation of foods like *sofki:* and wild onions. The goal of Creek ritual life is not a collapse of differences, but their careful articulation in a way that maintains a good balance. This ritual process has served the Creeks well, enabling them to appropriate new peoples and ideas, without losing their separate identities.[37]

---

36. Lester E. Robbins, "The Persistence of Traditional Religious Practices among Creek Indians" (Ph.D. diss., Southern Methodist University, 1976).

37. Bell, "Creek Ritual," 89–93, 143, 146.

There are thirty thousand Creeks and nine thousand Seminoles in Oklahoma carrying forward the Creek religious tradition. The tradition exists in communities outside of Oklahoma as well. In the eighteenth and nineteenth centuries, many Creeks migrated to Florida while others moved west to Texas. In Florida, they became known as the Seminoles. Most were removed to Oklahoma but two hundred remained behind. Today numbering two thousand, many Florida Seminoles continue to speak Creek, perform the green corn ceremony, and organize themselves by clans. Meanwhile in Texas, Alabama-Koasatis also carry forward many ancestral traditions from the days when they belonged to the historic Creek Confederacy. The story is somewhat different among the Creeks remaining in Alabama, numbering around two thousand. Long surrounded by a hostile white majority, they have been subject to nearly two centuries of pressure to acculturate. Today most of them are Christians, participating in a wide variety of Protestant denominations, including Free Will Baptist, Holiness, and Episcopal churches. Nevertheless, in the past two decades, Alabama Creeks have begun to recover their ancestral religious traditions. They have attended meetings of national Indian organizations, resumed the wearing of traditional clothing during an annual powwow, learned how to make war dance costumes, performed sweat bath rituals, and conducted Native American Church services (connected to the peyote religion). Alabama Creeks have also deepened their connections to Oklahoma Creeks and to classic Creek religion.

They hired a traditionalist Oklahoma Creek to teach Native heritage and Creek language classes, have attended Creek religious ceremonies in Oklahoma, and have discussed "reestablishing in Alabama a traditional 'square ground' with a properly sanctified 'fire.' "[38] Perhaps one day the green corn ceremony will be danced again where it was first performed, near a river in Alabama. If this happens, it may signal the end of a long phase of colonialism and exile, and the beginning of a new chapter in the history of one of the most persistent and dynamic living traditions in the New World.

---

38. J. Anthony Paredes, "Tribal Recognition and the Poarch Creek Indians," in *Indians of the Southeastern United States in the Late 20th Century*, ed. J. Anthony Paredes (Tuscaloosa: University of Alabama Press, 1992), 137–38. See also James H. Howard and Willie Lena, *Oklahoma Seminoles: Medicines, Magic, and Religion* (Norman: University of Oklahoma Press, 1984).

᪥ **F O U R** ᪥

Wiping the Tears: Lakota Religion in the Twenty-first Century

William K. Powers

More popularly known by the derogatory term *Sioux*, the Lakota are the western division of the *Oceti Sakowin*, or Seven Fireplaces, who after migrating to the region of Minnesota from the south, formed a confederacy of politically and linguistically related nations.[1] They lived in semisedentary villages; cultivated corn, squash, and beans; and engaged in seasonal buffalo hunting. After losing battles with Algonquian-speakers to the east, defeats brought about by their enemies' acquisition of guns from the British, the Lakota migrated westward, occupying what are now the states of North and South Dakota, and parts of Montana, Wyoming, Nebraska, and Colorado. They earned the reputation of being formidable warriors and quickly dispersed other tribes living in the region of the Black Hills, namely, the Kiowa, and within 150 years became the most famous equestrian, buffalo-hunting Indians of the northern Plains. After their encounters with whites, particularly the famous Red Cloud Wars of the 1860s, they signed a treaty with the United States in 1868 at Fort Laramie, Wyoming, after which they were placed on the Great Sioux Reservation in what was then Dakota Territory. More notoriety came after they defeated George Armstrong

---

1. *Sioux* is a French corruption of the Algonquian *nadowesiih*, meaning snakes. Since 1970, Lakotas have consciously attempted, with some success, to replace it with their rightful appellation (Lakota, Nakota, Dakota). However, most literature continues to refer to them as "Sioux." The major divisions of the Seven Fireplaces are the Mdewakantunwan, Sissitunwan, Wahpetunwan, and Wahpekute, collectively known as Santee, who speak the dialect Dakota; the Ihanktunwan and Ihanktunwanna, collectively known as Yankton, who speak Nakota; and Titunwan, also known as Teton, the largest and westernmost division, who speak Lakota. Over time, each of the Seven Fireplaces in turn divided into seven components. The Lakota, from which most of the material for this article is drawn, divided into the Oglala, Sicangu, Mnikowoju, Hunkpapa, Oohenunpa, Itazipco, and Sihasapa. For a detailed account of the political and linguistic structure, see W. K. Powers 1977.

Custer at the Battle of the Little Big Horn on June 25, 1876, and again because of their involvement in the Ghost Dance movement which ended with the assassination of Sitting Bull on December 7, 1890, and the wanton killing of 260 Lakota men, women, and children at Wounded Knee, South Dakota on December 29 of the same year.[2]

The shift from an essential Great Lakes culture to Plains hunting economy had a dramatic effect on Lakota religion in the sense that even today we find in their myths and rituals some residual artifacts of an earlier agricultural way of life. However, Lakota religion, which paid homage and respect to the main source of life, the buffalo, as well as the tumultuous Plains environment, took on a character of its own with only minimal references to its woodlands origins. The buffalo continues to be a major symbol of Lakota religion today, and its attendant myths and rituals have emerged as a sine qua non of Plains Indian belief. Not only has the tenacity of Lakota religion tended to influence the religions of other tribes, many non-Indian people have developed a fascination for its ceremonial life, especially the Lakota version of the vision quest, sweat lodge, and Sun Dance. Indeed, the Lakota Way has even reached Europe, where Lakota medicine men frequently travel and conduct sacred ceremonies in Paris, Vienna, Berlin, and Moscow, to name just a few cities.[3]

The persistence of Lakota religion and culture against overwhelming odds has been the subject of my own interest over the past half century. Not only have Lakota ceremonies been retained over a long period of time albeit changed to meet the needs of their worshipers, the Lakota have the ability to incorporate religious ideas from other tribes and even non-Indians, thus preventing Lakotas from becoming totally Christianized even though some live quite comfortably between more than one (sometimes more than two) religious systems. This process of transforming "foreign" ideas into their own religious structure is a phenomenon I have called "Lakotification."[4]

The concept of individual and community renewal eventuated by the proper performance of sacred rituals is a common theme in Lakota religion. Recognizing that their beliefs and rituals have been constantly

2. For the definitive work on the Ghost Dance, see Mooney 1896. For a translation of Ghost Dance songs, see W. K. Powers 1990a.

3. I have treated this far-ranging influence of Lakota religion on other tribes and non-Indians in "Beyond the Vision: Trends toward Ecumenicism in American Indian Religions," Powers 1987.

4. Particularly in my "Dual Religious Participation: Stratagems of Conversion among the Lakota," Powers 1987.

challenged by Christianity, Lakotas see themselves continuously fighting the influences of non-Lakota religion and culture, much of which
has brought about what they perceive to be the cause of their current state of living, one besieged with hardship. One important point
of cultural reference is the suffering caused at the hands of the U.S.
government at Wounded Knee. In an effort to memorialize the fateful
event, some Lakota spiritual leaders began a reenactment of the fateful
ride of Big Foot and his followers from the Cheyenne River reservation
to Wounded Knee Creek in an effort to deal with the wrongs of the
past. The prayers offered up at the end of the ride in which Lakotas
participated in ceremonies acknowledging the massacre of Lakota men,
women, and children, as well as subsequent rituals that seek to assuage
the sorrow associated with the loss of innocent life, have been deemed
Istamniyan pakintapi, "Wiping the Tears." It has been a regular focus
of all contemporary Lakota rituals, one that is likely to become even
stronger in the twenty-first century.

Creation

According to Lakota mythology, before humans were created a pantheon of supernatural beings lived in a vague undifferentiated celestial
space.[5] The paramount creative force is Takuskanskan ("Something
That Moves"), also known as Tobtob ("Four Times Four," in reference
to the sixteen categories of supernatural powers that control the universe), and later as Wakantanka, which since missionary intervention
has become the generic gloss for "God." In the beginning, the chief
god is the Sun, who is married to the Moon. They have one daughter,
Wohpe ("Falling Star"). Old Man is married to Old Woman, and they
have one daughter Ite ("Face") who is married to Tate ("Wind"). They
also have four sons who are known as the Four Winds. The devious
trickster Inktomi ("Spider") conspires with Old Man and Old Woman
to increase their daughter's status by arranging an assignation between
Ite and the Sun in the Moon's absence. Once the Moon discovers the
affair, she tells Takuskanskan, who ordains a series of rewards and punishments for those involved. He gives Moon her own domain, and the
separation of the Sun and the Moon creates both night and day and

---

5. The authorities for this attenuated form of the creation story are M. N. Powers 1986; W. K.
Powers 1977; and Walker 1917.

the monthly cycle. He also rewards Tate by giving him and his sons their own domain: the Lodge of the Wind, a metaphor for the earth itself, which is created when each of the four sons is assigned his own quarter, thus establishing not only the firmament but also the year. From that time on, conceptually and linguistically, time and space are integrally related.

Takuskanskan then punishes Ite by giving her a second ugly face, thereafter to be known as Anukite ("Face on Both Sides").[6] She and her parents are ostracized from the heavens and forced to live on the edge of the earth. The Sun, because he is chief, cannot be punished, but Inktomi also is sent to the world, where he will forever deceive its inhabitants. Soon after the earth is established, the Four Winds are joined by a fifth wind, Wamniomni ("Whirlwind"), the presumed offspring of an illicit affair between Sun and Ite, who is not given his own direction. Wohpe falls to earth and lives with the South Wind. The South Wind and Wohpe adopt Wamniomni and come to symbolize the ideal Lakota marriage.

The ostracized supernaturals soon become bored with their life on earth, and Ite, now Anukite, prevails upon Inktomi to find her relations, whom she calls the Buffalo Nation. Transformed into a wolf, Inktomi travels to the bowels of the earth, where he discovers a village of humans. He convinces one of the leaders Tokahe ("First") to accompany him to the surface of the earth, where he shall reveal to him the wonders of the real world. Although some of the people are skeptical, Tokahe agrees to follow Inktomi to the surface. The two finally reach the earth through a cave now believed to be Wind Cave in the Black Hills.

Once upon the earth, Inktomi shows Tokahe the green grass and blue sky and all the animals, birds, insects, plants, and marvels of the

---

6. The duplicity of Anukite, also symbolized by Winyan Nunpapika "Double Woman," serves as a strong metaphor for choice. The appearance of either in a vision requires the visionary to make an important decision in his or her life. For example, Double Woman frequently appears to a man holding a burden strap in one hand and a bow and arrows in the other. If the man chooses the burden strap he forevermore is required to behave as a winkte ("two-spirit person," or *berdache*). The idea of choice is further strengthened by the fact that Double Women are frequently shown in pictographic drawings as being connected by a thong tied around their waists in the center of which dangles either a baby or a medicine bag. The evil aspect of Double Woman is equated with Sintesapelawin ("Black-tailed Deer Woman"), who seduces hunters on a lonely trail and then reveals her horrible face, causing them to go insane. The point here is that the representation of Double Woman as inseparable underscores that a person's destiny is more or less of his or her own choosing. For further discussion of Double Woman see Theisz 1988 and DeMallie 1983.

earthly universe. He shows him how to make fire, boil water, hunt animals, and cook food. Tokahe tastes buffalo soup and all the savory food that the earth produces and is amazed. Inktomi also teaches him how to build and raise a tipi and how to make moccasins and other clothing, as well as bows and arrows for the hunt. Impressed by his introduction by Inktomi to culture, Tokahe returns to his subterranean village and convinces his people to follow him back to the earth to witness its wonders for themselves. Despite the admonitions of an old woman not to follow Tokahe, six other men and their families join him for the expedition back to the earth. However, when they arrive, buffalo are scarce, the season has turned cold, and they live in hardship. Anukite shows them her ugly face. Unable to find their way back, they remain on earth to found the Seven Fireplaces.

The Sacred Pipe

In the transition from myth to reality, Wohpe, the Falling Star, is transformed into Ptehincalasanwin ("White Buffalo Calf Woman"), who is recognized as the essential mediator between the Creator and the common people. Historically mentioned in at least three winter counts for the year 1797–98, this mysterious woman appears to two Lakota hunters who are searching for buffalo during a period of famine.[7] As they survey the landscape they see in the distance a figure approaching them. As it comes closer, they recognize the figure as a beautiful woman wearing no clothes but carrying an object wrapped in fur. One of the two hunters immediately is desirous of her and advances toward her; at that point he is instantly enveloped in a mist, which when it lifts reveals him lying on the ground, a skeleton through which snakes are crawling. She tells the other hunter not to be afraid and to return to the village and tell the chief that he should prepare a council lodge and that she will arrive on the next morning. The second scout hurries back and tells of the mysterious woman and at once the people prepare the lodge.[8]

---

7. These accounts may be found in the Colhoff winter count (W. K. Powers 1963); Baptiste Good count (Mallery 1986); and the Ben Kindle count (Beckwith 1930).

8. There are several versions of the coming of the pipe. See Densmore 1918; M. N. Powers 1986. Although the original story states that the White Buffalo Calf Woman was nude, more recent "missionary" versions have her attired in a dress, either white or red buckskin. For a discussion of the White Buffalo Calf Woman as culture heroine see M. N. Powers 1990.

The next morning they all assemble and she appears carrying the object. She enters in a clockwise direction and takes her seat at the place of honor at the back of the lodge.[9] She tells the people that she has brought them something very important and that in time of need they must pray with it. She unwraps the bundle, revealing a sacred pipe. She instructs the people how to fill the pipe bowl and smoke it whenever they require help from Wakantanka. She then commences to teach them the Wicoh'an Wakan Sakowin ("Seven Sacred Ceremonies"), which will become the foundation of Lakota religion.

After teaching the people, she tells them to take a good look at her and that she is leaving. She leaves the council lodge, continuing her clockwise direction as she bids the village farewell. As she ascends a small knoll, she suddenly turns into a black buffalo calf. As she progresses farther up the hill, she turns into a red buffalo calf, then a yellow buffalo calf. When she reaches the summit she turns into a white buffalo calf, looks back at the people, and then disappears. The colors of the buffalo calves are symbolic of the Four Winds: black for the West, the direction at which all ceremonies begin; red for the North; yellow for the East; and white for the South. Forever, she will be known as the White Buffalo Calf Woman, the original pipe will be called the Calf Pipe, and sacred ceremonies always will be performed in a circular, clockwise direction. Above all, the White Buffalo Calf Woman emerges as a model of Lakota virtue.

Ritual Specialists

Both men and women serve as ritual specialists and as such mediate between the supernaturals and the common people. However, far more men than women direct or otherwise participate in religious ceremonies.

The conventional terms *wicasa wakan* ("holy man") and *winyan wakan* ("holy woman"), routinely translated as "medicine man" and "medicine woman," are actually class markers for a number of men and women endowed with supernatural powers who conduct various types of rituals the differences and similarities of which are largely dependent on the source of their special powers, to wit, visions. For ex-

---

9. Since the doorway of every lodge faces east, the honored place called catku is at the west thus underscoring the importance of the first direction.

ample, among the various *wicasa wakan* we find men who cure (*wapiye*)
illnesses with supernatural aid from animals and birds, such as bear doctors and eagle doctors. Also there are those called *Yuwipi*, men who in
a darkened room cure patients afflicted with "Indian sickness." Others
cure by sucking out the source of evil in the patient's body by means of
a hollow bone. And still others called *Pejuta wicasa* ("medicine men")
cure their patients with herbs.

Also included in the class are those who perform sacred im-
personations (*Wakan kaga*) acting out their visions publicly. These
performances, depending on their sources, are called by such names
as *Mato kaga* ("bear impersonation" or "performance") or *Heyoka kaga*
("clown performance," the well-known "contrarians" of the Plains who
acted in an antinatural manner), and *Hehaka kaga* ("elk performance,"
a well-known society of dreamers who had power over women). Others
of this class included the lesser-known *wicahmunga* ("wizards"), who
cause harm to people by casting spells that travel over sound waves
(the verb *hmunga* means "to buzz"). Finally, there were the equally
well-known *winkte*, or "would-be women" — men who, as a result of
a vision from the Double Woman, dressed like women and engage in
female activities.[10]

Women's classes are similar in that some serve exclusively as curers
(*wapiye*), mediating through supernatural means as well as by herbal
curing (*pejuta winyan*, literally "medicine woman"). Lesser known are
the female contraries, heyoka and the *wihmunga* or "witches."

Most medicine men and women have similar childhood experiences
that lead them ultimately to the religious life. Most start with a mystical experience when they are still prepubescent, followed by some
personal misfortune. After consulting with another medicine man or
woman the initiate is instructed to go on a vision quest. The vision is
then interpreted, and depending on the nature of the vision, the initiate is informed that it is his calling to become a sacred person. After
this period, the candidate serves as an apprentice with an established
medicine man or woman after which time he or she becomes an established practitioner of major rituals such as the Sun Dance or, more
usually, curing rituals.

---

10. For a description of these sacred performances, see Wissler 1912, who erroneously calls
them "dream cults." The term *woihanble* means both "dream" and "vision" in Lakota. However,
dreams are experienced in sleep and visions, while fully awake.

In order to maintain powers, ritual specialists are required to go on vision quests, usually at some prominent place such as Bear Butte in the Black Hills to renew their power. There they learn new songs and receive instructions from their supernatural helpers with whom they speak in a sacred language.[11] Medicine men and women are frequently competitive with each other, and sooner or later as the medicine man or woman gets old, he or she abdicates his or her position and retires to a more secular life, thus making way for a new and younger medicine man or woman to intervene.

Today, the generic *wicasa / winyan wakan* are better translated as spiritual leader or spiritual adviser, even though the Native terms remain the same.

The Seven Sacred Ceremonies

Although the U.S. government attempted to halt or at least severely constrict Lakota religion at the end of the nineteenth century, the Seven Sacred Ceremonies have survived until the present day as the substrate of Lakota religion.[12] There is no record of the order in which the White Buffalo Calf Woman taught the ceremonies to the Lakota, but there is a general agreement that the Sweat Lodge and Vision Quest are the oldest.[13]

The Sweat Lodge, called *Initipi* ("life lodge") or *Oinikagapi* ("place where they renew life"), serves as a prelude to all other ceremonies and stands as an important ritual unto itself. The Sweat Lodge itself is constructed from sixteen willow saplings whose ends are inserted into the ground and tops tied together to form a domal shape symbolic of the Lakota universe. The Sweat Lodge as such is called the Lodge of the Wind. The saplings were originally covered with buffalo robes to form a shelter completely light-proof, but now they are covered with blankets or canvases. In the center of the Sweat Lodge, the medicine man digs a pit about three feet deep. An opening faces the East, and a

11. Sacred language is used by spiritual leaders in prayer as well as in philosophical discourse about religion. For examples of sacred language called wakaniye, see W. K. Powers 1986.

12. Details of these ceremonies may be found in Brown 1953; Neihardt 1932; M. N. Powers 1986; W. K. Powers, 1977; and Walker 1917, 1980. For a lengthy discussion of Neihardt's creation of Black Elk, see DeMallie 1984. For a critique of Neihardt's omissions in Black Elk's life, see W. K. Powers 1990b.

13. The Seven Sacred Ceremonies have been described by a number of historians and anthropologists. See particularly Brown 1953; Densmore 1918; Neihardt 1932; W. K. Powers 1977, 1982, 1986; Walker 1917, 1980, among others.

trail of earth leading several feet from the opening ends with a sacred hill upon which a sacred pipe is placed. Nearby, a fire tender builds a fire of pine on which stones collected from a creek bed are placed and heated until white-hot. When the ceremony is about to begin, the naked adepts enter the space and sit shoulder to shoulder. The medicine man then enters and sits at the north side of the doorway with a bucket of water and dipper. When all have entered, the fire tender hands the heated stones to the medicine man, who places them in the center hole. The first four rocks symbolize the Four Winds; the next two, the zenith and nadir, the seventh, the center of the universe. After the seven stones have been so placed more stones are handed in until the hole is filled. Sometimes as many as thirty stones are set in place.

In the old days, adepts would carry buffalo tail switches, which they used to slap their bodies to increase circulation. Once all were seated, and the stones were in place, the medicine man would instruct the fireman[14] to close the door flap of the lodge, thus rendering the space totally dark. It was during this phase that the medicine man would sprinkle water from the bucket onto the heated stones, thereby creating a rush of steam. In the darkness the spirits would be invoked and some would enter the Sweat Lodge where they would help the medicine man and participants in curing sickness or otherwise fulfilling their requests.

The medicine man called for the doorway of the lodge to be opened four times during the ceremony, and each time the fireman would hand in the pipe for all to smoke. When all had finished smoking and praying with the pipe, the doorway was closed and more songs were sung. At the conclusion of the ceremony, all the participants exited, dried themselves off with fresh sage, and gave thanks for the aid of the spirit helpers.

The Vision Quest, called *Hanbleceya* ("Crying for a Vision"), originally was a ceremony for males that first was conducted at pubescence and that carried over throughout their lives. Since the 1970s, females also participate. It is incumbent upon all medicine men to embark on the Vision Quest because it is one of the most important sources of their continued power.

---

14. "Fireman" is the English term for a man who builds the fire, heats the stones, and hands them into the medicine man using a pair of paddles, or more recently, a pitchfork or shovel. He also opens and closes the doorway and keeps the pipe when it is not in use. The general Lakota term is *wawokiya* ("helper").

Although Vision Quests characteristically take place on a hill, where a medicine man places the initiate for one to four days, some Vision Quests have taken place along dry creek beds and other isolated places. During the Vision Quest, a man or woman fasts for a predetermined number of days. The space upon which he or she stands is demarcated with offerings to the Four Winds. Since about 1900 the favorite place for a Vision Quest has been on a hill where a shallow pit has been dug. During the quest the adept is cautioned to take refuge in the pit during the nighttime and reappears only to pray with the pipe to the four directions until a vision is received. Once the vision appears, the adept is removed from the hill by the medicine man, and the latter interprets the significance of the vision to the adept.

The nature of the vision is normally kept private between the adept and his adviser. However, it is clear that visions are experienced during the candidate's waking hours and not while asleep.[15]

The Ghost-Keeping Ceremony, known as *Wanagi Wicagluhapi*, is performed for a loved one who has died. Although reportedly restricted as a ceremony to honor the spirit of a favorite son by a mother, the ceremony has been performed widely by any member of a family who is willing to take on the ordeal of *wasigla* ("mourning"). It is believed that a spirit lingers near the place of death for one year. During this time, a relative must keep a lock of hair wrapped in a soft buckskin. On nice days the spirit bundle must be placed in the sun and removed if there are any strong winds on which it is believed spirits travel. The spirit is fed every day. After one year, the spirit is fed for the last time and is thus freed to travel to the hereafter. Those keeping the spirit must dedicate all their time to guarding the spirit tipi and thus cannot hunt or leave the vicinity for any reason. On the day of the spirit's release, the family in mourning provides a great feast for its relatives, and those who helped the mourner over the year are given gifts.

Today, the elaborate and time-consuming Ghost-Keeping Ceremony has been supplanted with the Memorial Feast (*Wokiksuye Wohanpi*). In principle, the spirit is kept for the same length of time but normally is fed in the family kitchen or dining room. At the end of the year, the relatives invite their entire *tiyospaye*[16] to a feast, and the spirit is

---

15. See Neihardt 1932 for Black Elk's famous vision; also W. K. Powers 1982 and Walker 1980.

16. *Tiyospaye* is a unit of social organization comprising persons who are related consanguineally. Thus one is born into a *tiyospaye* and forever remains affiliated with it. Since in early days persons were required to marry outside their own *tiyospaye*, it is probably a residual of an

fed for the last time. One of the characteristics of the contemporary Memorial Feast is the rather elaborate meal and giveaway, the latter of which can cost several thousand dollars.

Today a smaller ceremony may be held after the wake and burial. Mourners usually bring food to the place of the wake, where they sit and sometimes ostensibly mourn over the casket. The body is most frequently buried in a Christian cemetery, in which case the Lakota ceremony is augmented with Christian burial. Frequently there is yet another ceremony when the tombstone is erected. Star quilts are tied around the tombstone, and close friends are designated to untie the quilts, which are given to them for performing the honor.

Although there are no puberty ceremonies for boys, girls undergo the *Awicalowanpi* ("they sing over them") at the onset of menstruation. The girl's family erects a lodge and the medicine man sings songs while waving wands over her. The medicine man then engages in a mock courtship with the girl, imitating the behaviors of a buffalo. The girl then removes her child's dress and replaces it with that of a woman. She is then ever after instructed to sit in the manner of a woman with her legs together and feet to one side. During her reproductive years she will be forbidden to perform sacred rituals, and during her monthly menses she will be required to stay in seclusion in a specially built lodge called *isnatipi* ("alone lodge"). After the ceremony, her family gives away gifts in her honor. The ceremony was reinstated in the 1980s and continues to be an important part of the female life cycle.[17]

Another ceremony reinstated in the 1990s is the *Tapa wankaiyeyapi* ("Throwing the Ball Ceremony") in which a small girl is given a ball made of buffalo skin stuffed with grass and told to throw it to a group of people standing at each of the four directions. Starting at the West, she throws it to the groups and the one who catches it will have good luck for the ensuing year. Because the young girl is innocent, she will not throw the ball to a favored person.

The *Hunka*, or "Making of Relatives," was probably learned from the Pawnee and originally was a ceremony in which two tribes were united in peace. The Lakota version, however, is intended as a form

older clan system. Today the term is frequently translated as "community," "extended family," or "band," none of which is technically correct. For further discussion see W. K. Powers 1977.

17. For a discussion of the relationship between ritual, reproduction, and menstruation see M. N. Powers 1980.

of adoption between an elder and younger member of the same sex. The bond created between the two is stronger than a blood tie, and the elder is expected to look after the welfare of the child for the rest of his or her life. The modern-day version of the *Hunka*, which continues to incorporate all the old songs and prayers, serves as a kind of initiation into the tribe as an adult. Names are bestowed upon the young adoptees resulting in the *Hunka* also being referred to as *Castunpi* ("naming ceremony"). An important part of the ceremony is the tying of a feather by the elder to the younger's hair, a symbol of the newfound tribal status of the adoptee.[18]

The *Wiwanyang Wacipi* ("Sun Dance," literally, "They Gaze at the Sun") is often considered the most important religious ceremony, and the only calendrical one being held sometime between June and August each year. At one time only one Sun Dance was held for the entire Lakota Nation and sometimes included Dakota and Nakota relatives as well as Arapahoes and Cheyennes. As such, the Sun Dance traditionally took place before the summer buffalo hunt, and part of its importance was to ensure that the hunt would be successful and unencumbered by the presence of enemies.

A cottonwood tree serves as a sacred pole in the center of an arbor. Certain men pledge to perform the Sun Dance, particularly if their lives have been spared in war or if their prayers for the welfare of a sick relative have been answered. There are essentially four major ways in which a man can participate. He can dance simply gazing in the direction of the Sun. He might also pledge to have the flesh over his breast pierced and be attached to the sacred pole by means of ropes. He might also opt to have the flesh over his scapula pierced to which skewers are inserted and buffalo skulls attached. In the last version, he might request to be pierced over both his breasts and scapula and be entirely suspended from four poles. In each of the latter three methods, he dances until his flesh tears loose. It is believed that one's body is the only thing that a person owns and thus is the only appropriate offering to Wakantanka. The act of being pierced symbolizes ignorance, and the breaking free, wisdom.

Women also participate by offering minute pieces of flesh from their arms. And during the Sun Dance, medicine men pierce the ears of

---

18. A description of a modern-day *Hunka* may be found in M. N. Powers 1991.

little children. In the past, those in mourning had their arms or legs gashed, or a finger amputated.

Since 1973, as a result of the Wounded Knee Occupation, the num-ber of Sun Dances has proliferated and many of them are by invitation only. Most of the Sun Dances are held in the respective reservation districts in which the medicine men live.

Other Ceremonies

Although not considered one of the Seven Sacred Ceremonies, smok-ing the pipe is a prologue to all other ceremonies. The pipe, which may be made and kept by anyone, is filled in a sacred manner. First the bowl and stem are joined. Tobacco made from *cansasa* (red willow bark) is then placed one pinch at a time into the bowl beginning with an offering to the West Wind, then progressively to the remainder of the winds, the sky, the earth, and the center of the universe. The bowl of the pipe is then capped with sage until it is ready to smoke. Typ-ically, the pipe is passed from one person to the other until all have smoked. Sometimes, the pipe remains capped until the conclusion of a ceremony. The joining of the stem and bowl of a pipe is sometimes likened to a loaded gun, referring to its inherent power. When smoked, the tobacco smoke rises, carrying the prayers of the participants.[19]

Yuwipi lowanpi ("Yuwipi Sing") is an important ceremony for the pur-pose of curing Indian sickness. A Yuwipi man conducts the ceremony in a darkened room and invokes the spirits of humans, animals, and birds to aid him in curing a patient. During the ceremony, the Yuwipi man is tied up and wrapped in a blanket or quilt symbolic both of life (when he is swaddled as a baby) and death (when his body is wrapped in preparation for the now defunct tree or scaffold burial). Singers lead the people in a variety of songs all learned by the medicine man in a vision and intended to propitiate the spirits who ultimately arrive, causing a great deal of noise. The Yuwipi man then communes with the spirits and determines the best way to cure the patient. Some-times multiple cures take place during the same sing. As a thanks to the spirits, whom only the Yuwipi man can see in the darkness, they are given offerings of tobacco. As they begin to leave, they emit blue

---

19. The original Calf Pipe is kept at Green Grass on the Cheyenne River reservation. For a history of the Calf Pipe see Smith 1967 [1994].

sparks every time they pick up an offering. The ceremony ends with a feast, smoking the pipe, and the formulaic prayer *Mitak'oyas'in* ("all my relations") symbolic of the communal nature of the curing.

In the late 1970s and early 1980s, some of the ceremonies associated with Christianity were appropriated by medicine men. Although typically most Lakotas were and still are baptized and buried in church rituals, many burials are now ministered by medicine men on family land rather than in church cemeteries. The graves are frequently noticeable by their distinct flags staked at the Four Winds bearing the sacred colors. Medicine men also officiate over "Indian" weddings in which a bride and groom wrap themselves in a single star quilt while the medicine man prays with the sacred pipe. The ceremony is concluded with the bride and groom feeding each other *wasna* and chokecherry juice.[20]

Although the Ghost Dance still is remembered particularly in association with the 1890 Wounded Knee Massacre, there have been only one or two feeble attempts to reinstate it and for all practical purposes Lakotas are more interested in what they regard as their traditional religion.

Although the Native American Church has a presence on the reservation, less than 10 percent of the population participates. One can identify Peyotist homes by the addition of a tipi in the yard which is used on Saturday nights for services. They also have their own wakes and funerals, and their followers are buried in a Native American Church cemetery.[21]

Approximately thirteen Christian denominations proselytize on the reservations, the most popular being Roman Catholic and Episcopalian, whom the Lakota distinguish as *Sapaun* ("black wearers") and *Skaun* ("white wearers"). Presbyterians are called *Ogleptecela* ("short coats") and Pentecostals, of which there are many, are referred to as *Ceya wacekiye* ("crying church").

Birth and Death

Traditional Lakotas call a newborn *icimani* ("traveler"), underscoring that life is ephemeral and that soon everyone returns to his or her beginnings. Before leaving the spirit world the grandfather and grand-

---

20. *Wasna* is the Lakota equivalent of pemmican, meat and wild fruit pounded together with lard. It is considered extremely sacred and may be eaten only during the daytime lest it attract troublesome ghosts. Chokecherry juice also is sacred. Both are ingested at Naming Ceremonies as well as weddings. For a discussion of sacred foods see Powers and Powers 1990.

21. For a discussion of the Native American Church among the Oglala see Steinmetz 1990.

mother instruct the infant-to-be that it should not take anything extra with it, that all it owns is its own body. (Hence, the only appropriate offering in the Sun Dance is one's own flesh.)

Each person is born with four aspects of "soul." The first, *sicun*, is that potency that allows the body and soul to form and is immortal. It is invested in a person at conception. At death, the *sicun* returns to somewhere in the North, where it awaits a future conception. Twins and sacred men and women are particularly susceptible to reincarnation, and both are believed to be born with intellectual maturity.

The second, *tun*, refers to the power to transform energy from visible to invisible, and vice versa. Life and death are *wakan* ("sacred") because in the former the invisible *tun* is transformed into the latter, and in death the transformation is reversed.

Life is manifested in *ni*, the third aspect of soul, which also means "breath" or "life" and which leaves a person at death.

The fourth, *nagi* ("shade," "shadow," "ghost"), is that aspect of soul which at death departs along the *Wanagi Tacanku* ("ghost road," i.e., the Milky Way) en route to the *Wanagi Oti* ("ghost village"), where it joins its deceased relatives and resumes traditional life. An old woman waits at the fork of the road and assesses each person's earthly virtue. The good are allowed to continue on the road; the bad are remanded to earth to live as evil spirits. Every *wanagi* dwells on earth for a year before departing. Thus most *wanagis* are beneficial.

The circle is sacred, and everything in Lakota myth and ritual is performed in sets of fours and sevens. Life is thus cyclical, the newborn enters life from the South, moving clockwise to the West (childhood), North (adolescence), East (maturity), and South (old age). All rituals begin with an offering to the West Wind and proceed to the South, thus reflecting the order in which the Four Winds were born. Prayers are also offered to the Sky, Earth, and Center of the Universe, thus completing the ritual pattern. When a pipe is filled with seven pinches of tobacco, the pipe is thus symbolic of all creation and all time. Lighting the pipe activates the spiritual potency of the universe.[22]

22. There is an obvious relationship between the concept of "soul," filling the pipe, and other ceremonies, in particular, the Sweat Lodge. The idea of activating spiritual potency by lighting the pipe is mirrored in the Sweat Lodge by the heating of the stones to which water is added. The pit is a replication of the subterranean beginnings of the Lakota people. Stones, the most sacred of ritual objects, are the oldest things on earth. Water animates the stones. Steam arising from the heated rocks is called *ni* ("breath, life"), which like smoke carries prayers to the Above. Metaphorically speaking, the four aspects of "soul" may be seen as a process rather than objects.

Inktomi continues to deceive the Lakotas, and stories about him called *ohunkankan* are told to children on winter nights as guides to morality.

Two myths are told about the end of the world. One describes an old woman sitting alone making porcupine quillwork as she cooks meat. Every time she rises to stir the pot, her dog unravels her work. If the dog should ever unravel the entire work, the world will end.

Another describes the beginning of time when a buffalo was placed in the West to hold back the waters. Every year, the buffalo loses a hair, and every age he loses a leg. As the Lakotas enter the twenty-first century, they believe that the buffalo is very nearly bald and that he is standing on one leg.

Always fearful that their religion is dying, Lakotas have responded in the twentieth century with a new and tenacious vitality. As they enter into the twenty-first century, most prevalent is the doctrine of the Seventh Generation, originally a prophecy of Red Cloud. Today, the elders represent the fifth generation; their children, the sixth; and their grandchildren, the seventh. According to Red Cloud, Lakota culture, language, and religion will be totally independent of the white man's influence and will flourish without end when the fifth and sixth generations have died off, and the Seventh Generation reaches maturity.

Bibliography

Beckwith, Martha W. 1930. "Mythology of the Oglala Dakota." *Journal of American Folklore* 43:339–442.

Brown, Joseph Epes. 1953. *The Sacred Pipe*. Baltimore: Penguin Books.

DeMallie, Raymond J. 1983. "Male and Female in Traditional Lakota Culture." In Patricia Albers and Beatrice Medicine (eds.), *The Hidden Half: Studies of Plains Indian Women*. Washington, D.C.: University Press of America, 237–65.

———— (ed.). 1984. *The Sixth Grandfather*. Lincoln: University of Nebraska Press.

Densmore, Frances. 1918. *Teton Sioux Music*. Bulletin of the Bureau of American Ethnology, no. 61. Washington, D.C.

Feraca, Stephen E. 1961. *Wakinyan: Contemporary Teton Dakota Religion*. Browning, Mont.: Museum of the Plains Indian.

Kemnitzer, Luis. 1968. "Yuwipi: A Modern Day Healing Ritual." Ph.D. diss., University of Pennsylvania.

To use a Euro-American analogy, the *sicun* is like tinder, the *tun* like a spark, the *ni* like a flame, and the nagi like smoke.

Mallery, Garrick. 1886. "The Dakota Winter Counts and the Corbusie Winter Counts." Fourth Annual Report of the Bureau of American Ethnology. Washington, D.C., 89–146.

Mooney, James. 1896. Ghost Dance Religion and the Sioux Outbreak. Chicago: University of Chicago Press [1965].

Neihardt, John G. 1932. Black Elk Speaks. New York: William Morrow.

Powers, Marla N. 1980. "Menstruation and Reproduction: An Oglala Case." Signs 6:54–65.

———. 1986. Oglala Women in Myth, Ritual, and Reality. Chicago: University of Chicago Press.

———. 1990. "Mistress, Mother, Visionary Spirit: The Lakota Culture Heroine." In Christopher Vecsey (ed.), Religion in Native North America. Moscow: University of Idaho Press, 36–48.

———. 1991. Lakota Naming: A Modern-Day Hunka Ceremony. Kendall Park, N.J.: Lakota Books.

Powers, William K. 1963. "A Winter Count of the Oglala." American Indian Tradition 52:27–37.

———. 1977. Oglala Religion. Lincoln: University of Nebraska Press.

———. 1982. Yuwipi: Vision and Experience in Oglala Ritual. Lincoln: University of Nebraska Press.

———. 1986. Sacred Language: The Nature of Supernatural Discourse in Lakota. Norman: University of Oklahoma Press.

———. 1987. Beyond the Vision: Essays on American Indians. Norman: University of Oklahoma Press.

———. 1990a. Voices from the Spirit World. Kendall Park, N.J.: Lakota Books.

———. 1990b. "When Black Elk Speaks, Everybody Listens." In Christopher Vecsey (ed.), Religion in Native North America. Moscow: University of Idaho Press, 136–51.

Powers, William K., and Marla N. Powers. 1990. Sacred Foods of the Lakota. Kendall Park, N.J.: Lakota Books.

Riggs, Stephen Return. 1869. Tah-koo Wah-kan: or, The Gospel among the Dakotas. Boston: Congregational Sabbath-School and Publishing Society.

Smith, John L. 1967. A Short History of the Sacred Calf Pipe of the Teton Dakota. Kendall Park, N.J.: Lakota Books [1994].

Steinmetz, Paul B., S.J. 1990. Pipe, Bible, and Peyote among the Oglala Lakota. Knoxville: University of Tennessee Press.

Theisz, R. D. 1988. "Multifaceted Double Woman: Legend, Song, Dream, and Meaning." European Review of Native American Studies 2, no. 2:9–16.

Walker, J. R. 1917. "The Sun Dance and Other Ceremonies of the Oglala Division of the Teton-Dakota." Anthropological Papers of the American Museum of Natural History, vol. 16, pt. 2, 53–221.

———. 1980. Lakota Belief and Ritual. Edited by Raymond J. DeMallie and Elaine Jahner. Lincoln: University of Nebraska Press.

Wissler, Clark. 1912. "Societies and Ceremonial Associations in the Oglala Division of Teton Dakota." Anthropological Papers of the American Museum of Natural History, vol. 11, pt. , 1–99.

ᥑ F I V E ᥑ

The Continuous Renewal of
Sacred Relations: Navajo Religion

Trudy Griffin-Pierce

The Four Corners area of the southwestern United States — where the states of Arizona, New Mexico, Utah, and Colorado join each other (Fig. 1) — is a place of great natural beauty: endless space and brilliant light set the Colorado Plateau country apart, inspiring awe and wonder. Rolling clouds in a vast sky cast racing shadows across the valley floor; dramatic sandstone spires, towering red cliffs, great expanses of sagebrush steppelands, and mountains that touch the sky remind humans of their place in the whole of creation.

For the Navajo people, the beauty of this land is but the outer manifestation of its sacredness. All aspects of the natural world are imbued with sacredness and life: every mesa, mountain, animal, and direction is alive and has its own name and personal history; each must be approached in the proper way to maintain balanced relationships in the universe. This article explores the reciprocal relationships between humans and the natural and supernatural worlds, relationships which underlie the rigorous philosophical and ritual system that is Navajo religion.

The *Diné*

The *Diné* — The People, as the Navajo call themselves — are the largest Native American nation, both in territory and in population: their seventeen-million-acre reservation is roughly the size of the state of West Virginia or the Central American country of Belize. By the year 2000, their population is estimated to reach a quarter of a million people.

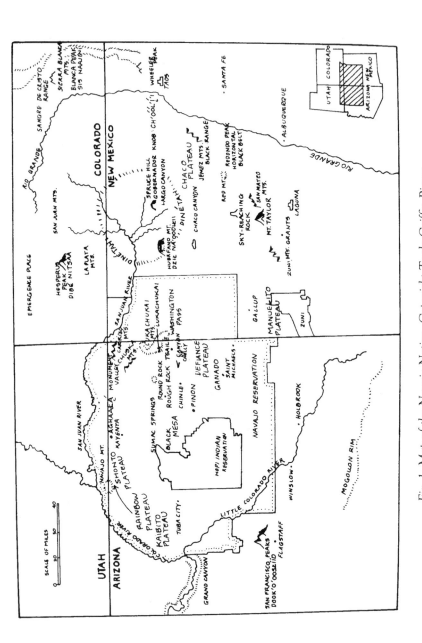

Fig. 1. Map of the Navajo Nation. Copyright Trudy Griffin-Pierce.

Relative latecomers to the Southwest, the Navajo speak an Athabas-can language, which they share with their southwestern cousins, the Apache, as well as with Native Americans living in Canada, Alaska, Oregon, and California.

Although towns exist today on the Navajo reservation, traditionally, the Navajo lived in small, isolated family groups. The same individu-alistic tradition, a legacy of their Athabascan heritage, underlies their ceremonial practices and beliefs, in contrast to the more communal, calendrical ceremonies of their Puebloan neighbors. Although the great winter ceremonials are timed to occur "after the first frost" and "be-fore the first thunder," Navajo ceremonies are scheduled according to individual needs. While Puebloan ceremonies emphasize communal well-being and are sponsored by priesthoods or societies, Navajo cere-monies are held in response to the illness of an individual, known as the patient, under the direction of a ceremonial practitioner, or singer, who is not part of an organized priesthood. Furthermore, instead of occurring in a communally shared structure, such as the Pueblo kiva, Navajo ceremonies are held in the hogan — the "place home" — of the patient's family.

The Dynamic Nature of the Sacred

Wind — swirling gusts and fresh breezes, blustery gales and turbulent air — more than any other natural force, embodies the energy of change and a sense of dynamic force. The Navajo view of the world, which is based on movement, change, and flux, is most evident in a central concept of Navajo philosophy — the Holy Wind. *Nílch'i* is the subtle breath of life which suffuses all of nature, giving "life, thought, speech, and the power of motion to all living things" (McNeley 1982:1).

Movement is emphasized in language, sandpaintings, and myth. The Navajo language requires specification of the nature, direction, and status of movement in considerable detail (Hoijer 1964:146). Sand-paintings are full of symbolically expressed motion: swirling snakes, rotating logs, streaming head plumes, whirling rainbows; sandpainting figures also carry feathered travel hoops, their magical means of travel. Travel is an essential part of sacred stories as heroes constantly journey from one holy place to the next.

The concept of dynamic order is of tremendous importance to Navajo philosophy. Creation occurred *nizhónígo* or "in an orderly and

Fig. 2. "Prayers to the Dawn": a traditional Navajo greets each sunrise with prayers and a pollen blessing to pray to the Holy People who are present at this time of day. Copyright Trudy Griffin-Pierce.

proper way." The enclitic "-go" at the and of the word denotes an ongoing process and stresses the need for the continuous re-creation of order.

Ceremonials both re-create and restore this ongoing state of order-liness, but such orderliness, or holiness, is never a static, permanent condition. Before a nine-night ceremonial can be held in a family's hogan, the hogan must be cleared of household items and sanctified so that it is *hodiyiin*, a word which translates not as "sacred" but rather as "at this moment in time this space is holy." By establishing con-ditions which are *hodiyiin*, one shows respect to the *diyin dine'é*, the Holy People, thus inviting their presence, the first step toward restoring proper relations with them.

The conception of the universe as a place of motion and process means that no state of being is permanently fixed. To ensure that the universe continually reanimates itself, humans have a daily responsibility to renew the proper balance of the universe through songs, prayers, offerings, and proper thought and actions. Humans must constantly be aware of and work to maintain proper relations with all aspects of the universe.

This is why a traditional Navajo greets the Holy People who come with the sunrise with prayers and a pollen blessing (Fig. 2). The East, where the day begins, is associated with Talking God; by praying in the direction of the initial rays of light, a person takes on Talking God's spiritual strength to see him or her through the course of the day.

"We Are All Related"

The universe is an all-inclusive whole in which every being has its own place and beneficial relationship to all other living things. In traditional Navajo thinking, *hózhǫ́* — harmonious conditions — results from living life in a way that acknowledges all parts of the universe as alive and interdependent, a way of life that maintains proper relations.

This emphasis on relationships is evident in the fact that the phrase "We are all related" has no direct equivalent in Navajo; instead, each relationship must be specified. Relationships cannot be glossed over in the Navajo language as they can in the English translation.

In order to say "We are related" in the Navajo language, one must say:

Nahasdzáán — Nanise altaas'éí	Earth — growth of all different kinds
Yádiłhił — Yótáhnaazléí	Sky — and everything in the sky
Nohokáá' dine'é	Earth People
T'áa'altsoh shik'éí.	All are related to me.

The theme of proper relationships is a constant thread that runs through all myths in the great complex of Navajo oral literature, including the myths that sanction the Navajo chantway (ceremonial) system. Every mountain, animal, Holy Person, and ceremony has its own story of mystical creation, spiritual powers, and its purpose in relation to the *Diné.*

Everything in the Navajo universe has an inner and an outer form. One's physical being — the outer form — exists independently of one's indwelling consciousness — the inner form. After the Emergence, the

Holy Wind (*nílch'i*) and inner forms — (*bii'gistíín*) were placed within all things, endowing them with life, movement, speech, and sentience. When the soil from the four Sacred Mountains was brought up from the previous worlds at the time of Emergence, this soil was placed in each of the four directions; however, these mountains were not alive until each had an inner form placed within it (Fig. 3).

The Holy Wind — the vital energy that animates the universe — unites all forms of life by virtue of its omnipresence inside and outside all life forms. Unlike the Western concept of the soul, the Holy Wind is not an independent spiritual agency which exists in a unique form within each individual. Instead, it is a single entity that exists everywhere, an all-pervading substance in which all living beings participate.

The act of breathing is a sacred act which unites all beings and phenomena — humans, deer, mountains, stars, and the Holy People. This understanding embues the Navajo with a profound sense of connection and responsibility to all other species and beings. Thus, to exploit or destroy any aspect of creation is also to harm oneself.

The *Diyin Dine'é*

"Every creature, every aspect of nature has its holy people. . . . They are represented, some of them, by colors: the blue sky, the evening dusk, the night — these are holy people and one prays to them. . . . There are dawn people, twilight people, air, thunder, and cloud people." (Medicine man, Mike Mitchell [in Page 1989:87–88]).

The most familiar Holy People — *diyin dine'é* — are Changing Woman, who embodies the powers of renewal inherent in the earth; the Sun; and their children, the Sacred Twins, Monster Slayer and Born-for-Water. Other important *diyin dine'é* include Earth; Moon; Sky; Wind; First Man; First Woman; helpers of the Holy People; and intermediaries between the sacred and secular realms, such as Big Fly, who relay messages to the heroes of many myths, guiding them out of their predicaments and saving their lives. Another group of Holy People, the Yé'ii are called *hasch'ééh* — the Failed-to-Speak People — because they are capable of uttering only calls, not words.

What Euro-Americans call "nature" or "natural phenomena" is not a discrete category for traditional Navajos. Mountains, animals, plants, and natural forces are considered to be *diyin dine'é,* or People, as medi-

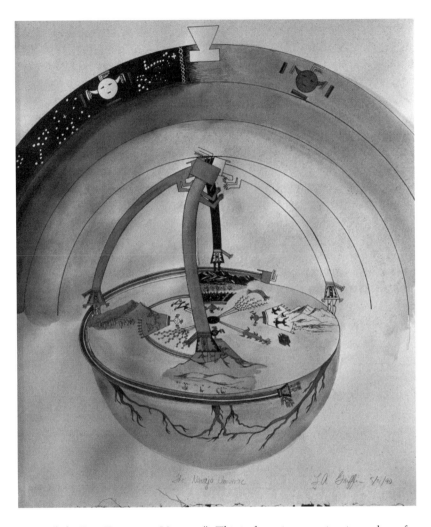

Fig. 3. "The Post-Emergence Universe": This is the universe as it exists today, after the Emergence from a series of underworlds. The Four Cardinal Light Phenomena are depicted as pillars of different colored light in each direction: white in the East, blue in the South, yellow in the West, and black in the North. Each pillar emerges from its Sacred Mountain and has roots that reach deep with the earth. Copyright Trudy Griffin-Pierce.

cine man Mike Mitchell explained. Because of their divinity, stars, plants, and certain animals are often depicted as people in sandpaintings. This visual personification also reminds humans of their proper relationship to them.

Ritual observances are designed to enlist the aid of the *diyin dine'é* with whom the Earth Surface People (ordinary humans) share the universe. Although the customary translation of *diyin dine'é* is "Holy People," a more accurate translation would be "superbeings" because their most salient trait is the possession of special powers (Young in Aberle 1967:16). But because "nature" and "supernature" are not discrete categories in Navajo thought, the Navajo do not think of the *diyin dine'é* as "supernaturals," but rather as "greater-than-human configurations of reality who are actually encountered in the Navajo environment" (Luckert in Wyman 1983:556–57).

Unlike the separation between gods and humans which exists in many Western religions, the Holy People are closely linked to human beings. The term Holy People is also misleading because it implies a state of moral perfection. In the great body of oral literature that sanctions all Navajo ceremonials, the *diyin dine'é* do not display exemplary behavior; instead, they are described as having human emotions such as jealousy, worry, greed, and anger. A Navajo scholar (Consultant A) explained that the *diyin dine'é* have human emotions "writ large in order to show us the results of our actions when we let our emotions get away with us."

Furthermore, in addition to emotional closeness, the *diyin dine'é* share both spatial proximity and genealogical closeness with humans. Through the clan organization, the *diyin dine'é* are linked to the Earth Surface People (Reichard 1950:58–59). The *diyin dine'é* are omnipresent as well: "Navajo Holy People aren't far away...they never make themselves visible but you interact with them on a daily basis, and they make your day go right" (Consultant B).

The Ritual Power of Knowledge

The boundary between the *diyin dine'é* and humanity is fluid because the acquisition of knowledge can lead to personal holiness. Each chantway myth recounts the story of a hero who enters supernatural realms and, through the course of his journey, acquires ritual knowledge.

To obtain the help of the *diyin dine'é*, the hero must first learn how to properly approach them (how to establish proper relations with them). He then gains knowledge of how to acquire and use the *jish* — medicine bundle (see Frisbie 1987) — for that particular ceremonial; this knowledge then belongs to him as his tangible (the *jish*) and intangible (procedures and prayers) property. Such knowledge is power, the power to control adverse circumstances and to compel the *diyin dine'é* to assist in healing. The hero then returns with his new knowledge and teaches the ceremony to the *Diné* (the People). However, after his contact with the *diyin dine'é*, the hero no longer feels comfortable with humanity and ultimately departs to live with the Holy People (Spencer 1957:34–35; Reichard 1950:55–56).

The power that comes through knowledge, therefore, is available not only to *diyin dine'é* but also to humans. Holiness is not an attribute of a separate class of beings who are rigidly bound in space and time, but rather something attainable; with the progressive acquisition of knowledge, a person becomes more and more like the *diyin dine'é* (Farella 1984:29).

At the time of Creation, the *diyin dine'é* thought and prayed the world into existence (Wheelwright 1942:57–60; Wyman 1970b: 115). Knowledge, the inner form of thought, preceded thought; thought led to its outer form, speech. Speech then led to physical action, which created physical reality. Thus, thought is creative and ultimately manifests in physical reality; the Navajo conception of thought attributes great power to thinking (see Witherspoon 1977).

The concept that the progressive acquisition of knowledge leads to greater personal holiness gives knowledge a definite kind of power that it does not possess in the Euro-American worldview. The words of a Blessingway prayer, which tell the story of Creation, express the power of knowledge: "Of Earth's origin I have full knowledge ... of long life's, now of happiness's origin I have full knowledge ... I had full knowledge from the very beginning" (Chanter Slim Curley in Wyman 1970a: 113–14). Knowledge is thus the first step toward Creation.

Knowledge leads to the spiritual powers of the *diyin dine'é*. The *diyin dine'é* are empowered by their complete (full) knowledge of how to attain *hózhǫ́* — ideal and desired conditions; they are composed of pure energy because of this knowledge. Throughout the course of their lives, humans endeavor to stay on the path of *hózhǫ́*, but constantly fall off because it is so difficult to follow; unknowingly, they commit violations

Fig. 4. "Navajo Stargazer": Stargazing, hand-trembling, listening, and crystal-gazing are a means of diagnosing illness. After diagnosis, the patient seeks out a chanter to perform the appropriate ceremonial. Copyright Trudy Griffin-Pierce.

against the *diyin dine'é*. Thus, humans can only strive to attain the degree of knowledge which leads to the physical and mental perfection of the *diyin dine'é*.

The ideal state is expressed in the sacred and complex phrase, *sąʼa naagháii bikʼe hózhǫ́*. On a literal level, *Sąʼa Naagháii* refers to Young Man, while *Bikʼe Hózhǫ́* represents Young Woman; they personify Thought and Speech, respectively (Witherspoon 1977:17–46). Originating from the medicine bundle of First Man, Thought and Speech are the sources of life for the inner forms of all living beings. *Sąʼa naagháii bikʼe hózhǫ́* expresses the goal of living to old age by following the path of *hózhǫ́* — "journeying into old age by way of spiritual beauty" (Gold

1994:4) — and then, upon death, being reincorporated into the life force that will animate future generations of living beings.

The Cause of Illness

Each person has a responsibility to abide by the prescriptions and pro-scriptions of the *diyin dine'é*. Because thought is creative, individuals reap the results of their thoughts and actions through illness or health, misfortune or well-being.

In the Navajo world, each state of being is balanced by its comple-ment. At the other end of the continuum from *hózhǫ́* — the state of desired, blessed conditions — exists *hóchxǫ* — the state of worthless, evil conditions.

One experiences illness or misfortune (*hóchxǫ'*) by committing vio-lations, that is, by disregarding proper relations with the *diyin dine'é*, animals, the ghosts of Navajos or non-Navajos, or witches. As a Navajo father told folklorist Barre Toelken (1979:96), "We have to relate our lives to the stars and the sun, the animals, and to all of nature or else we will go crazy, or get sick."

After a diagnostician — a hand-trembler or stargazer (Fig. 4) — has identified the cause of illness, the patient and his or her family seek out a singer who specializes in that particular kind of illness. Navajo ceremonies heal by restoring harmonious conditions and right rela-tions in all realms of a patient's life: physically, spiritually, mentally, and socially. The patient is responsible for following the singer's in-structions regarding personal behavior and thought before and during the ceremonial. The patient further demonstrates the strength of his or her commitment to healing through careful adherence to ritual re-strictions, which last four days after the close of the ceremonial; such actions continue the patient's restoration to *hózhǫ́*, a state of balance and proper relations with all aspects of the natural and supernatural worlds.

Navajo Religion: "Moving about Ceremonially"

"The Navajo religion is *being* Navajo.... Religion is something that you live everyday.... We are much like the Amish, whose religion dic-tates their way of life" (Navajo educator and medical anthropologist, Jennie Joe [in Trimble 1993:122]). The inseparability of spirituality from other aspects of life is reflected in the lack of a Navajo word for "religion." The closest approximation is *diné binahagha'*, which means "moving about ceremonially," a linguistic subset of *diné yee hináanii*, "That by means of which Navajos live" (Werner, Manning, and Begishe 1983:589).

Navajo ceremonials are conducted by a "singer" or "chanter" — *hataałii* — a trained specialist who, through apprenticeship to an older singer, has learned the appropriate songs, medicines, and ritual actions for curing patients. The *hataałii* derives his name from the *hataał*, or "sing," which is the name for a performance of one of the chantways, the major group of ceremonials.

Chantways used for curing or preventing illness are performed according to one of three rituals, or patterns of behavior governing procedure: Holyway, Evilway, and Lifeway. Holyway ritual is concerned with the attraction of good and the restoration of the patient; most chantways are in this category. Evilway ritual employs techniques for exorcising Native ghosts and their evil influences. Lifeway ritual treats injuries resulting from accidents.

There were once some twenty-four chantways, but by the 1970s, only eight were well known and performed frequently (Wyman 1983:542). Shootingway is the only chantway today which can still be done according to Holyway, Evilway, and Lifeway rituals.

Each chant, which may last two, five, or nine nights, is composed of discrete units called ceremonies which are set off by pauses in activity. Most of the principal ceremonies of the first half of the ritual performance — such as the consecration of the hogan, the sweat-emetic, and the unraveling — are exorcistic and protective, invoking the powers of specific *diyin dine'é* to drive out all disruptive forces and to protect the patient. The patient also leaves offerings to invite the *diyin dine'é* to be present at the ceremonial.

At the midpoint of the ceremonial — around the afternoon of the fourth day in a nine-night ceremonial — activities shift to invocation and blessing. The sandpainting, figure painting-token tying, and all-night singing are examples of invocatory ceremonies. Scholar Leland Wyman (1983:543) proposed that the Athabascans may have brought the exorcistic pattern of ritual behavior with them to the Southwest; after their arrival, they probably derived the sandpainting practices, and other invocatory rites, from the Pueblo Indians, reworking these practices into uniquely Navajo ceremonies.

The Restoration of Proper Relations

The Navajo universe, as described above, is not static, nor is it inhabited by discrete classes of beings with fixed boundaries who never
interact with each other. Instead, the Navajo universe is a dynamic
place, with fluid boundaries between the natural and supernatural, between humans and the Holy People. By its very nature, the world
is a place of ever-changing relationships that need constant renewal
through ritual enactments. Folklorist Barre Toelken (1977:81) describes
the Navajo philosophical and ritual system as one "which places demands on individuals that most non-Navajos would find it difficult to
cope with."

The goal of Navajo ceremonial practices is the restoration of proper
relations — between the *Diné* and other human beings and between
the *Diné* and the *diyin dine'é*. Each ceremonial addresses a specific relationship as well as restoring the overall balance to all other relationships
in the patient's life.

For example, the Enemyway heals relations between the *Diné* and
other human beings. This ceremony protects warriors from the ghosts of
slain enemies; today, it is also used to cure any illness resulting from the
ghosts of non-Navajos. Many World War II and Vietnam War veterans
found that the Enemyway helped to stop or decrease their nightmares
and recurrent flashbacks, which were considered to be the symptoms
of contact with ghosts.

In contrast, Mountainway focuses more on the patient's relationships with the group of *diyin dine'é* that Euro-Americans call "nature."
More specifically, Mountainway treats illness caused by improper contact with the animals who live in the mountains, especially the bear;
bear sickness is associated with arthritis and mental disturbances. This
chantway also cures illness caused by contact with other mountain
dwellers, such as the porcupine, which causes gastrointestinal trouble
or kidney and bladder disturbances; the nasal discomfort or coughing
resulting from killing squirrels is also treated with the Mountainway.
The symptoms cease once the patient's proper relationship to one or
more of these animals has been reestablished.

Nightway concentrates on healing relationships between the patient
and the group of *diyin dine'é* known as the *Yé'ii*, the Failed-to-Speak
Ones. When an individual experiences stiffness, paralysis, or blindness
because he or she has offended the *Yé'ii*, the Nightway is given. This

ceremony is also known as the *Yeibichai* — from the leader of the *Yé'ii*, Talking God, *Yé'ii Bicheii* or "Grandfather of the Gods." On each of the final four days, an immense sandpainting, often measuring twenty feet in diameter, and, on the final night, teams of masked dancers, bring life to the *Yé'ii*. Through the course of this elaborate nine-night ceremonial, health is restored to the patient as his or her proper relations to the *Yé'ii* are reestablished.

Balancing Male and Female, Unifying Earth and Sky

Together, Mother Earth and Father Sky embody complementarity, the basic relational principle of Navajo philosophy. In Western thought, the monad is considered to be the basic and strongest unit; in Navajo thought, a dyad is the irreducible minimum.

All aspects of "nature" have male and female qualities: there is male rain, which comes down in a deluge, while female rain is a light mist. Rather than being associated with sex, the distinctions relate to a contrast between that which is aggressive, strong, and active and its counterpart, which is submissive, gentle, and passive. Neither is considered to be morally better than the other; both are necessary to the state of balance and wholeness. The contrast between the two defines and gives meaning to each component of the pair. Each provides what is lacking in the other; together, they create a complete whole. Furthermore, the whole is considered to be much greater than the sum of its parts. Thus, a painting of Mother Earth accompanied by Father Sky is much more powerful than individual depictions of each figure.

Male and female pairing is also seen in the four Sacred Mountains, which are actually two pairs of mountains, with a male and female in each pair. Blanca Peak (the eastern, male mountain) faces San Francisco Peak (the western, female mountain), while Mt. Taylor (the southern, female mountain) is paired with Hesperus Peak (the northern, male mountain) (Fig. 5). According to Navajo educator Harry Walters (in Griffin-Pierce 1992:71–72), each mountain faces its complementary mountain so that they "keep each other in check," leading to *"alch'isilá,* which means balance."

Each person has this unity of male and female within him or her. The left side of the human body represents maleness and physicality (the left hand holds the bow and arrow in ceremonies) while the right side

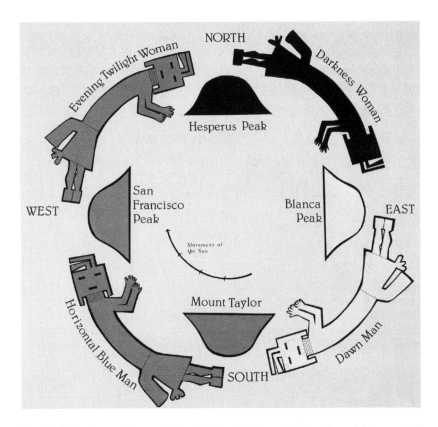

*Fig. 5. "The Inner Forms of the Cardinal Points with the Sacred Mountains":
Each of the Sacred Mountains has an inner form by which it breathes and lives.
Dawn Man is in the East with Blanca Peak; Horizontal Blue Man is in the South
with Mount Taylor; Evening Twilight Woman is in the West with San Francisco
Peaks; and Darkness Woman is in the North with Hesperus Peak. Copyright Trudy
Griffin-Pierce.*

is the female, emotional side (the right hand holds the corn pollen, a
symbol of life and peace).

Sʼą'a naaghái bikʼe hózhǫ́ can refer to the inner forms of the Earth
and the Sky combined; a common view is that sʼą'a naaghái is "sky's
inner form" and that bikʼe hózhǫ́ is "earth's inner form." Sʼą'a naaghái
bikʼe hózhǫ́ — the desired state of balance and wholeness — is why
Mother Earth is always drawn with Father Sky and why these two forms
must also be carefully measured so that they are absolutely symmetrical
(Fig. 6). Chanter Bitter Water explained, "Mother Earth and Father Sky

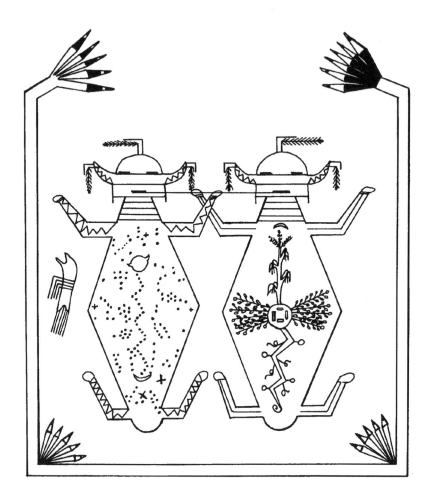

Fig. 6. Diagram of a sand painting of Mother Earth and Father Sky. Copyright Trudy Griffin-Pierce.

must be identical in shape and size, since they are the two halves of a whole creation laid side by side, like the two halves of an evenly cut melon" (Wyman 1970b: 34).

Significantly, Bitter Water does not use two equally sized objects which are whole by themselves for his simile. Instead, he describes Earth and Sky as two halves of the *same* melon; the state of wholeness — holiness — is achieved only because each half fits perfectly into the other, supplying what is lacking in the other for the completion of the whole.

The "Mother Earth, Father Sky" sandpainting, which depicts the entirety of the universe, is a particularly powerful painting because it is the visual embodiment of humanity's relations to all creation as well as the balancing of maleness and femaleness. Unlike most sandpaintings, which symbolize events, objects, or beings in their accompanying chantway myth, this painting does not relate specifically to the symbols of the Male Shootingway myth to which it belongs. Instead, this painting draws down the powers of the heavens and brings up the powers of the earth to heal the patient. Through its correct ritual use, the patient's proper relations are restored with other humans and with the *diyin dine'é* of the Earth and Sky.

The "Mother Earth, Father Sky" sandpainting is thus a metaphoric and literal depiction of *sa'a naagháii bik'e hózhǫ́*, living into old age through balanced and perfect conditions. Both the goal of proper relations and the means by which to achieve this goal are encoded in the sandpainting imagery. On the most basic level, the sandpainting is a statement of balance — the ideal relational state — between Mother Earth and Father Sky, the two halves of creation. At a more subtle level, each of the symbols on Mother Earth is a visual reminder of *diyin dine'é* with which one must interact in the proper manner. Each constellation on the body of Father Sky indexes a moral story about how to achieve proper relations with other people and with the *diyin dine'é*.

On the body of Mother Earth, the plant symbols serve as visual reminders of the sacredness of all plants. Although these are the four sacred plants — corn, beans, squash, and tobacco — rather than specific medicine (of these four plants, only tobacco is used in a ritual manner), by extension, they represent all plants. Chanter George Blueeyes calls plants "Plant People" (i.e., they are Holy People). He explains: "They are our food and our medicine and the medicine for our livestock. From the Plant People we have *Inaaji Azee* — the medicines of the Life Way, and other medicines" (Arthur:23). Each plant must be approached and obtained in a special manner to ensure that reciprocal relations are respected. Humans have a responsibility to show respect by singing the right plant-gathering songs and leaving offerings; in exchange, the plants will provide efficacious medicine.

On Father Sky, each of the depicted constellations encodes an allegory about the way one should live in order to ensure proper relations and thus, a long and peaceful life. *Náhookǫs bika'ii* (the Big Dipper) and *Ná'hookǫs ba'áadii* (Cassiopeia) are a paired set of constellations as they revolve around Polaris. Together, they serve as a visual metaphor for the balance of maleness and femaleness within the Navajo home or hogan; Polaris is the fire in the center cf the hogan. Chanter A (in Griffin-Pierce 1992:153) said, "They tell us to stay at home, to stay around your fire." Here, the implication is that these constellations set a moral example for the *Diné* to remain at home with their families to carry out familial responsibilities.

The hogan itself is a powerful Navajo symbol, which is personified in myth as a deity and as a living entity. There are both male (the old-style forked-stick hogan) and female (the more commonly seen round hogan). The hogan is a home and place of security and is equated with maturity and a willingness to settle down (Frisbie 1980:165–66). "Without a hogan you cannot plan...you have to build a hogan first. Within that you sit down and begin to plan" (Frisbie and McAllester 1978:244).

Dilyéhé (the Pleiades) is an injunction against disharmony and disorder. Chanter A (in Griffin-Pierce 1992:156–57) interpreted this constellation as two sequential events: seven old men playing a dice game and the loser of the game, who drags his wife and children home in a fit of anger. The principle of order and harmony in human relations is a basic premise of Navajo culture; the story indexed by this constellation is an allegory which cautions against disruptive behavior, specifically toward those outside one's family group.

Black God, the *diyin dine'é* in charge of all the heavens, selected *Dilyéhé* to represent all constellations; this star cluster appears on the temple of his mask. Thus, *Dilyéhé* is a visual example of ritual synecdoche — part representing the whole — and an example of the Navajo concern for the same state of wholeness and completion inherent in the paired bodies of Mother Earth and Father Sky.

Both *Dilyéhé* and *'Atsé'ets'ózí* (Orion) are seasonal markers and represent the continuity of time on an annual basis. One aspect of reciprocal relationships with the natural world is a respect for seasonal timing, both on a ritual and on an agricultural basis. The appearance of *Dilyéhé* begins the proper season for the Nightway ceremonial; this also marks the end of planting season because it is then too late to plant and still be able to harvest before the first frost. Planting begins when *'Atsé'ets'ózí* sets at twilight in early May.

Hastiin Sik'ai'í (Corvus) embodies the value of concentration, wisdom, and knowledge, greatly respected attributes in Navajo culture. This constellation, whose name means "Man with Legs Ajar," represents a man standing above the earth with his feet firmly planted as he searches the earth and sees everything that occurs (Chanter B in Griffin-Pierce 1992:166).

The name *'Atsé'etsoh* (the front part of Scorpius) means "The First Big One"; this star grouping is an old man who must rely on his cane for balance. This figure embodies old age, the desired end of a long life which can only be achieved by maintaining proper relationships with the natural and supernatural worlds.

Rabbit Tracks — *Gah heet'e'ii* (the tail of Scorpius) — symbolizes proper relations to all game animals. T'ááschí'í Sani is one of the few men left who still know the ancient songs and ceremonies of the hunt and the ways of the Deer People. He said that before leaving on the hunt, sacred songs must be sung and hunters "must keep holy thoughts . . . the hunter talks about the game in a special language. . . . Do everything correctly in the holy way and the game will be waiting for you" (in Arthur 1982:42). He also described rules for skinning and butchering the kill and the proper songs which should be sung on the return home. Everything must eaten because the *diyin dine'é* decreed that nothing can be wasted or they will send no more game.

The Milky Way — *Yikáísdáhí* — is known as "Awaits-the-Dawn" and reminds people to say their prayers to the dawn, an act which helps to ensure temporal continuity. This ritual enactment compels the relationship to work between humans and the *diyin dine'é*. All relationships in the Navajo world are reciprocal; by fulfilling one's ritual responsibilities, the *diyin dine'é* will respond.

Thus we see that the "Mother Earth, Father Sky" sandpainting not only embodies the balance between male and female necessary to the restoration of *sǫ'a naagháí bik'e hózhǫ́*, but the constellations on the body of Father Sky also serve as a cultural text — "rules for living" (Newcomb 1967:83) — which guide an individual toward the attainment of this desired state. *Náhookǫs bika'ii* (the Big Dipper) and *Ná'hookǫs ba'áadii* (Cassiopeia) embody the balance of male and female within the home. *Dilyéhé* (the Pleiades) serves both as an injunction against disharmony and as a reminder of the balance and beauty inherent in wholeness. Together, *Dilyéhé* and *'Atsé'ets'ózí* (Orion) reflect the dynamic nature of the universe as they mark seasonal transitions. Wisdom and knowledge are embodied in *Hastiin Sik'ai'í* (Corvus). '*Atsé'etsoh* (the front part of Scorpius) represents the desired goal of old age. Balancing the plants on the body of Mother Earth is *Gah heet'e'ii* (the tail of Scorpius), which symbolizes the rabbit and game animals; together the plant and animal symbols serve as visual reminders of reverence for the plants and animals who provide nourishment and life.

The "Mother Earth, Father Sky" sandpainting visually embodies the principle of *sʠ'a naagháii bik'e hózhʠ*, a phrase which is spoken in almost every Navajo prayer and which lies at the heart of Navajo ceremonialism and belief. These words, layered with multiple levels of meaning, are both life's goal and the means by which one reaches that goal. Inherent in this often-heard phrase is the continuous renewal of right relationships among all aspects of existence, relationships that were established by the Holy People at the time of Creation. This sense of connectedness and proper relationship to all other living beings are the essence of Navajo religion.

References Cited

Aberle, David F. 1967. "The Navajo Singer's Fee: Payment or Presentation." In *Studies in Southwestern Ethnolinguistics,* ed. D. H. Hymes and W. E. Bittle, 15–32. The Hague: Mouton.

Arthur, Claudeen, et al. 1982. *Between Sacred Mountains: Navajo Stories and Lessons from the Land.* Tucson: Sun Tracks and the University of Arizona Press.

Farella, John. 1984. *The Main Stalk.* Tucson: University of Arizona Press.

Frisbie, Charlotte J. 1980. "Ritual Drama in the Navajo House Blessing Ceremony." In *Southwestern Indian Ritual Drama,* ed. C. J. Frisbie, 161–98. Albuquerque: School of American Research, University of New Mexico Press.

———. 1987. *Navajo Medicine Bundles or Jish: Acquisition, Transmission, and Disposition in the Past and Present.* Albuquerque: University of New Mexico Press.

Frisbie, Charlotte J., and David P. McAllester, eds. 1978. *Navajo Blessingway Singer: The Autobiography of Frank Mitchell 1881–1967.* Tucson: University of Arizona Press.

Gold, Peter. 1994. *Navajo and Tibetan Sacred Wisdom: The Circle of the Spirit.* Rochester, Vt.: Inner Traditions.

Griffin-Pierce, Trudy. 1992. *Earth Is My Mother, Sky Is My Father: Space, Time, and Astronomy in Navajo Sandpainting.* Albuquerque: University of New Mexico Press.

Hoijer, Harry. 1964. "Cultural Implications of Some Navaho Linguistic Categories." In *Language and Society,* ed. D. Hymes, 142–53. New York: Harper & Row.

McNeley, James K. 1982 [1981]. *Holy Wind in Navajo Philosophy.* Tucson: University of Arizona Press.

Newcomb, Franc Johnson. 1967. *Navaho Folk Tales.* Santa Fe, N.Mex.: Museum of Navajo Ceremonial Art.

Page, Suzanne. 1989. *A Celebration of Being: Photographs of the Hopi and Navajo.* Flagstaff, Ariz.: Northland Press.

Reichard, Gladys A. 1950. *Navaho Religion: A Study of Symbolism.* Bollingen Series 18. Princeton: Princeton University Press.

Spencer, Katherine Halpern. 1957. *Mythology and Values: An Analysis of Navaho Chantway Myths.* Philadelphia: Memoirs of the American Folklore Society 48.

Toelken, Barre. 1977. "The Demands of Harmony: An Appreciation of Navajo Relations." *Parabola* 2:74–81.

———. 1979. *The Dynamics of Folklore.* Boston: Houghton Mifflin.

Trimble, Stephen. 1993. *The People: Indians of the American Southwest.* Santa Fe, N.Mex.: School of American Research Press.

Werner, Oswald, Allen Manning, and Kenneth Yazzie Begishe. 1983. "A Taxonomic View of the Traditional Navajo Universe." In *The Handbook of the American Indians.* Vol. 10, ed. W. C. Sturtevant, 579–91. Washington, D.C.: Smithsonian Institution Press.

Wheelwright, Mary Cabot. 1942. *Navajo Creation Myth.* Santa Fe, N.Mex.: Rydal Press.

Witherspoon, Gary. 1977. *Language and Art in the Navajo Universe.* Ann Arbor: University of Michigan Press.

Wyman, Leland C. 1970a. *Blessingway.* Tucson: University of Arizona Press.

Wyman, Leland C. 1970b. *Sandpaintings of the Navajo Shootingway and the Walcott Collection.* Smithsonian Contributions of Anthropology 13. Washington, D.C.: Government Printing Office.

———. 1983. *Southwest Indian Drypainting.* Santa Fe: School of American Research, and Albuquerque: University of New Mexico Press.

Personal Communications

Consultant A 1990
Consultant B 1991

⚙ S I X ⚙

In the Space between Earth and Sky: Contemporary Mescalero Apache Ceremonialism

Inés Talamantez

In Mescalero Apache cosmology, 'Isánáklésh is described as one of the five divine deities present at the time of creation. In those first days, she appeared with the lower half of her face painted with white earth clay and her body completely covered with yellow cattail pollen; she wore a necklace of abalone shell as she watched over all things growing on earth. Using her power, *diye,* she ripened trees, plants, the flowers of the fields, fruits, and medicinal herbs. Her compassion and creative wisdom as healer provided information from the beginning of time about the animals, plants, and people, in order to aid those who suffered from disease, injury, or distress. Before this time, healing knowledge did not exist. This chapter introduces a myth critical for understanding the young woman's initiation ceremony of the Mescalero Apache and their religious values. The myth was given to the Apache people by 'Isánáklésh herself, and it is important because it provides the framework for the ceremony which is practiced today. In addition, if we reflect upon the myth, we begin to see the religious, intellectual, and aesthetic climate in which the ceremony takes its beginnings and how these beginnings continue to influence the community today, despite slight changes in the ceremony over time.

From a theoretical perspective, Grenville Goodwin's monograph, *Social Organization of the Western Apache,* has been useful in this analysis. In his work on Apache female initiation, Goodwin recognizes pubescent Apache girls as central figures who become charged through the ceremony with power which can be utilized by the community for the growth of crops, good health, and long life.[1] Similarly, Van Gennep, in a classic analysis of rites of passage, echoes this idea, elaborating also on how the female sponsor explains the relationship between ritual behavior and the dynamics of individual and group life to the initiate, he argues that women's fertility is frequently associated with creative thinking.[2] In Mescalero culture, religious creative thinking is spoken, sung, or chanted by ritual specialists in intricate patterns, often using esoteric language. The impetus for these traditions stems from the visible patterns observed in nature which are often seen to be ordered and sustained as well as cyclical, and which in this case are ultimately heard and ceremonialized. Nature's seasonal renewal is studied by Apache religious specialists as the most consistent visible pattern which people can associate with the life cycle of an initiate. In other words, people's beliefs regarding the transformations that occur in nature are associated with the ritual transformations that a young girl experiences in her rite of passage from girlhood to female deity to womanhood.

Bruce Lincoln, in *Emerging from the Chrysalis*, writes, "Each time a woman is initiated, the world is saved from chaos, for the fundamental power of creativity is renewed in her being."[3] Mescalero Apache believe that, as each initiate is transformed into 'Isánáklésh, our mother, the earth, the world itself is again created. Each time a girl's life is celebrated through the ceremony, the earth is celebrated as well. Mescaleros view the initiate's changing body in the same way they view the changes that occur in the springtime in the natural world. What is important in both cases is that the balance, symmetry, and harmony seen in the natural world are the most important criteria for the ways in which human bodies, and especially the bodies of the female initiates are intimately related and seen as one.

One of the classic examples of this idea can be found in Harry Hoijer's version of the Apache creation myth, collected from an Apache named Charlie Smith. In this version of the myth, Life Giver and Child of Water, the culture hero and son of 'Isánáklésh, creates what he feels is necessary for the people's well-being. He realizes that something is still missing and asks 'Isánáklésh for help. She appears and provides knowledge of what will be needed for healing and maintaining balance.

---

1. Grenville Goodwin, *Social Organization of the Western Apache* (Tucson: University of Arizona Press, 1969).

2. Arnold Van Gennep, *Rites of Passage* (Chicago: University of Chicago Press, 1960).

3. Bruce Lincoln, *Emerging from the Chrysalis* (Chicago: University of Chicago Press), 107.

She tells about plants, minerals, grasses, and herbs, because she knows there will be diseases among the people that will need to be cured.[4] In the contemporary ceremony, the initiate's sponsor, the *nadekleshen*, provides the girl with traditional healing knowledge which is still used as medicine today. The young initiate is instructed where and when to collect plants and herbs used in healing, how to store them, and how to use them. These are examples of knowledge provided through the myth that is still recounted and relevant, especially for the women as they seek to live balanced lives.

The work of Driver, Hoijer, Opler, Basso, Goodwin, and Ball reflects a variety of concerns with young girls as a primary source for cultural continuity.[5] This female initiation ceremony is based on a mythological figure who was the first to be initiated into womanhood and is involved in a continual ritual transformation which, when completed, rewards the community with a new woman, if all the rituals are performed correctly. In this myth, the female deity never grows old. 'Isánáklésh gives her womanhood and knowledge to the initiate, and in exchange the girl gives her youth to 'Isánáklésh, who is once again made young. Since the girl is young, it is said that her body is soft like clay, and like clay, she is capable of being molded into the body of the female deity. But it is the deity's power which she acquires that allows her to grow into womanhood, continuing the cycle of life.

This critical time of female transformation is ceremonialized in many societies. Warner has pointed out that the life cycle is "punctuated by a number of critical moments of transition which all societies ritualize and publicly mark with suitable observances to impress the significance of the individual and the group or living members of the community."[6] What Van Gennep identified as female puberty ceremonies, because they elaborately delineate initiation into adult life at menarche, is still practiced in many places, although not always at menarche. These

---

4. Harry Hoijer, *Mescalero and Chiricahua Apache Texts* (Chicago: University of Chicago Press, 1937).

5. See Harold Driver, "Culture Element Distributions: 16 Girls' Puberty Rites in Western North America," *Comparative Studies by Harold Driver and Essays in His Honor,* ed. Joseph G. Jorgenson (New Haven: HRAF Press, 1974): 149–61; Hoijer (1937); Morris E. Opler, *An Apache Lifeway: the Economic, Social, and Religious Institutions of the Chiricahua Indians* (Chicago: University of Chicago Press, 1941); Keith Basso, "The Gift of Changing Woman," *Bulletin of the Bureau of American Ethnology* 196 (Washington, D.C.: U.S. Government Printing Office, 1966); Goodwin (1969); and Eve Ball, *Indeh: An Apache Odyssey* (Albuquerque: University of New Mexico Press, 1980).

6. Lloyd Warner, *The Living and the Dead: A Study of the Symbolic Life of Americans* (New Haven: Yale University Press, 1959), 303.

ceremonies are also usually guided by corresponding myths, whenever they are still available.

Since the cultures and landscapes differ in various natural areas, symbolism in the myths differs as well, according to geographical differences and different eco-systems. What remains the same is the way the people create their sacred symbolism from their immediate environment. For example, Seri girls are bathed in the coastal salt water and their hair is washed in it. Marine animals figure largely in Seri initiation songs. Similarly at Mescalero, the lower half of initiates' faces are painted with white clay, utilizing the appropriate nature symbolism mentioned in the myth. A special ceremonial dress, made from natural materials gathered in the area, is provided and the singers use deer hoof rattles, all materials collected from the natural environment in which they live.

J. Stephen Lansing's book *Three Worlds of Bali* provides an example from another part of the world. Lansing refers to ritual as "the window to another world." He argues that the divine is in everything, even the body of a dancer or singer. Further, he points to the role of the ceremonial participants in understanding that they must maintain balance. Cycles of growth and decay must be kept under control. Lansing quotes one Balinese as saying, "We will not let the forces of change overwhelm us. We will not let our culture die."[7] This, of course, is the argument for why these ceremonies persist in many indigenous cultures striving to live balanced lives in a world seen as out of balance. Threatened cultures recognize the continuity of these ceremonies for their survival. In American society today, the new interest in female initiation reflects concerns with the cycle of a woman's life, especially the lives of young girls, human rights, as well as current concerns with environmental issues. Just as social changes in this society affect the lives of women, technological development and pollution affect the cycles of nature. There is much work to be done to achieve and maintain balance in women's lives as well as the earth's life.

At Mescalero, cultural continuity today is also reflected in the way that myths are told. When chanter Willetto Antonio, my mentor, was interrupted while telling the myth of creation, he would keep in mind and remember where he left off, and then start over from the beginning of the myth. Repeatedly he emphasized the importance of the correct

---

7. John Stephen Lansing, *The Three Worlds of Bali* (New York: Praeger, 1983).

continuity of the story line. Once, many years ago, I made the mistake of asking him a question during a pause. Nonverbally he communicated to me that I had distracted him. For the duration of the telling, I decided to keep quiet and only listen. Following his lead, I saved my questions for later. The next day, when I asked him to retell a portion of the myth that I was unable to understand, he agreed to help. He did this by starting all over again from the beginning of the myth, which took three hours to tell.

While there are always a series of versions of any myth, at Mescalero all versions are honored. Someone else's version is never questioned. At Mescalero the creation myth provides the framework for the elaborate song cycle and rituals which bring about the transformations of the young girls during their initiation ceremonies. This process of transforming the young initiate into 'Isánáklésh through song, and her corresponding movement into the role of deity and then woman, is elaborated in Talamantez and Shapiro, from a ceremony held on July 4, 1984.[8]

This work is based on the Mescalero Apache version of the myth as sung by the chanter mentioned earlier, Willetto Antonio. For the past twenty-five years, Mr. Antonio has guided me in studying and analyzing this myth and its corresponding set of songs and rituals celebrated in 'Isánáklésh Gotal. The following portion of the myth was related to me and two of my graduate students in the forest at Mescalero on a most remarkable summer day.[9]

Willetto told me that in the beginning each singer sang about a different part of 'Isánáklésh as they observed her for the first time, emerging out of a body of water somewhere to the north of where we live today in the state of New Mexico. Each singer created a different song according to what he saw. Singers gathered together and told what they observed of 'Isánáklésh, and that's how the songs came into being. The songs refer to the different parts of the body and characteristics of 'Isánáklésh. Willetto goes on to tell the sacred story:

---

8. Inés Talamantez with Anne Dhu McLucas, "The Mescalero Apache Girls' Puberty Ceremony: A Consideration of the Role of Music in Structuring Ritual Time and Transformation," *Yearbook of the International Council for Traditional Music* 18 (1986): 17–90.

9. This took six hours because I wrote it all out in longhand. At the time I was not allowed to use a tape recorder. This restriction has changed for me over the years that we have worked together. I first had to establish my sincerity in wanting to study the ceremony, and I had to prove that I was willing to work toward that end. Once I had established this trust, I could use the tape recorder.

When she first appeared, that is, when she began to come up out of the water, with early morning light, they could see only the lower half of her face painted with white clay. Yellow cattail pollen was all around in the air and on the water. The water had a shoreline. Where we are now, here at Mescalero, all was underwater at that time. People were living on the earth, but they were different from us. The Holy People who were present then sent the water away so that people could live here safely. When the big water receded, a flood came from the north. Everything was once again covered with water. That floodwater was different from the water we use now, it was clean and pure. Toward the east, you can still see those white high-water marks on the mountains, they are clearly marked. At that time when that water was here, the earth was here, also, only it was below that first water. Again when the water receded, from there they created the first songs about this land, about what they experienced and exactly what they saw. With beautiful language they described everything in great detail.

It took a long time as the people wandered all over the earth to find a safe place to live where they would have food and shelter. Suddenly one day the Holy People saw something in the water and they called to the others, and they came and together tried to help the being out of the water. Only half of the face was out of the water when they first saw this being, yet it is said that they thought about it and that they said that it looked like them. The hair was black and covered with yellow pollen, and matted from being in the water for such a long, long time. The dark skin was shimmering with pollen dust from the cattails all around the water's edge. But yet as they watched they were aware that it was different from them somehow. There was something about it that made it different. Some were scared and wanted to leave it alone. Some wanted to take it in and get it out of the water. They couldn't figure it out! You see, it was underwater from the nose down, so it could not talk to them.

They sent someone to check on it for four days. Those days were different, not as we know them. We don't know how long those days were. Before they decided that they should help it out of the water, they thought about it for a long time. On the fourth day, they checked as the sun came up: the face was out of the water and the hair was dry enough for it to be recognized as a person. The lower half of the face, from below the eyes, was stained white from the minerals in the water, just as minerals mark the mountains or a river bank when the water recedes, creating a stain as it is dried by the air and the sunlight.

From where I am now, the sun rises over the mountains to the east. It travels across the southern sky during the daylight, and sets in the western horizon during the night. It travels across the northern sky in the dark, and we don't see it again until the early morning, when once more it rises.

On the fourth day of the sun's movement across the sky, they decided to try to get it out of the water. They helped it out very slowly by asking it to hold on to the tip of an eagle feather (tip end), which they held out to it. Each of those men as they helped it saw a different part of it as they tried to help it out of the water. One of them saw one side of the face; another saw the forehead; another saw the ears. One saw a little farther down to the white chin. In between they created songs for her. It took time for the water to go down. Finally, when the water went down to the chin from the eyes, they waited another four days. The white markings on the chin represented the rocks close to the tops of hills around here, the rock cliffs. It was at the same time as the water receded and uncovered the rocks that this being was getting born or coming out of the water. Next time the water receded again, the water went down and uncovered her shoulders, and in between we don't know how long it took for all of this to happen. The singers realized finally that it was a young girl. They sang songs for her as this being came out of the water. Songs are sung on the last night of the ceremony today because that's when the girl *is* 'Isánáklésh coming out of the water. The girl is going through what 'Isánáklésh went through. The girl is becoming 'Isánáklésh, and on the last morning they paint half of her face white like 'Isánáklésh's face when they found her in the primordial waters, her face stained white from the minerals in the water.

Down to her breasts, she was exposed now. They got that far, then the Holy People decided she should be covered nice and warm like other women. That's when they put buckskin on her to cover her breasts. We don't know how long it took after they covered her breasts. The water went down some more.

They killed an antelope. Antelope was dangerous to people then. They prayed to it that they could get some medicine from the antelope. They wanted the antelope to be good to the people. They split his toes so he would not run so fast and be mean to people. He then provided food for the people. They used it for meat. They also took the antelope medicine. They took the things that hang down from the antelope, the dew laps. They put these on the girl for earrings so that she would be beautiful. And then the same medicine antelope didn't want to share his meat. He said, "If you eat my hide you will die." After a while they said, "No, we only want your flesh." So he said, "Okay, you can have my flesh." The people gave thanks and they were grateful.

They fed 'Isánáklésh meat, and they all moved down a little farther south. They found a buffalo, which had more meat than the antelope. He, too, was mean. He would not allow himself to be caught or killed. Hunters couldn't keep up with the buffalo. In the mornings they could see him. Then they would lose sight of him. They would hunt for days. One day this man got lost. Tired, he stopped to rest. He put his head on an anthill for a headrest, and he received some important information from the ant world about directions and where to find food.

When he awoke ants came out and asked why he was sad and crying. He told an ant he was hungry and lost. The fog had settled very low for a long time and he lost all sense of direction. Ant told him, "When we all bring food home to the anthill we always come in from the east side. So if you find an anthill you will find your direction." Today it is still true. Ant gave him directions and told him where to find food, so he took off and found another place to spend the night before getting home.

The next morning Prairie Dog came out and asked the man why he was crying. "I'm crying because I'm hungry and thirsty." Prairie Dog went in his hole and came out with a little leaf with drops of water. "What do I do with this drop of water?"

"Put it underground, there is water there. Now eat this leaf." And he never could eat it all. That's where he got some food. Then he dug for water, and he was ready to go on his way again.

Then he told Prairie Dog, "I need to get hold of Buffalo, that man up there. I know he sees me and smells me, but I can't get him." Then Prairie Dog bore a hole straight down, it was an escape hole. Then he bore up to Buffalo. He pulled some hair off his left side under his arm. Buffalo got mad. Prairie Dog said, "Don't get mad. I just need a little fur to keep my babies warm."

Prairie Dog went back to the man and told him how to get to Buffalo and where to shoot him, and then he dropped down his escape hole, straight down. The man shot Buffalo straight through the heart. The man also dropped down Prairie Dog's escape hole. Buffalo dug down, and at the end, he died. Today Buffalo has a hole on his left side where he has no hair. That's where he got shot. Prairie Dog escape holes are twenty-two feet deep. After that he knew how to get buffaloes. He needed the buffalo for its meat, hide, and intestines. He took buffalo meat back to the people. They took the buffalo intestines and filled them with blood to go get Eagle, who was a manhunter at that time. They filled the intestines with blood and wrapped them around the man to lure eagle. Eagle killed with the power of its eyes then. Eagle saw the man and shot at him with its eyes. Eagle picked up the intestines full of blood and took it to its chicks. The man was still tied to the eagle and alive, so he made noises and the chicks heard: "Shhh, shhh, shhh, shhh." Eagle asked the eagle chicks why they had not eaten. The chicks were afraid. The man shook off some of the weight of the intestines, and some of the chicks got some food. Eagle came back and started to roost. The man shot Eagle right under the chin. Today eagles have a little hole there from the man's arrow.

Eagle got excited. The man jumped up and got on the back of the Eagle, then Eagle took off. The man was on his back and Eagle twisted him back and forth and finally had him land close to his camp.

By this time, back where the girl was, she is uncovered down to her knees, she is almost ready to come out of the water. So while the man was hunting Eagle, the other men covered her breasts with hide. Across her chest was a red earth mark. There should be a red mark there on the initiate's dress today. They trimmed her dress with deer hoof rattles, like the singer's rattle. This made a nice soft rattling sound. Under the red mark on her chest, they put a rattle there of shells. So the dress should have a red line and shells attached to the red line. The red line and the shells are Apache symbols of earth minerals, stained by the water.

From then on they conquered Eagle and told him to behave. They told him not to act so big and not to be mean to the people. They would always use his feathers. Today they use two layers of tail feathers for decoration on [the initiate's] hair at the top of her head. They always use only top-layer feathers for the girl's hair. They use the fourth feather of the left side for a feather fan for fanning the girl.

Now she is down to her skirt markings. The skirt fringes came from the antelope. They put the two pieces of buffalo hide on her, down to her ankle. They prayed to Eagle and took number one and two left-side eagle feathers and gave it to her across the water so that she could walk out onto the land. The singer held the tail end in his right hand, and the girl held the tip end with her left hand, as they led her out. We still do that in the tipi to bring the young girl into the tipi on the first night, just as the singers brought 'Isánáklésh out of the primordial waters. Finally they sang again for her and pulled her very carefully out of the water. We don't know how long it took to do this. She had great trouble walking.

After she had eaten deer meat to make sure she was alive, they decided to put moccasins on her. They made her moccasins of buffalo hide for the bottom, buckskin for the top, and deer sinew to tie them together. The top part of her dress is from buffalo hide. Doeskin is used for the skirt because it's softer. They let her stand there so that she would dry out. They led her off onto the earth where she would dry off and get warm. They tried to give her some water, but she didn't know how to drink water, so they took a dry tule reed, put water on her hand, and she sucked it up, refreshing herself. 'Isánáklésh today, during the ceremony, must also drink water through a reed. She had her mouth closed for so long and her mouth was very dry. Today the initiate must make sure water does not touch her lips because the water may rise and cause flooding. Sun Clan girls have an eagle fan on the right side of the dress skirt, above the knee, tied to the fringes. They use them for fanning with a feather. The feather is for warding off any bad dreams.

They talked about all of this for a long time, and decided to
have a ceremony for her. They decided, "Let's have a *gotal* [cere-
mony]." They selected a special place that was nice and flat and
beautiful as nature can be. There they set up tipis but they wanted
hers to be special and different from the other tipis. That place
where they were had the evergreen sugar fir, which was chosen
for all the poles for her tipi.

Bitl guh iyah, my daughter [addressing me], always remember
that she worked her way up from the bottom of the water, and we
were the ones to help her out so that as she came up she could see
clearly. As everything on the earth leveled off she made it to the
top, to the earth's surface. You know what's going on. Today we
still have 'Isánáklésh's ceremony for all the people. We pray for
all people, even though you have not been here we have prayed
for you. At the end of the ceremony she runs to the east to the
sun so that we will all live on. We live in the space between the
earth and the sky.

At the end of the ceremony, it got cloudy, sprinkling rain, misty.
A man with Eagle Rower came on the scene. So he sat and prayed
for the girl and for advice to let him know if it's okay to do what
he was about to do. He asked if he could have all these different
groups of Indians who were present recognized and blessed. He
prayed again and again, and he was answered with lightning.

He prayed to the east, where the sun comes up. The answer
was yes, you may do it.

He prayed to the south, where the sun moves across the sky.
The answer was yes, you may do it.

He prayed to the west, where the sun goes down. the answer
was yes, you may do it.

He prayed to the north, where it is dark. The answer was yes,
you may do it.

North Lightning came on, and he said yes, and that's when
Thunder spoke. So today we have lightning, and if you see four
lightnings, one after the other, it's a blessing.

He turned around and grabbed a thunder and lightning in the
palm of his hand. He turned around and put it on her shoulder.
This is medicine full of power. Then it rained very heavy to bless
the people. Rain from the south. Hail from the north. This is the
first morning prayer.

He did that again, then the wind came from the south. Wind here still comes from the south to the north. From the north came the snow. All four seasons were present during that time of the ceremony.

He prayed again, arms up to the sun, and everything quit. Rainbow and Sun came out. Then he brought the eagle. Still in the morning of the first day, Lightning Man blessed the bird again. He gave out all of the eagles' chest feathers to all the peoples of the world who were gathered there. They all have eagle feathers up to today. All different tribes are related to the beginning tipi in this way by the eagle feathers. All who came to 'Isánáklésh's *gotal,* all got blessed with red clay and pollen and all went home with feathers. *Ako sha.* And so, that's when all the different tribes developed their own ways of doing things.

They kept on moving south. Different generations interpreted things differently, according to what they saw, but all that time while 'Isánáklésh was getting created, she was never out of the evergreens. There were also oak, pine, aspen, and spruce trees. She was at home in the trees, she loved the forest. She never went back to the lowlands for water, and so it is.

Evergreen trees have to be prayed over, cut and carried to other places where there are not appropriate trees for creating the ceremonial tipi. After everyone leaves the ceremony, 'Isánáklésh the initiate turned into a deity, and now a new Apache woman has to stay and help her people clear the camp before leaving. This is all done in a quiet reflective mood. Since there are many people and they come from long distances, she has to work with her mind to wish them safe journeys home and with her body to help them break camp. For a long time before the ceremony the initiate is trained for ceremonial running. She wears heavy clothing and learns that it's not easy to have a strong body. Sometimes it takes years of planning for 'Isánáklésh Gotal.[10] People have to go to the flats to collects Indian foods. Some years earlier, when the Pacific Ocean was still in New Mexico, that's when the Gahe, or Mountain Spirits, came, and people saw them for the first time. They came with the flood; the time is unknown. They are now

---

10. The ceremony is referred to as 'Isánáklésh Gotal among the medicine people.

also part of the ceremony. With their power they bless the initiate, the fire, the ceremonial area, the tipi, and the people.

Right after the water went down, they came from the south on top of the water. A blind man and a crippled man found them on the Guadalupe Mountains. The blind man carried the crippled man. We do know the Gahe are very old. They came long before the white man came.

When they brought her out of the water, 'Isánáklésh didn't know how to walk. She came out on the shore, shaking and cold. That was the way she walked, the way the young girls dance on the hide today. The hide she dances on represents the silky sandy beach she came on. The jumping step, hands on hips with a kicking forward step, she learned later, because she was proud that she had learned how to walk and kick her legs with her arms on her hips in a strong way.

Where we found her could be near the Canadian border, some-where on the other side of North Dakota near Regina. As the water is draining, and the ice is melting. From cold weather we go to warm weather in one day. Like the making of the North American continent. You know what I mean. We did our share.

Change at Mescalero is inevitable, as it is in any culture, and there are many examples of diversity among the Apache. Yet in discussing 'Isánáklésh Gotal with some older women, they insisted that the cere-mony is still the same as when they were girls; as a matter of fact, one of them claimed that it is unchanged from the very beginning. Each of these women had different descriptions of their experience, yet they all agreed that the ceremony was the same. The changes were in the minute details of practice rather than in the overall ritual process. The running of the first and last mornings of the ceremony was done for a much greater distance (over a mile) and, usually, young children ran with the initiate. Today, in private ceremonies the girl usually runs alone, although Willetto Antonio, going along with the earlier tradi-tion, instructs young children to run with 'Isánáklésh. Some of the dietary restrictions and other practices, such as the use of the scratch-ing stick and the drinking reed, are still observed. In the face painting there is some variation depending on the style of the singer. Willetto Antonio insists that only the lower half of the face is to be painted. The painting of the whole face implies ghostlike qualities.

The most obvious change that I have noticed has to do with the four days of quiet meditative isolation after the four days of ritual activity. Here the strict lines of conduct are often relaxed. The constant visits and supervision of the *nadekleshen* (sponsor) are required for this process to be effective. The taxing constraints of the eight days of ceremonial activity on the sponsors away from their homes and jobs have implications for this process. Ceremonial drinking and gift giving are often commented on as being different from the way things used to be. According to individual reactions by consultants, and also in informal conversations, these minor changes have not altered 'Isánáklésh Gotal from the beginning of mythological times.

Interviews with female Apaches ranging in age from ten to seventy-five years reveal how they feel about 'Isánáklésh as being most important for their identity as women and the survival of the Apache people. The older women agree that as long as 'Isánáklésh Gotal is practiced, the Apache people will continue as a viable culture. Although cultural change due to non-Indian and Christian influences is obvious on the reservation, the ceremony continues to emphasize Apache values and to instruct the people that it is also possible to continue to apply Apache concepts to the inevitability of having to live in a changing world. Today, young initiates are instructed to apply the teachings of the ceremony in preparing themselves for careers as well as for family life and as members of Apache culture. Just as the ceremony moves her from one stage of life to another, the young woman must realize that the tribe is also undergoing a transitional stage. The ceremony is a symbolic representation of transformation and a behavioral model for how to handle change, whether it be personal, familial, or social. Many people are caught between the traditional Apache lifeway with its ideals and values and the values imposed on them by non-Indian teachers, preachers, counselors, and government bureaucrats. In defiance of rapid societal and religious changes introduced by others to the area, 'Isánáklésh Gotal, in its re-creation of sacred myth into contemporary religious practice, functions as the most significant factor in preserving traditional Apache values and giving them meaning in present-day Apache life.

The people are aware of the power this ceremony has for stabilizing their identity, religious beliefs, and cultural practices. Although many ceremonies and their corresponding myths have become obsolete, there is a revival of some of the almost-forgotten practices with a renewed zeal that resists acculturation and religious conversion. This resistance implies a symbolic thrust in the direction of cultural preservation. The insistence of the women on preserving and maintaining this ceremony for their daughters and granddaughters is the best assurance for its continuity. Women know that survival implies preserving culture as well as the Earth Mother, 'Isánáklésh. In this sense, 'Isánáklésh Gotal is seen as both preventive and curative.

It is 'Isánáklésh who instructed her son, Child of Water, on how to use the many herbs and minerals that will cure diseases. If a plant's root is used, then there are explicit instructions on what to do with the other parts of the plant. They are not to be left behind in a careless way.

Herbal medicine, she instructs, will cure if it is breathed in four times in a ceremonial manner. Things of a ceremonial nature are usually repeated four times and in a prescribed directional manner, starting with the place where the sun rises in the east, then recognizing the way the sun moves over the southern sky, then where it sets in the west, and finally the direction in which it does not appear at all (the north) until it again rises in the east.

Cattail pollen, known as the pollen of the earth, is the symbol for the generative life-giving powers of the earth as they go out to the four directions through chants and prayers. To live in the pollen way means to live in balance and harmony. This symmetry is learned by observing the balance and harmony that we see in nature. Nature teaches in the most perfect way what it is that we as people need to learn to live in an aesthetic, sustainable manner.

Even the rocks used to crush herbs and the various minerals are to be used in a sacred manner, so that nothing is wasted. If anything is mixed with pollen, then 'Isánáklésh will give it the power to heal. She goes on to speak of the herbs, trees, and mineral substances vital to the people's well-being, all of the things necessary to sustain life and cure humankind so that people may live in a peaceful, harmonious way. In the creation myth, 'Isánáklésh gives to the Mescaleros the ceremony for counteracting the disease and imbalances that provoke disharmony. Through continued use of these rites, the women and men of the tribe make it clear that they still see 'Isánáklésh as the model of heroic and virtuous womanhood.

For pubescent girls, having a ceremony requires spiritual, physical, and psychological preparation far ahead of their menarche. Although the symbols that are used to influence them vary considerably in function, their overall purpose is to convince the girls that they will undergo good and positive changes if they participate fully in the ceremony, putting forth their best efforts. Some have been told from a very young age about the importance of the ceremony for a good, healthy, long life, and they are continually encouraged by female kin so that they begin to anticipate their ceremony. Often prepubescent girls will come to observe the ceremony of other initiates primarily as a way of knowing what to expect. Many times I have heard mothers of young girls say, "Go up toward the front of the Big Tipi where you can see and hear everything better."

Since at this young age the girls are thought of as soft and moldable, this implies that they can still be conditioned and influenced by female kin. Some girls are easier to convince to participate in the ceremony than others. Some need to be awakened to their female identity; others need to be calmed down and taught to be more feminine, following the ritual design of the ceremony. Two Apache concepts are at work: awakening the initiate to the world around her and calming the unrestrained nature of adolescence. Both concepts, as well as the symbols that imply and strengthen the concept of self within the community, are central to the transformative process. These symbols are engaged over and over again, demonstrating the multiplicity of rituals concerned with the life cycle as individuals face the critical periods of transition in their lives, from birth to a wise old age.

In the Americas, the ritual transformation of initiate to divinity to woman is a powerful rite of passage. In many of these ceremonies the female deities are models for perfect appropriate female behavior; the young girls are told to concentrate, focus, and work hard so that they too can become the perfect paradigmatic figure of the female deity, our mother the earth. In the Mescalero ritual transformation, "becoming" the deity is clearly distinct from "imitating" the deity.

Analysis of these transformative changes within the ceremony allows us to understand that there is no one moment in which the transformation occurs. It takes place over the entire eight-day period as the initiate's childhood identity is transformed into 'Isánáklésh and then ultimately into womanhood through the power generated by a complexity of ritual actions brought into effect by the correct ceremonial order. Great attention is paid to the structural details of the ritual activity, symbols, and their corresponding meanings. Explanations given to the initiate by her sponsor allow her to understand how to incorporate the important cultural elements that she will now be charged with maintaining. After her ceremony she will be a keeper of Apache traditions and the community in which the traditions continue to endure. This knowledge can also provide meaningful paradigms for the young women of mainstream America, as we move into the new millennium.

When Arnold Van Gennep wrote about rites of passage, he commented that rarely do physical and social puberty converge. I propose that this rare convergence does occur as it is ritually performed by the Mescalero Apache in 'Isánáklésh Gotal. In this example the physiological changes in a girl as she reaches menarche are marked and accompanied by a change in social status. The meaning of this ceremony is embedded in the ritual transformation of the pubescent girl as she moves through the door of adolescence from one state of mind or spiritual being into the transformative state in which she incorporates the deity into herself and becomes 'Isánáklésh. If the ceremony is successful, she then leaves behind the ways of childhood and emerges as a responsible young Apache woman, able to carry on the Apache traditions as well as to bestow the gift of life.

In this ritual sequence, the tripartite schema of separation, transition, and incorporation that Van Gennep identified as features of rites of passage collapses into the one ceremony. Initially, the young girl is *separated* from her family and her usual daily activities to live in her own private tipi specifically constructed for the ceremony. In the preliminal rites of this stage of separation, she is without social status, no longer a child but not yet a woman.

During the process of ritual transformation, she is in *transition*. In this state of liminality, the rites are designed to inscribe in her the traditional Apache knowledge and wisdom as she changes from girl to deity and then into transformation. After this stage, she is *incorporated* back into the community with a new social status. The postliminal rites involve using her new power by blessing those in the community who so request it. She is also allowed time to reflect back on the ceremony and the powerful changes she has just undergone.

Each of these stages is accompanied with sacred songs which generate *diye*, power. They are used to distort the present time and return us to mythological time, when the deities lived on the earth. They then bring time forward to the present by reenacting the myth which becomes ceremony with its designated sacred rituals. Through song, the young girl is transformed into the deity and finally into a new Apache woman. This complex system is nourished through the rituals that are composed of symbols as the smallest component of the ceremony. The sacred meaning of ceremonies that have persisted over time is transferred to the Apache through these sacred symbols of power, which are used to distinguish ritual reality from everyday life. Without such symbols, the primary participants could not enter into the state of ritual, and thus be properly prepared for ceremonial transformation.

For the past twenty years there has been a concerted effort by feminist writers and thinkers to focus their research on the struggle for female identity. This Apache ceremony is especially timely as contemporary women question what it means to be a woman at this time in history. As we move forward to create our place in a society that has ignored and consistently coerced women into either imitating male social order or living silently in their shadows, we are ambivalent and uncertain. We search for female models and rites of initiation, and, yes, we search for the deity.

In the creation myth, 'Isánáklésh describes the importance of having this beautiful ceremony for all of the young girls of the tribe. She describes the singing of many songs whose power will bless and guide the young girls into strong women who will live a long life. These women instructed in the sacred knowledge of the tribe will assure its cultural survival. Here in the space between the earth and the sky every time we have the ceremony we pray for all women, the earth, and all of its entities, as well as for all men. Even though you have never been there you have been prayed over.

⚡ S E V E N ⚡

Synchretism, Revival, and Reinvention: Tlingit Religion, Pre- and Postcontact

Richard Dauenhauer

The Tlingit Indians live in southeast Alaska from Yakutat to Dixon Entrance, predominantly on the coast, but with inland communities along the Chilkat and Stikine Rivers in Alaska, and in southwest Yukon and northwest British Columbia. A variety of evidence as well as Tlingit tradition suggests that the Tlingits migrated to the coast at a very early date and spread along the coast from the southern range of their territory to the north, where they were expanding toward the Copper River at the time of European contact. This part of Alaska is an archipelago roughly the same size and shape as Italy, with few communities connected by road, so that contact is primarily by ferry or air. Native people live in scattered, predominantly Native villages of several hundred people, and also in larger cities such as Juneau, Ketchikan, and Sitka. In the past one hundred years there has been significant intermarriage with other Native people and with non-Natives. From the point of view of religion, it is important to remember that all communities are now ethnically mixed to some degree, and that most American religious denominations are present (especially in the larger communities), but not all have equally significant Tlingit membership, and not all have had the same historical influence.

Coastal Tlingits live in and on the edge of a rain forest — the most extensive temperate rain forest in the world, reaching from Puget Sound to Kodiak Island — and this environment has shaped their lifestyle and material culture, along with those of other cultures of the region. With their immediate neighbors to the south, the Haida and Tsimshian, the Tlingit comprise a northern subgroup of Northwest

Coast culture. Native American culture of the Northwest Coast has captured the imagination of explorers since first contact. These are the people of totem poles, elaborately carved wooden bowls and bentwood boxes, plank houses, oceangoing canoes, Chilkat robes, button blankets, and other well-known cultural features, especially the ceremony known in English as "potlatch." To the extent that the visual art and its role in potlatch was connected with traditional religion, both art and potlatch became targets of attack by some (but not all) missionaries.

Because this region is famous for its totem poles, a few words about them are in order. Totem poles were equated with "graven images" by many missionaries, but totem poles were never worshiped or prayed to. They were and are essentially heraldic and refer to the genealogy of the person or group that commissioned the pole to be carved and erected. The images do not "tell" a story as much as allude to stories already known, much as the Christian cross does not "tell the Easter story" but alludes to a story familiar from other sources.

The most significant impact on the history and contemporary practice of Tlingit religion is contact first with Russians (1794–1867) and then with Euro-Americans (following the sale of Alaska by the Russians to the United States in 1867). In general, descriptions of Native American religion can be divided into two groups: those that recognize and incorporate dynamic interaction with postcontact religion as part of the complete picture of the religion of the community today, and those that do not, but insist on an isolated "purity" of the precontact culture and either ignore Christianity or view postcontact influences as "contamination." I think it is unrealistic to describe only precontact or reconstructed memory culture as if it were a static "golden age" and to ignore or deny the presence of contemporary religion and worldview. The historical and living dynamics of mission and contact are very complex and are an important part of Tlingit intellectual history. In this overview I will address precontact Tlingit religion, major postcontact religious influences, and some contemporary interactions of the two. As this is a complex topic with substantial documentation, I also note principal sources for further reading and more detailed information.

Precontact Tlingit Religion

It is impossible to reconstruct the precontact Tlingit religious system in complete detail with absolute certainty. But we do know much about

its basic principles from the patterns and examples that survive today in practice, in memory, and in earlier documentation. The central
belief was that everything has spirit; not only humans, but animals,
plants, and features of the natural world such as water, mountains, and
glaciers. Rules of personal behavior emphasized the importance of being respectful, not only to other humans, but to the nonhuman forms
as well, which were also instilled with spirit life. Religious thought was
linked with ritual action. It was important to speak and even think
kindly and respectfully of and to nonhuman forms. Especially in hunting, fishing, and proper treatment of the bodies, food, and remains of
fish and animals proper behavior was essential. The belief was that fish
and animals give themselves to humans, who must remain in a proper
spiritual state and frame of mind to benefit from the relationship. Very
often, the mythical covenants for the present relationship stem from
an incident of disrespectful behavior in the past, as a result of which
ancestors or progenitors of the modern people either gave their lives or
survived out-of-body experiences after which the rules for proper behavior and ritual protocol were handed down. This is a major genre of
Tlingit and neighboring Northwest Coast oral literature (Dauenhauer
and Dauenhauer 1987).

It seems that in many shamanic traditions the right to hunt is
typically established in ancient covenants (myth); continuing luck
or success is confirmed through ritual observances and correct personal thought and behavior (Hamayon 1992). (For Tlingit examples,
see Dauenhauer and Dauenhauer 1987:166–93 regarding brown bear;
Swanton 1909:301–20 for salmon.) Myth is the single event in the
past that establishes the covenant; the ritual is the ongoing imitation,
remembrance, or representation, such as the Jewish seder, Christian
communion, and the Tlingit ḵoo.éex' (or "potlatch," described in a later
section), and other personal or private observances. (For examples of
Tlingit texts of myth and ritual see Dauenhauer and Dauenhauer 1987
and 1990, respectively; also Dauenhauer and Dauenhauer 1994b for a
set of texts paired to demonstrate this relationship.)

Many situations could be considered spiritually dangerous. Therefore
conduct was governed by a system of taboos and rewards. Disrespectful
conduct could cause "bad luck" (*ligaas*). Human beings who avoided
disrespectful acts and followed the rules of personal purity were re-
warded with *laxeitl*, "good fortune" or "luck," manifested in successful
fishing and hunting, wealth, good health, and so on. Thus the non-

human beings of the world were seen as reciprocating with *laxeitl* in return for respectful treatment by human beings. In addition, many persons had their own luck-bringing objects, which no translation does justice, but which would be called in English "good luck charms" or "good luck medicine" or "magic charms." These powerful objects were themselves often the gifts of the nonhuman spirits and were kept in boxes or bundles. The generic Tlingit term for the objects as well as the attendant special physical and spiritual exercises and purification rites is *héixwaa,* often translated as "magic" or "good luck medicine." More technique-specific terms are described by elders (Dauenhauer and Dauenhauer 1987:174–75).

The important point is this: in precontact Tlingit religion, the moral order of the universe was maintained not by a single and omnipotent god, spirit, or deity, but by a set of rules for proper thinking, speaking, and behaving, vis-à-vis its nonhuman inhabitants, from the especially powerful spirits to the smallest creatures. This concept of moral order and "respect" certainly survived for most conservative elders following conversion to Christianity. The basic concepts are congruent with Russian Orthodoxy, whose prayer to the Holy Spirit begins, "O Heavenly King, the Comforter, the Spirit of Truth, Who art everywhere present and fillest all things." The concept of the presence of God in all creation is also acceptable to many Protestant denominations. As an ecological aesthetic, it is acceptable to many secular Americans. But these traditional rules and worldview of the precontact era and nineteenth century, although they may survive to some extent for some people, are no longer the prevailing concepts of moral order or the central organizing feature of contemporary Tlingit religion and society.

In addition to the spirit world, each individual seems to have had a personal guardian or tutelary spirit, residing right above the head and threatening to depart from an unclean or immoral person. This concept of one's *kinaa yéigi* (spirit above) was most likely an aboriginal one, although undoubtedly augmented in the postcontact era by the Russian Orthodox concept of the guardian angel. The Tlingit term is well documented and appears with a required possessive pronoun (my, his/her, one's). In the oldest documentation, the possessor is always singular, but in the twentieth century, the term appears with the plural possessive "our" (*haa kinaa yéigi*), and some Tlingit people have compared the concept to the Christian God. We do not know for certain whether this is pre-Christian or not, but it is possible that at least a vaguely defined concept of a spirit-protector of individual kinship groups existed prior to contact. The question of the presence of other, more monotheistic concepts in the pre-Christian Tlingit worldview is more complex. Both Kan (1999) and de Laguna (1972:813) report that neither the pre-1867 Russian sources nor Emmons mention the concept of "my savior" to whom the Tlingit appealed for help in cases of life-threatening danger, but their elderly teachers insisted that such a notion did exist in traditional Tlingit thought and was not a product of Christian proselytizing. The Tlingit term for this is *shageinyaa*, and some elders have described it as "more like God," but insist that, unlike the God of the Christians, "my" or "our" *shageinyaa* was rarely addressed, and then in a very personal rather than collective prayer. This notion fits in with the general picture of much of the pre-Christian Tlingit religion being individually practiced and individually oriented.

In the twentieth century, some Tlingit people have compared the word *shageinyaa* with *shagóon*. This word has a range of translations, at one end of which is "ancestor." The more complex end of the translation range includes the ideas of the collective origin and destiny or fate of an individual and his or her matrilineal group, and the "sacred heritage and destiny" or "moral order" of a group. Thus, the term *shagóon* seems at one end of its range to be similar to the concepts of *kinaa yéigi* and *shageinyaa*, and seems to be gravitating in modern Tlingit thought toward a more collective concept.

Kan (1999) reports and concurs that none of the early European observers found any evidence of collective worship of any spirit or deity, including Raven (*Yéil*). Nor was there a hierarchized and centralized pantheon of spirits. Instead, much of the traditional religion was focused on acquiring and maintaining spirit power for and by the individual.

Traditional, precontact Tlingit religion was shamanism "of a classical circumpolar type" or "Siberian type" (Kan 1991:365; de Laguna 1987:87). All nineteenth-century observers stressed the centrality of the shaman to the entire Tlingit sociocultural order (Kan 1999; Veniaminov 1984:400). Swanton considered that among all the Northwest Coast people, shamanism reached its climax among the Tlingit (1908:463). The source of the shaman's power was his control over powerful spirits, called *yéik*, who served as his helpers. Each *yéik* has a personal name, a special song and associated ceremonial objects (bone amulets, rattles, masks, etc.). The spirits had the capacity to choose the person whose helpers they wished to become, and it was extremely dangerous to refuse such a call.

As in other shamanic religions, candidates were not ordained into a preexisting religion as much as they became recipients of personal spirits who revealed themselves to the individual. Where Tlingit shamanism seems unique or significantly different is that the spirits are not "owned" by the entire community, but only by the clan of the shaman. Individual revelation of shaman spirits is common, but for spirits to be perceived as clan property is unusual. Shamanism is typically individualistic and unstructured, and sedentary cultures with complex social structures tend to have more codified religious systems. Tlingit traditional religion is characterized by an unusual combination of shamanism and complex social structure. Because Tlingit religion is inseparable from the social structure, a few words of introduction are in order.

Tlingit society is divided into two moieties, most generally called Raven and Eagle. The word *moiety* is a word meaning "half," and the term is appropriate. Each moiety also includes many clans. The clan was the major traditional unit of social, political, and ceremonial identity and interaction, but this system has weakened in the past one hundred years. A person is born into his or her mother's moiety and clan, and traditionally one married a person of the opposite moiety. Each clan had its leader and an autonomous "foreign policy," and owned a variety of real and intellectual property. Stories, songs, dances, and art designs are included in the concept of property, as are a range of spirits. Often the spirits are depicted in visual art or referenced in song, dance, and oratory. Stories remember the history of acquisition of certain spirits by clan ancestors. Song, dance, and oratory are vehicles for recalling the spirits to the present time and place in a ceremonial context. These concepts of ownership and prerogative are common to most of the Northwest Coast. The Tlingit term for this is *at.óow,* which means "a purchased object." Purchase was frequently through the death of an ancestor.

Because each clan has its own spirits and no single clan owns the total or collected spirits of the community, the concept of reciprocity becomes very important. The best example of this is the Tlingit memorial for the departed, commonly called "potlatch" in English, to which each moiety brings half of the spirits or provides access to half of the spirits needed for the removal of grief. The memorial is hosted by the clan of the departed, with support from other clans of the same moiety. They invite guests of clans of the opposite moiety. The Tlingit term for "potlatch" is *koo.éex'*, which means "to invite." Food and gifts are distributed to guests of the opposite moiety. The traditional belief is that by sharing food and gifts such as blankets with the living, we can also share them with the spirits of the departed. In fact, only by sharing with the living can we share with the departed. Traditional regalia is displayed, and traditional songs and dances are performed in turn by hosts and guests. Thus the potlatch represents several levels of mediation: between the living members of a community; between the living and the spirits of the human departed; and between humans and the disembodied shaman spirits of the spirit world. Thus, while much of precontact Tlingit religious life was individual-oriented and there was apparently no collective worship of powerful spirits or deities, extremely elaborate death-related ritual activities such as the *koo.éex'* formed the traditional core of the entire sociocultural order and continue to do so, although to a lesser degree and in changing ways.

Hamayon (1984) presents a different configuration of the clan-shaman-spirit relationship. Her evidence suggests that the concept of clan ownership or clan residence of spirits may be widespread, but is resolved differently in each culture-specific situation, according to social structure, gender roles, and the extent to which social structure and shamanic structure are congruent or conflicting in a given culture. For example, both the Tlingit and the Buriat (of Siberia) have female shamans; but in Tlingit society, which is matrilineal, with women being full members of their clans, the structures are congruent. In Buriat society, which is patrilineal and in which women "cannot be members in any clan" (Hamayon 1984:317), the structures are in conflict and there is considerable anxiety over potential loss of spirits, which may abandon one clan (without a male shaman) and move to another that has a male shaman. This anxiety does not exist in Tlingit, where women share full membership in the owning clan.

In Tlingit tradition, shamanism was ideally positive, benevolent, and focused on healing. But the spirits were ambivalent (like fire or explosives) and were potentially dangerous. Therefore, extreme caution was exercised in dealing with the spirits. Reciprocity with a clan of the opposite moiety is part of this traditional protocol. The popular Tlingit term is *balance*. The spirits of clans of the opposite moieties balance each other out and keep the supplicants from harm.

In contrast to shamanism, witchcraft was negative and malevolent. Like shamanism, beliefs about the witch, called *nakws'aatí* ("master of medicine"), *nukws'aatí*, or *neekws'aatí* ("master of sickness or master of pain"), were central to the pre-Christian Tlingit worldview, and vestiges survive today. The terms for witches refer to the belief that they cause sickness and death by casting spells on other persons. Part of the job of the shaman was to combat witchcraft. Protestant missionaries confused these roles. These are, of course, ideal categories; as in all world religions, we can assume the occasional presence of personally corrupt "professional" clergy. Historical evidence suggests that many accusations of witchcraft, as in other cultures, targeted weak or marginal persons or were linked to personal rivalries in the community. (For more detail and discussion on the traditional spirit world and both pre- and postcontact potlatch, see Dauenhauer and Dauenhauer 1987, 1990, 1994b; de Laguna 1972, 1987; Emmons 1991; Kan 1987, 1989, 1999; McClellan 1954, 1975; and Swanton 1908.)

Earlier Contact: Pre-1867

The Roman Catholic Church

The first Roman Catholic mass in Alaska was celebrated by Spanish explorers in 1779 near the present-day community of Craig, which celebrated the bicentennial of this event in 1979. Thus, the Catholic Church has a long history in southeast Alaska, but has had a limited and more local influence on Tlingit life, in contrast to the Orthodox and Presbyterian churches, because its presence was not continuous but was reestablished following the gold rush. Among its activities, the church operated the Pius X mission school in Skagway and St. Ann's hospital in Juneau (where many Juneau residents were born), now a nursing home. The Catholic Church has many Tlingit communicants, and during the 1930s and in the postwar period this was reinforced through intermarriage between Tlingit women and Filipino men, with many of the mestizo families being Catholic.

The Lutheran Church

The Lutheran church comprises a fascinating but little-known and often-forgotten chapter in the history of religion in Alaska. The Lutheran presence was important during the Russian period as the religion of the Finnish community in Sitka, including some of the governors of the colony. The first pastor and builder of the church was the Finnish educator Uno Cygnaeus. Although important historically as the first Lutheran church on the west coast of North America and the first Protestant church in Alaska, it had no impact on Tlingit religious life, and Lutheran continuity was broken after 1867.

The Russian Orthodox Church

The Russian Orthodox Church was the first to have significant and lasting influence on the Tlingit community. Although the first recorded contact between Tlingits and Europeans (the Russian Chirikov) occurred on July 15, 1741, and the Russians traded with Tlingits at Lituya Bay in 1788 (Izmailov and Bocharov), lasting contact did not begin until the 1790s, with the founding of settlements at Yakutat (1796) and Sitka (1799). The Sitka fort was destroyed by the Tlingit in 1802, but the Russians returned with reinforcements and recaptured Sitka in 1804. The Tlingit evacuated Sitka, but gradually returned and resettled over the following decades. A delicate and uneasy truce existed for the remainder of the Russian period in Alaska, until the sale of Alaska to the United States in 1867. After 1867, the Orthodox Church continued with support from Russia until the Bolshevik Revolution of 1917, after which it was maintained largely through the efforts of the indigenous faithful. Alaska is a diocese of the Orthodox Church in America (OCA), which received autocephaly (independence) from the Orthodox Church of Russia in 1970.

The most dynamic figure during the Russian-American period was Ioann (John) Veniaminov (1797–1879), who spent many years in Alaska, first as a priest and later as bishop. He was eventually elected Patriarch of Moscow, the head of the Russian Orthodox Church, and he was canonized by the Russian Orthodox Church in 1977. Although he designed an alphabet for Tlingit and began to translate prayers and a catechism, the impact of literacy in Tlingit culture was not as profound as on Aleut, where it became indigenized and was used by subsequent generations of writers and translators. The main reasons for his limited success in Tlingit were the greater complexity of Tlingit phonology and grammar, and Veniaminov's shorter stay in Sitka, characterized by more limited contact and politically strained relations with the Tlingit community.

Perhaps the most dramatic example of Veniaminov's missionary attitude toward Alaska Native culture is his famous 1828 encounter with the Aleut elder Smirennikov, regarded locally as a shaman because of his familiarity with spirits. (For details on this, see Mousalimas 1995:155–62; Oleksa 1987:132–55, 346–48; 1992:130–32; Veniaminov 1993:78.) What is remarkable is Veniaminov's positive assessment of Smirennikov and his spiritual condition, and his total lack of pride and arrogance of assumed spiritual superiority. Veniaminov was bewildered by the presence of Christian teaching prior to his arrival, but his bishop essentially reminded him that the Holy Spirit goes where the Holy Spirit wants to. Perhaps the most important lessons of the encounter are Veniaminov's respect for the elder and his willingness to take the advice of St. John and examine the spirits (1 John 4:1). This was in sharp contrast to the attitudes of the late-nineteenth-century American Protestant mission to southeast Alaska.

Veniaminov's personal example and pastoral directives called for maximum positive attitudes toward traditional language and culture. Thus, he encouraged bilingual education and translation of scripture, and use of Tlingit language in the church services. This legacy survives today in the form of Tlingit prayers and festal hymns, including the Lord's Prayer and the Hail Mary. He also encouraged minimal interference with traditional Tlingit cultural practices. It is important to note here that not all pre- and post-1867 Russian missionaries were as enlightened as Veniaminov and that Veniaminov was also critical of Tlingit shamans.

Later Contact: Post-1867

The Presbyterian Church

The most far-reaching impact on traditional Tlingit religion, culture, and language was made by the Presbyterian church, especially under the leadership of S. Hall Young (1847–1927) and Sheldon Jackson (1834–1909). Young landed in Wrangell, Alaska, in 1878 and gradually developed a system of missions and boarding schools to include Sitka and Haines. One of his most famous fellow travelers on his early missionary journeys was the naturalist John Muir. Jackson was the General Agent of Education in Alaska from 1885 until 1906. At the time of his death, he was the Moderator of the General Assembly of the

Presbyterian Church in the United States, the highest position in the church. The careers of Veniaminov and Jackson are remarkably parallel in many respects, but they had conflicting visions of mission and education. As a deliberate strategy, Jackson divided the territory of Alaska into spheres of missionary influence and established a major Protestant denomination in each former Orthodox center: the Methodists at Unalaska, the Baptists in Kodiak, the Presbyterians in Sitka, and so on. It is important to remember that in the Russian-American colony the Orthodox Church was officially responsible for education, and in Alaska after the 1880s, despite the nominal separation of church and state, the educational system was politically affiliated with the Presbyterian and other Protestant churches.

The American Protestant attitudes toward Tlingit language and culture were the opposite of and directly in conflict with those of the Russian Orthodox Church. Within two years of their arrival, the Presbyterian missionaries abandoned the idea of Bible translation, arguing that the Tlingit, Haida, and Tsimshian languages were full of superstition and sin and were inadequate for expressing Christian thought; they felt these languages should be left to die, the sooner the better, to be replaced by the language of Christian civilization. To this end, the Presbyterian missionaries rigorously enforced policies of using only English in their schools. The modern Presbyterian Church rejects these Victorian ideas, but these policies dominated American education in Alaska for several generations and had a devastating impact on language survival in Southeast Alaska. Haida now has an estimated fifteen speakers in Alaska, and Tlingit perhaps five hundred. It is important to note that this decision not to translate scripture and develop indigenous literacy is in direct conflict with the history, theology, and spirit of Calvinism and the Reformation.

Another significant contrast was in the Protestant attitude toward traditional Tlingit religion. Veniaminov was born and raised in Siberia, where shamanism was (and still is) a viable religion and was familiar to him and his colleagues. Jackson came from Schenectady, New York, and he and his fellow Presbyterian missionaries arrived in Alaska with a different frame of reference regarding shamanism. Young his colleagues considered the shamans to be "fiends incarnate." There was aggressive persecution and public physical and psychological humiliation of shamans by the missionaries and the U.S. military. In southeast Alaska, one village cut down and burned all its totem poles, and drove a spike in the boardwalk to symbolize the rejection of all Tlingit cultural tradition. In other places, traditional villages were abandoned and new communities formed around the Presbyterian church and government school.

There was considerable conflict between Russian Orthodox and Presbyterians from the 1880s on. The Tlingit population was by no means passive in its adoption of either Orthodoxy or Presbyterianism; there is ample documentation of people affiliating with one faith or the other according to a number of social and political agendas. There are records of massive conversions back and forth, with the social, linguistic, and politically conservative Tlingit families and individuals tending toward Orthodoxy, and the innovative, English-language-oriented Tlingit toward Presbyterianism. (For more on this, see Kan 1985, 1987, 1996, 1999.) Whereas during the Russian period shamanism remained a religious option and was not interfered with, as the American administration intensified and the link of secular and religious power grew closer, shamanism was aggressively persecuted in southeast Alaska, continued for a while in secret, and eventually died out.

The Episcopal Church

The Episcopal Church has had comparatively minimal impact on Tlingit culture. Historically, its greatest impact has been on the Tsimshian community of Metlakatla, which was founded in 1887 by Father William Duncan, who split with the Anglican Church in Canada and led his followers to Alaska, where they founded a new community.

The Salvation Army

The Salvation Army is among the older churches that have had substantial impact on the Tlingit population. Since the beginning of the twentieth century, the church has been strong in most communities, with significant Tlingit membership and leadership. Drumming and singing were certainly a major attraction in the beginning, and the Salvation Army remains well known for its lively tradition of hymn singing and testimonial giving in the Tlingit language. It has played an important role in the sobriety movement. I should note here that many Tlingit people, especially in smaller communities, often went and still go to services of several churches, especially the Salvation Army, Russian Orthodox, and Presbyterian. (For more on the historical contact between the Tlingit and Christian missionaries, see Black 1996; Black and Arndt 1997; Black and Pierce 1990; Dauenhauer 1996, 1997; Dauenhauer and Dauenhauer 1994a; Emmons 1991; Garrett 1979; Hinckley 1996; Kan 1985, 1987, 1988, 1996, 1999; Mousalimas 1995; Oleksa 1987, 1992; and Wyatt 1996.)

More Recent Contact

Pentecostalism

The greatest recent impact on Tlingit religion has been the arrival of various Pentecostal or "fundamentalist" churches since the end of World War II. By Pentecostal, I refer here to a variety of "classical" Pentecostal denominations dating from around 1886–1914 and not to the "charismatic revival" elements of the Catholic, Orthodox, or "mainstream" Protestant churches. Differing in doctrinal emphasis and concepts of organization, these include the Assembly of God, Church of God, Church of Christ, United Pentecostal, and various nondenominational, "Bible," or "Full Gospel" churches and prayer groups. In southeast Alaska today there are one or more of these groups in every village, with the Assembly of God most numerically widespread, but with Church of Christ, Church of God, and United Pentecostal also present, along with various unaffiliated congregations. These groups vary widely in their attitudes toward Tlingit language and traditional culture (such as singing, dancing, and ceremonial wearing of regalia). Attitudes range from active endorsement to tacit tolerance to prohibition and active protest against teaching the language in school, calling it "demonic." From time to time, individual preachers have held rallies and revivals in villages and urged people to burn their tribal regalia, arguing that "there are no Chilkat blankets in heaven." As noted above, the Presbyterian Church today has abandoned and reversed its nineteenth-century policies of this kind, but some of the fundamentalist groups have taken up the old position, arguing that Tlingit language and culture are incompatible with Christianity. The popularity of the Pentecostal movement parallels or is certainly congruent with the increasing shift in Tlingit society away from traditional clan-oriented cultural identity to the wider culture of American individualism, and many communities and families are bitterly divided over this issue. (For a helpful overview of the Pentecostal movement, see Burgess et al. 1988.)

Other Religions

Other familiar American religions, although they have congregations in major southeast Alaska communities, have had negligible historical impact on Tlingit society and have relatively insignificant Tlingit membership. Among these are the Baptist, Methodist, Nazarene, Jehovah's Witness, Christian Science, and Seventh Day Adventist churches. The Mormons (Church of Jesus Christ of Latter-day Saints) have congregations in most communities, with increasing Tlingit membership. Also increasing is the Baha'i faith, which has a relatively small but energetic Tlingit membership very active in alcohol and substance abuse recovery not only at home, but also among the indigenous people of Siberia.

Syncretism

ANB Memorials

The best examples of syncretism (the blending of pre- and post-contact religious traditions) may be observed in contemporary Tlingit funeral customs such as the ANB memorial, potlatch, and the forty-day party. The Alaska Native Brotherhood (ANB) was founded in 1912 by a group of Tlingit men and women most of whom were affiliated with Sheldon Jackson School. The Alaska Native Sisterhood (ANS) was founded a few years later. Their models were the Orthodox Church brotherhoods and the Presbyterian sodalities. Their purpose was the advancement of Tlingit, Haida, and Tsimshian civil rights. Their strategies called for the adoption of the English language and Euro-American dress and customs, and the abandoning of Tlingit language and tradition, especially potlatching. Regardless of a member's religious affiliation, it is now the general custom to hold a memorial service for departed members on the evening before the church funeral. The ANB or ANS service may be combined with a church service ranging from an Orthodox *Panikhida* (requiem) to a more Pentecostal-like prayer-group service. The ANB/ANS portion is very secular and "pan-Protestant" in tone, with scripture readings, but following the form of a business meeting, conducted according to Robert's Rules of Order. As the roll is called, and the departed fails to respond, a motion is made to remove his or her name from the active membership to the book of memory. This is a very moving moment in the service. Later in the service is the ceremony for the transferring of the departed's member-ship pin, hat, and sash to a member of the younger generation of the family. Tlingit fondness for Robert's Rules of Order reflects traditional concern with protocol and diplomacy, and the transfer of ANB/ANS insignia parallels the traditional passing of clan regalia at a potlatch, a custom that many people had abandoned. The memorial/meeting ends with a call for new members.

Synthesis of pre- and postcontact religion creates other funeral vari-ations. A 1998 funeral in Juneau for two young men who died by accident had no ANB component because the deceased were not members. The afternoon funeral was clearly divided into the "cultural part" and the Russian Orthodox requiem, which followed. The "cul-tural part" was so identified by speakers and was perceived as the time and place for ritual display of clan regalia and traditional oratory. The traditional rhetoric was strong, but the traditional clan context and the concept of cross-moiety reciprocity were confused or lost for sev-eral speakers, indicating an ongoing change in cultural patterns. The perception of Orthodoxy was also interesting. In this family, neither the deceased nor the parent generation had attended church since the baptism of the deceased, yet the family insisted on an Orthodox burial service. Ironically, this Christian component is not perceived as part of "the culture" although it is clearly operating as such and as a power-ful element of contemporary Tlingit folk religion. An extended family member of the grandparent generation of one of the young men ex-plained, "They put the oil on you at baptism and it's good for life." The bishops disagree, of course, arguing that membership is defined by active communion. (This is not to imply that other Tlingit families and individuals are not more spiritually involved with the church.) As one theologian commented, "It's hard to separate what comes from God and what comes from Grandma." Most contemporary Tlingit fu-nerals exemplify some aspect of this constantly evolving synthesis of precontact religion and Christianity.

Potlatch

Potlatch was abandoned in many communities under pressure of the Protestant missionaries and civil authorities (although it was not out-lawed in Alaska as it was in Canada). The practice survived most strongly in Orthodox areas such as Angoon, Hoonah, Juneau, and Sitka, and it is experiencing a general revival today. It is interesting to

note that as traditional shamanism was gradually replaced by various
Christian denominations, all of the hosts and participants of potlatch
in the twentieth century have been and are practicing (or at least nominal) Christians. This is certainly the situation today, where the most
active hosts may also be the most active in Salvation Army, Orthodox,
Presbyterian, or even Pentecostal churches. Much of the visual and verbal art alludes to or calls upon traditional spirits of the pre-Christian
era for comfort and healing. Thus traditional practices of healing and
removal of grief survive along with those of Christianity. Also, some
Presbyterian and Catholic congregations have incorporated elements
of traditional Tlingit spiritual healing into their services for healing
and the removal of grief.

Forty-Day Parties

The forty-day party is an interesting example of synthesis. In most
Tlingit communities, forty days after a person's death, a banquet is
given in memory of the departed. The giving of gifts and money is
reserved for the potlatch, which is usually held a year or more after a
person's death, typically in the fall and after sufficient resources can
be gathered for distribution. The forty-day party is on a much smaller
scale and usually involves only food. Most people believe that it derives
from Russian Orthodox practice, but it fit so well into the traditional
Tlingit pattern of postfuneral memorials, feasting, and gift giving that
it captured popular imagination and spread into areas that were not
Orthodox. It is thoroughly indigenized today. (See Kan 1987 and 1999.)

Revival and Reinvention

Creation of New Objects

The most recent phenomena in contemporary Tlingit religion are revival and reinvention. This is evident in two areas: the creation of new
or neo rituals and regalia and the spiritual and political recontextuali-
zation of historical objects being returned to communities under the
Native American Graves Protection and Repatriation Act of 1990
(NAGPRA). Recent years have witnessed the creation of a "Healing
Blanket," a "Healing Drum,"and a "Healing Totem." For many persons
of the younger generations, the traditional regalia are encumbered with
cultural or political restrictions. The traditional regalia (*at.óow*) are inseparable from the traditional clan system, which is increasingly alien

to many people. In some cases, the stewards of the objects may not permit their use outside of traditional ceremonials. The newly evolving system is community and individually based and is not linked to the clan system and ceremonial reciprocity. The clan system has been on the decline for more than a century; the genius of the ANB was to re-place it with Western protocol for political purposes. The new religious phenomena seem to be a parallel development to address growing spiritual needs such as drug and alcohol abuse, AIDS, teen suicide, family violence, and other contemporary problems at the most personal and individual level. This suggests that neither conventional Christianity nor the traditional Tlingit clan system is functional for a significant number of Tlingit individuals, and that some new synthesis is in for-mation. The contemporary Tlingit revival includes an extension of pan-Indian, pan-Native American healing into Alaska that operates on a more personal, charismatic level than traditional Tlingit ceremony. This seems to be more immediately accessible to an increasing num-ber of people today, whereas the workings of Tlingit tradition become increasingly incomprehensible with each passing generation, require more study and learning, and are often topics of political dispute.

NAGPRA and the Recontextualization of Objects

With the passage and implementation of NAGPRA, many objects such as hats are being returned to Tlingit clans and communities from mu-seums where they have been stored for at least three generations. This is a complex issue. Some tribes and clans are grateful to museums for preserving and protecting these objects that would otherwise have been lost or destroyed; other individuals and groups are very confronta-tional, viewing museums as enemies and thieves. As the objects return to the community, they need to be recontextualized. Many persons no longer understand the social and spiritual context in which the objects were created and traditionally functioned, and the genealogi-cal inheritance lines along which they were and are owned, cared for, and transmitted. Thus, the objects acquire a sense of immediate po-litical power as well as less-understood spiritual power. The effort to understand the traditional spiritual context is characterized by a com-bination of revival, invention, and reinvention. The surface rhetoric of repatriation is typically in terms of an ancestral pre-Christian or non-Christian (or anti-Christian) ancestral religion, but the deeper patterns and categories of thought are typically Western and Christian, and often follow patrilineal descent rather than matrilineal. A linguistic analogy would be using a neotraditional vocabulary but retaining a Western / Christian grammar. The irony here is that while one expects (and accepts) postcontact Christian thinking and practice to be influenced by pre-Christian indigenous thinking and practice, it is not politically correct to suggest that revitalized traditional spirituality should show influence of a century of active and self-conscious assimilation. This is certainly one of the unfolding dynamics of Tlingit religion today.

Shamanic Revival

A final word is in order about the revival of shamanism in contemporary Tlingit culture. The objective, critical, serious study of shamanism, whether "classical" or contemporary is hindered by vestiges of prejudice. Reactions range from cynicism or skepticism to antishamanic, postmissionary hysteria, to proshamanic, New Age romanticism. The most knowledgeable tradition bearers have been reluctant to discuss particulars, for example, to help write a biography of one of the last well-known female shamans. Another initial barrier is simply vocabulary: how to define the range of traditional and contemporary shamanic activities and determine the extent to which they are the same. There is a well-known, middle-aged Tlingit man who has studied extensively with recognized non-Tlingit Native American healers and who is a serious and respected practitioner. He conducts private healing and public ceremonies of purification. No one regards him as a charlatan. He has been described variously as a "shaman" (*íxt'*) and a healer. But it remains unclear the extent to which others identify him, and he identifies himself, with the full range of traditional, "classical" nineteenth-century shamanic activity. Is he the same or different? What spirits does he control? Even if the shaman is the same, his clients exist in a different social, intellectual, and spiritual context than a century ago.

The situation is not unique to Tlingit. The same and similar concepts and questions are being explored by Marjorie Mandelstam Balzer (1993a, b, 1995, and research in progress) for the new forms and contexts of shamanic revival in post-Soviet Yakutia (Sakha), especially ethnicity, nationalism, the politics of culture, and the ambiguous boundary, if any, between curers and shamans. Such new forms and phenomena compel us to reexamine our norms and frames of reference for defining shamanism and healing, and perhaps to challenge

Richard Dauenhauer

our understanding of "classical" as well as contemporary shamanism and healing. This is a new and exciting dimension in Tlingit religion, and at present it raises more questions than it answers. Therefore, the extent to which shamanism in the classic sense exists today in Tlingit remains unclear.

References

Balzer, Marjorie Mandelstam. 1993a. "Shamanism and the Politics of Culture: An Anthropological View of the 1992 International Conference on Shamanism, Yakutsk, the Sakha Republic." *Shaman* 1, no. 2 (Autumn 1993): 71–96.

———. 1993b. "Two Urban Shamans: Unmasking Leadership in Fin-de-Soviet Siberia." In George E. Marcus, ed., *Perilous States: Conversations on Culture, Politics, and Nation*. Chicago: University of Chicago Press, 131–64.

———. 1995. "The Poetry of Shamanism." In Tae-gon Kim and Mihály Hoppál, eds., *Shamanism in Performing Arts*. Budapest: Akadémia Kiadó, 171–87.

Black, Lydia T. 1996. "Ivan Pan'kov: Architect of Aleut Literacy." In Haycox and Mangusso, 43–65.

Black, Lydia T., and Katherine L. Arndt. 1997. *A Good and Faithful Servant: The Year of Saint Innocent*. An Exhibit Commemorating the Bicentennial of the Birth of Ioann Veniaminov 1797–1997. Fairbanks: University of Alaska Fairbanks and the Alaska State Veniaminov Bicentennial Committee.

Black, Lydia T., and Richard A. Pierce. 1990. "Russian America and the Finns." *Terra* 29:18–29.

Burgess, Stanley M., Gary B. McGee, and Patrick H. Alexander. 1988. *Dictionary of Pentecostal and Charismatic Movements*. Grand Rapids, Mich.: Zondervan.

Dauenhauer, Richard. 1996. "Two Missions to Alaska." In Haycox and Mangusso, 76–88.

———. 1997. *Conflicting Visions in Alaskan Education*. Fairbanks: University of Alaska Veniaminov Bicentennial Project.

Dauenhauer, Nora Marks, and Richard Dauenhauer. 1987. *Haa Shuká, Our Ancestors: Tlingit Oral Narratives*. Seattle: University of Washington Press.

———. 1990. *Haa Tuwunáagu Yís, for Healing Our Spirit: Tlingit Oratory*. Seattle: University of Washington Press.

———. 1994a. *Haa Kusteeyí, Our Culture: Tlingit Life Stories*. Seattle: University of Washington Press.

———. 1994b. "Glacier Bay History Told by Amy Marvin and Speech for the Removal of Grief delivered by Jessie Dalton." In Brian Swann, ed., *Coming to Light: Contemporary Translations of the Native Literatures of North America*. New York: Random House, 151–75.

de Laguna, Frederica. 1972. *Under Mount Saint Elias*. Washington, D.C.: Smithsonian Institution Press.

———. 1987. "Atna and Tlingit Shamanism: Witchcraft on the Northwest Coast." *Arctic Anthropology* 24, no. 1:84–100.

Emmons, George T. 1991. *The Tlingit Indians*. Edited with additions by Frederica de Laguna and a biography by Jean Low. Seattle: University of Washington Press.

Garrett, Paul D. 1979. *St. Innocent, Apostle to America*. Crestwood, N.Y.: St. Vladimir's Seminary Press.

Hamayon, R. 1984. "Is There a Typically Female Exercise of Shamanism in Patrilinear Societies Such as the Buryat?" In Mihály Hoppál, ed., *Shamanism in Eurasia*. Göttingen: Edition Herodot, 307–18.

———. 1992. "Game and Games, Fortune and Dualism in Siberian Shamanism." In Mihály Hoppál and Juha Pentikäinen, eds., *Northern Religions and Shamanism*. Budapest and Helsinki: Akadémiai Kiadó and Finnish Literature Society, 134–37.

Haycox, Stephen W., and Mary Childers Mangusso. 1996. *An Alaska Anthology: Interpreting the Past*. Seattle: University of Washington Press.

Hinckley, Ted C. 1996. "The Early Ministry of S. Hall Young, 1878–1888." In Haycox and Mangusso, 134–55.

Kan, Sergei. 1985. "Russian Orthodox Brotherhoods among the Tlingit: Missionary Goals and Native Response." *Ethnohistory* 32:196–223.

———. 1987. "Memory Eternal: Orthodox Christianity and the Tlingit Mortuary Complex." *Arctic Anthropology* 24:32–55.

———. 1988. "The Russian Orthodox Church in Alaska." In Wilcomb E. Washburn, ed., *Handbook of American Indians*, Vol. 4, *History of Indian-White Relations*. Washington, D.C.: Smithsonian Institution Press, 506–21.

———. 1989. *Symbolic Immortality: Tlingit Potlatch of the Nineteenth Century*. Washington, D.C.: Smithsonian Institution Press.

———. 1991. "Shamanism and Christianity: Modern-Day Tlingit Elders Look at the Past." *Ethnohistory* 38:363–87.

———. 1996. "Clan Mothers and Godmothers: Tlingit Women and Russian Orthodox Christianity, 1840–1940." In Harkin and Kan, *Native American Women's Responses to Christianity*. Special issue of *Ethnohistory* 43, no. 4 (Fall): 613–41.

———. 1999. *Memory Eternal: Tlingit Culture and Russian Orthodox Christianity through Two Centuries*. Seattle: University of Washington Press.

McClellan, Catharine. 1954. "The Interrelations of Social Structure with Northern Tlingit Ceremonialism." *Southwestern Journal of Anthropology* 10, no. 1:75–96.

———. 1975. *My Old People Say: An Ethnographic Survey of Southern Yukon Territory*. Ottawa: National Museums of Canada. National Museum of Man, Publications in Ethnology, no. 6.

———. 1987. *Part of the Land, Part of the Water: A History of the Yukon Indians*. Vancouver and Toronto: Douglas and McIntyre.

Mousalimas, S. A. 1995. *The Transition from Shamanism to Russian Orthodoxy in Alaska*. Providence, R.I., and Oxford, U.K.: Berghahn Books.

Oleksa, Michael. 1987. *Alaskan Missionary Spirituality*. Mahwah, N.J.: Paulist Press.

———. 1992. *Orthodox Alaska: A Theology of Mission*. Crestwood, N.Y.: St. Vladimir's Seminary Press.

Swanton, John. 1908. *Social Condition, Beliefs, and Linguistic Relationship of the Tlingit Indians*. Washington, D.C.: Smithsonian Institution. Reprinted 1970, New York: Johnson Reprint Corporation.

Veniaminov, Ioann. 1984 [1840]. *Notes on the Islands of the Unalaska District*. Translated by Lydia Black and R. M. Geoghegan. Edited, with an introduction by Richard A. Pierce. Kingston, Ontario: The Limestone Press.

————. 1993. *Journals of the Priest Ioann Veniaminov in Alaska, 1823 to 1836*. Translated by Jerome Kisslinger. Introduction and commentary by S. A. Mousalimas. Fairbanks: University of Alaska Press.

Wyatt, Victoria. 1996. "Female Native Teachers in Southeast Alaska: Sarah Dickinson, Tillie Paul, and Frances Willard." In Haycox and Mangusso, 156–75.

᚛ᚋ E I G H T ᚛ᚋ

Eye of the Dance:
Spiritual Life of the
Central Yup'ik Eskimos

Ann Fienup-Riordan

Much of what has been written concerning Arctic peoples emphasizes their ability to survive in a frigid and inhospitable environment. Relatively little has been said about the values that make such survival culturally meaningful (but see Briggs 1970). On the contrary, a close look at the value systems of the peoples of the Far North reveals less environmental determinism than cultural imagination. The following is an attempt to present the system of symbols and meanings that continue to guide the daily lives and ritual activities of the contemporary Yup'ik people of southwestern Alaska. The representations in this essay are derived in part from late-nineteenth- and early-twentieth-century reporters (e.g., Nelson 1899; Lantis 1947) but mostly from the author's own field observations from the present day (Fienup-Riordan 1994, 2000), along with recent work on ceremonialism by Phyllis Morrow (1984) and Elsie Mather (1985).

The loss of spiritual traditions in Siberia and some regions of Alaska by the time their cultures came to be recorded makes understanding of the rich, continuing culture and language of the Central Yup'ik people all the more important as a model for visualizing traditional belief systems and ideologies that were once more widely distributed in the North Pacific–Bering Sea region.

This article first appeared in *Crossroads of Continents: Cultures of Siberia and Alaska*, ed. William W. Fitzhugh and Aron Crowell (Washington, D.C.: Smithsonian Institution Press, 1988). Yup'ik translations were generously provided by David Chanar and Louise Leonard.

The Relationship between Humans and Animals

Unlike the coastal Iñupiaq to the north, the Yup'ik Eskimos relied on neither the bowhead whale nor the walrus for their sustenance. Although the shallow coastline precludes the presence of either of these larger sea mammals, the coastal waters of the Bering Sea abound with a variety of seals as well as beluga whales, occasional walrus, and sea lions. The daily lives of the men and women of the Bering Sea coast were centered on the conquest of these sea mammals, as well as of an impressive variety of fish, land mammals, and waterfowl. In their dealings with these animals, the Yup'ik Eskimos did not view themselves as dominant over dumb, mute beasts that served them. Neither did they see themselves as dependent on or subordinate to the animals. On the contrary, they viewed the relationship between humans and animals as collaborative reciprocity by which the animals gave themselves to the hunter in response to the hunter's respectful treatment of them as nonhuman persons (see also Brightman 1983; Fienup-Riordan 1994: 46–92; Hallowell 1960).

According to the worldview of the Yup'ik Eskimos, human and non-human persons shared a number of characteristics. First and foremost, the perishable flesh of both humans and animals belied the immortality of their souls. All living things participated in an endless cycle of birth and rebirth of which the souls of humans and animals were a part, contingent on right thought and action by others as well as self. For both humans and animals, the soul was identified as the principle that sustained life. For sea mammals, the soul had an anatomical locus (the bladder). For human and nonhuman persons, the soul remained in the vicinity of the body for a specified time after death before going to an extraterrestrial realm to await rebirth. For humans, an essential aspect of the person was reborn in the next generation. The newborn child regularly received both the name and with it the soul of a recently de-ceased relative in the ascending generation. Finally, inanimate objects were also believed to possess souls. Thus hunting implements were dec-orated not only to please or attract animals but also to impart life into and please the objects themselves.

Side by side with this belief in an essential spiritual continuity bridg-ing the gap between the past and the future, the Yup'ik people allowed that humans and animals alike possessed awareness. According to Joe Friday of Chevak:

We felt that all things were like us people. The small animals like the mouse and the things like wood we liken to people as having a sense of awareness. The wood is glad to the person who is using it, and the person using it is grateful to the wood for being there to be used. (Friday 1985)

As they gradually grew to maturity and gained awareness, both humans and animals were the recipients of a multitude of prescriptions (*alerquutet*) and proscriptions (*inerquutet*) for the culturally appropriate living of life. Three related ideas may be seen to underlie this elaborate detail: the power of a person's thought, the importance of thoughtful action in order not to injure another's mind, and, conversely, the danger inherent in "following one's own mind" (Fienup-Riordan 1987:8ff.).

As to the first point, the power of a person's thought, the clear message was that a person's attitude was as significant as action. Thus young men were admonished to "keep the thought of the seals" foremost in their minds as they performed daily duties. In all these acts, by the power of their minds they were said to be "making a way for the seals" whom they would someday hunt. In the same way, a pregnant woman must keep the thought of her unborn child first in her mind to assure its well-being.

Animals were also subject to this stricture. For example, oral tradition describes how young seals were admonished by their elders to "stay awake" to the rules, both literally and figuratively, so that their immortal souls might survive the hunter's blow. If they were asleep when they were hit they would "die dead, forever" (Fienup-Riordan 1983:179).

In all tasks undertaken, appropriate attitude was considered as important as action. Conversely, for humans and animals the "power of the mind of the elders" to affect their future was cited as reason both to give help to individual elders and to avoid their displeasure. One contemporary account admonished young people to be careful to perform these charitable tasks at night, so that no person would see them:

> Only at night he clears the path.
> If he does it during the day,
> letting the people see him,
> already then,
> through the people he has his reward.

But if he does that with no one watching him
and nobody is aware of him,
only the one watching him,
the ocean or the land....
the *ellam yua* [person of the universe]
will give him his reward.

Second, as proper thought could effect success in the domain of human and animal interaction, so careful thought must reign over thoughtless action in order not to injure the mind of the other person. Ideally, smoothness and agreeableness should mask a person's emotions. This rule was as important in animal-human as in intrahuman interaction. For example, it was out of consideration or respect for the animal's mind that the hunter was admonished never to brag about either his projected accomplishments or past success. This same consideration also motivated his verbal apology when dispatching his prey.

Last, a number of traditional tales recalled the consequences of people following their own minds as opposed to following the advice of their elders. The results were usually disastrous, with retribution often experienced by the wrongdoers as well as their companions. In the oral tradition, some animals are identified as descended from human beings who were transformed as a consequence of willfully disregarding the rules.

In the end, human and nonhuman persons can be seen to share two fundamental characteristics: an immortal soul and mind, or awareness. This essential similarity in turn creates the common ground on which their interaction is played out. Just as human hunters are capable of conscious decisions as to what and where to hunt, animals are likewise capable of conscious decisions that affect the success of individual hunters, e.g., the decision of a seal not to approach a hunter who appears to him as careless in either thought or action (Fienup-Riordan 1983:180; see also Brightman 1983).

The qualities of personhood shared by humans and animals established the basis for a mutual and necessary respect. One such instance of respectful action is the care given to animal bones. For example, great effort was made to remove every scrap of meat from seal bones. If this was not done, the seals would perceive the bones as loudly singing, warning them not to give themselves to those careless people. Traditionally bones were either buried, burned, or submerged. It was felt to be essential that bones not be left to lie around for fear they would be stepped on by men or chewed on by dogs. Moreover, the bones of food given away must be returned to the donor. The respect shown to animal bones was motivated by the desire that the animals be able to "cover their bones" in the future, that is, to return as edible game.

Although human-nonhuman interaction is made possible by the common possession of an immortal soul and a mind meriting respect, humans and animals are also clearly differentiated. Within the oral tradition, these differences are least evident in the traditional tales of time out of mind. Moreover, the reality of the mythical space-time they describe is still believed to be present, although largely invisible. In these tales, animals are often encountered who lift up their beaks or muzzles, transforming themselves into human form (e.g., Nelson 1899:394, 453). In the tale of Ayugutaar, a Nelson Island hunter who was visited by a wolf, the hunter's initial encounter with the wolf is described as follows:

> After doing something around its head .
> and doing something to its mouth
> when it faced him,
> it became this way
> taking its hood off.

In the same way, gaining awareness (*ellange-*) is sometimes equated with peeling back the skin of an animal, as when the puppies born to a Nelson Island woman who had married a dog peeled back their fur and revealed themselves to their mother in human form. Nineteenth-century transformation masks are a vivid portrayal of this perception of reality (Fitzhugh and Kaplan 1982:215).

Along with the depiction of animal-human transformations, the oral tradition also recalls the subsequent process of differentiation by which the physical and behavioral contrasts between humans and animals occurred. For example, the origin of the wolverine with its vicious personality is attributed to the frustration and subsequent transformation of a man following his desertion by his spirit wife (Tennant and Bitar 1981:263). In these tales, contemporary animal species are identified as descended from transformed human beings.

Perhaps the most vivid accounts of animal-human interaction, and those that best portray both the similarities and the differences between animal and human society, are tales that describe humans visiting ani-

mal society and animals living within human society. An example of
the first is the story of the boy who went to live with the seals (Fienup-
Riordan 2000:58ff.). On arriving in the seals' underwater home, the boy
perceives his hosts as humans of differing sizes and shapes, depending
on their species identity. Conversely, animals can enter human society,
as in the case of the wolf who takes human form and comes to dwell
with the hunter Ayugutaar. However, the animal nature of the former is always apparent, as in Ayugutaar's guest's propensity to crunch
bones when he eats.

Although these tales depict animals as humans and describe their
social interaction, they also serve to underline the differences between
them. For example, the story of the boy who went to live with the
seals describes the seals' experience with humans from the seals' point
of view. From the seals' perspective, humans who failed to live by the
rules would appear distorted in one way or another:

> People would be walking
> and one of the men on shore
> would be seen as
> having a necklace of many things
> such as old mukluks.
> Some men were encumbered as such.

> It is said that
> those are the ones
> who continually walk
> under everything that is hanging.

In the same way, after drinking from a bowl or dipper, a person was
required to make a stylized removal motion, in which the right hand
was passed back and forth across his face to clear his vision. If a man
failed to perform this removal motion, he would not be able to see
game even though it was well within his view. At the same time, the
animals would see him as having the bowl stuck in the front of his face.

In the end, the view persists that animals were once closer to humans
and used human clothing and speech, but were gradually differentiated
from their human counterparts. Their possession of mind as well as
their rebirth after being killed and eaten by humans are described as
essential aspects of their personhood, real yet unavailable to conventional observation. The ritual treatment given animals by Yup'ik people

in southwestern Alaska today presupposes these same shared aspects of personhood. To this day, animals are believed by some people to observe what is done to their carcasses, communicate with others of their kind, and experience rebirth after death. These aspects of the animal as a nonhuman person underlie and set the stage for everyday experience.

The Relationship between Men and Women

Just as differences exist between humans and animals, there are also differences between men and women. This distinction traditionally framed, and continues to frame today, activities in everyday life. At the same time, the domains of hunting and procreation are ultimately joined, and together are viewed as essential to assuring the reproduction of life.

To begin with, a well-documented sexual division of labor traditionally circumscribed daily activity in southwestern Alaska. Men hunted while their mothers, wives, and daughters processed their catch. Men were largely, although not wholly, responsible for the provision of raw materials, while women worked in the house to produce food and clothing. The moment the hunter reached home, he lost jurisdiction over his catch. Along with processing the kill, women were also largely responsible for its distribution.

Into the 1940s, this division of tasks was replicated in a significant residential division. Men lived together communally in a large central dwelling (*qasgiq*) in which they worked, ate, slept, instructed male children, entertained visitors, took sweat baths, and held elaborate celebrations. Women and children, on the other hand, lived and worked in smaller sod houses (*enet*).

The residential division of the sexes that characterized village life had important ritual as well as social significance. In a variety of contexts, the women's house was comparable to a womb in which biological, social, and spiritual production were accomplished. It was in this house that women worked to transform the raw materials supplied by their men into food and clothing for the people. When a woman was pregnant, her activity within and exit from the house were likened to that of the fetus within her own body. For instance, upon waking each morning a pregnant woman had to quickly rise and exit from the house, before she did anything else, so that her child's exit from the womb would be a speedy one (Fienup-Riordan 1983:184, 218).

Furthermore, both the woman's house and her womb were, under certain circumstances, equated with the moon, the home of the spirit keepers of land animals. Spring itself was marked by the cutting of a door in the side of the women's sod house to permit ready egress. A similar opening in the moon was necessary to release the land animals for the new harvest season. As part of their effort to insure success in the coming year, shamans would journey to the moon (also sometimes a euphemism for sexual intercourse), where they were said to use their power to induce land animals to visit the earth.

Not only was the women's house viewed in certain contexts as a symbolic womb, productive of animals as well as men. Women's activity and inactivity were also directly tied to a man's ability to succeed in the hunt. First and foremost, contact with women was carefully circumscribed so that a man could retain his power to pursue game. Traditionally, men and women had distinctive eating utensils reserved for their exclusive use. Women's bentwood bowls were made with a rim, and men's bowls were blunt-edged. In bed with his own wife, a man was warned never to sleep facing her, lest the braid of her hair appear hanging in front of his face and subsequently block his vision.

Women's air was also considered polluting to young hunters and dulled their senses. According to Paul John of Toksook Bay, a man's breath soul (anerneq) was particularly vulnerable to contamination from such contacts. That such proscriptions affected a man's ability to hunt is attested to in a description of a shaman's visit to the underwater home of the seals occurring during the celebration of the Bladder Festival at the coastal village of Chevak. When peeking in the skylight, the shaman overheard the conversation of the "bladder people":

> Some of them will say they had a good host and will go back to the same host. Some of them will say they had a bad host because the host always made him smell female odor and would say he is not going back to his former host. (Friday 1984)

At the same time that female odor repelled animals, the smell of the land was believed to attract them. For this reason, hunters fumigated themselves with the smoke of wild celery, Labrador tea, and blackberry bushes, among other things, to prepare for the hunt.

At the same time that a hunter had to protect himself from the depleting effects of unclean air, socially restricted sight was necessary to procure powerful supernatural vision. Likewise, young women were admonished against direct eye contact with hunters.

In all social as well as ritual situations direct eye contact was, and continues to be, considered rude for young people, male or female, whereas downcast eyes signify humility and respect. Sight is the prerogative of age, knowledge, and power. For example, the powerful man in the moon has a bright face, and people fear to look at him and must look downward. The powerful shades of the dead were traditionally said to hear and see nothing at first. However, by the time they reached the grave, they attained clairvoyance (Nelson 1899:425). Finally, powerful images and hunting fetishes were supposed to watch for game and, by clairvoyant powers, sight it at a great distance (Nelson 1899:436).

A material manifestation of vision imagery is seen in the nucleated circle that appears as decoration on many hunting charms as well as objects of everyday use. The circle-dot motif, so common in Eskimo iconography, is specifically designated *ellam iinga* (literally, "the eye of awareness") in the Central Yup'ik language. The nucleated circle has, in the literature, been designated as a joint mark and, as such, part of a skeletal motif. Alternately, it has been labeled a stylized woman's breast that might be substituted for a woman's face (Ray 1981:25; Himmelheber 1953:62). The sexual and skeletal motifs may well have been part of its significance. However, it was not merely that the nucleated circle marked joints but rather that joints were marked with circular eyes (Fienup-Riordan 1986, 1987). Here William Thalbitzer's (1908:447ff.) observation on the Greenland Inuit is particularly significant: "According to Eskimo notions, in every part of the human body (particularly every joint, as for instance, in every finger joint) there resides a little soul."

Throughout the Arctic, joint marking was associated with social transformation in various contexts. For example, in southwestern Alaska the wrists of young men and women were tattooed with dots on the occasion of their first kill or first menstruation, respectively. Ritual scarification has also been observed among the Siberian Yup'ik Eskimos (Bogoras 1904–9:408), and Waldemar Bogoras records that among the Maritime Chukchi of northeast Siberia tattooed joint marks once served as a tally of homicides. When these tattooing customs are considered in the context of the custom of applying eye-shaped markings to the joints, it strongly suggests that the tattooed joint mark is itself the rudiment of the eye motif (Schuster 1951:18).

As in the circle-dot motif as applied to material objects, the puberty tattoo denoted enhanced vision. In fact in the oral tradition, one mark of a transformed character is the appearance of black circles around the eyes. Dark circles also appear as goggles on Bering Sea Eskimo nineteenth-century objects. These goggles identify beings as supernatural, are puns for masking, and refer to their state of transformation. One contemporary Central Yup'ik hunter recalled his mother circling his eyes with soot when, at age nine, he returned to the village after killing his first bearded seal (Fienup-Riordan 1987:43).

Not only were joints marked with eyes as a sign of social transformation. Actually cutting an animal or human on the joints was also associated with spiritual transformation, as when the joints of dangerous animals were cut to prevent the animal's spirit from reanimating its body. In the same way, the shaman might be ritually dismembered prior to his journey to the spirit world. Traveling out through the smoke hole or down through a hole in the ice, he would visit the "persons" of the fish and game to entreat them to return the coming year. The nucleated circle, both an eye and a hole, thus recalls the ability to pass from one world to another, as well as the ability to see into another world.

An example of the relationship between socially restricted sight and powerful supernatural vision is contained in the traditional tale of the boy who lived and traveled with the seals for one year to gain extraordinary hunting knowledge and power:

And his host [the bearded seal] said to him,
"Watch him [the good hunter], watch his eyes, see what good
    vision he has.
When his eyes see us, see how strong his vision is.
When he sights us, our whole being will quake,
and this is from his powerful gaze.
When you go back to your village, the women,
some will see them, not looking sideways, but looking directly at
    their eyes.
The ones who live like that, looking like that,
looking at the eyes of women,
their vision will become less strong.
When you look at women your vision will lose its power.
Your sight gets weakened.

But the ones that don't look at people, at the center of the face,
the ones who use their sight sparingly,
as when you have little food, and use it little by little.
So, too, your vision, you must be stingy with your vision,
using it little by little, conserving it always.
These, then, when they start to go hunting,
and use their eyes only for looking at their quarry,
their eyes truly then are strong."

In the above the finite nature of human sight is especially significant. A hunter's vision, like his thought and breath, must not be squandered. Significantly, a man's ability to harvest animals as an infinitely renewable resource was contingent on his careful use of his own finite personal human resources. Moreover, a hunter's ability to succeed in the hunt was not only tied to his care of the animals but also to his relationship with women.

Not only did a woman's actions impact the power of the hunter to attract and overcome game, but also, in specific contexts, a woman's actions were believed to directly affect the actions of the fish and game the hunter sought. For instance, when her husband went in search of certain land animals at fall camp, a woman was required to remain at rest within the house, neither working nor coming outside. In some instances, she was equated with the hunter's prey, her inactivity directly related to the inactivity (and subsequent huntability) of the animals her husband sought. In other cases, the care with which she worked was felt to directly impact the willingness of animals to give themselves to her husband. For instance, if a man's wife was a sloppy seamstress, her irregular stitches would cause animals to run away. Finally, in the case of sea mammals, a woman was felt to attract or draw the animals by virtue of the fresh water she gave their thirsty souls immediately following their successful capture. While performing this action, the woman would talk to the seal, saying, "See our water here is tasty, very inviting."

At different stages in her life, a woman affected men differently. For a young woman, the most important event in her maturation was celebrated following her first menstruation. At this time, a girl was sequestered, her condition comparable to that of the fetus in her social invisibility, restriction of movement, and the prohibition against both childhood and adult activities:

Then in the spring time,
when they became aware that she had become a woman,
they let her sit down.
They put a grass mat in front of her,
and then behind her they made a door.
They didn't let her go out through the regular doorway.
Only through the back door....
And those girls who had become women,
they let them wear old clothes,
and their mittens had no thumbs.
And when they went to the bathroom they put their hood on
without looking around,
and their head bowed really low.
They go to the area where trash was taken.
They would urinate in the dumping place.
These are some of the things for those who had sat down.

Here a number of elements evoke the power of the menstruating woman to impact the harvest. These include the image of the thumb-less hand simultaneously signifying the idea of impaired grasp and its relation to game productivity (Nelson 1899:395), as well as the restricted sight and use of a hood described above as prerequisites for male hunting power.

On the occasion of her "standing up" after this period of isolation, the girl was required to give away her childhood playthings, including small dolls and their clothing, to other prepubescent females. The restrictions surrounding the use of these dolls are particularly meaningful. Young girls were forbidden from using their dolls during the winter or inside the house; their use was restricted to the outside after the return of the geese. Their dormancy in the interior of the house during the winter and their emergence in the summer replicate both the transformation of their owners through puberty restrictions into women capable of giving birth and the birth process itself (Fienup-Riordan 1983:218). It was believed that if a young girl was to play with a doll outside the house before the arrival of spring, the birds would pass by and winter would move into winter with no intervening season. Here again inappropriate female activity was directly tied to cosmological upset and subsequent human disaster.

Not surprisingly, one of the first women to impact a hunter's relationship with animals was his mother. While she carried the fetus, a woman's actions were believed to influence not only the immediate well-being of her child but also its future abilities as a hunter.

> And it was an *inerquun* [proscription] that never,
> through the window,
> was she to try to see what was going on.
> She was only to check by going through the door.

> And if she does that,
> when her son grows up
> and goes hunting,
> when the animals hear him and become curious,
> they would show themselves to him and be caught.

> All those things that she is doing
> to that baby of hers, if it's a boy,
> towards the times when he will be trying to do things
> the things she does or doesn't do while pregnant affect them.

> His mother then,
> like the one who makes his catch available,
> like the one who makes his catch visible,
> she will give to the one she is carrying.

A number of rules continue to tie the action of the mother and child (male or female) throughout its growing up. For instance, a woman was traditionally admonished never to breast-feed her child while lying down but rather to sit up and unabashedly bare her breast for him to make him tough and strong. Were she to be lazy, her careless attitude and action would directly undermine her child's future hunting ability. As he grew, a mother constantly taught her son the rules by which he would live. Significantly, her advice focused on the distance he must keep from women:

> A child,
> if it is a boy,
> he is never to go near a female.
> He is not to look at a female squarely in the face.
> And he was to pass on the lee side of a female,
> and he was never to be stepped over by a woman.

Then, finally, at the age of five or six he was ready to leave her: "Leaving his mother, moving out of his mother to those men, he joins them."

The Window between the Worlds: Houses, Holes, Eyes, and Passages

When young boys came to live in the men's house (*qasgiq*), they entered the social and ceremonial center of the Yup'ik world. It was in the men's house that they would receive technical training as well as careful instruction in the rules that they must follow to become successful hunters. Under the tutelage of their fathers and uncles, even very young boys were expected to rise early and work diligently on a number of manual tasks. It was the boys' job to keep the communal water bucket continually filled, as well as to keep the entryway and skylight of the men's house cleared of snow.

As in a woman's work, the performance of these tasks had both practical and ritual implications. For instance, the water bucket must be kept full at all times to attract the seals, who were always thirsty for fresh water. Likewise, boys were required to keep the water hole constantly free of ice and to take care to drink from it only in a prone position to please the animals who would subsequently send them good luck in hunting. Here the water hole was explicitly designated the window of the world below. In stories such as "The Boy Who Went to Live with the Seals," the seal people were depicted as living in an underwater men's house from within which they could view the attention of would-be hunters by watching the condition of the central smoke hole in their underwater abode. If hunters were giving them proper thought and care, the smoke hole would appear clear. If not, the hole would be covered with snow and nothing would be visible. When their visibility was obstructed in this way, the seals would not emerge from their underwater world or allow themselves to be hunted. It was this vision that young men sought to maintain as they carefully cleared ice from skylights and water holes (Fienup-Riordan 1983:178).

The performance of a number of important ceremonies in the men's house dramatically reinforced the notion of the ice hole and smoke hole as passageways between the human and nonhuman worlds. For instance, one of the most important traditional ceremonies was the Bladder Festival, held annually to insure the rebirth of the *yuit*, or persons of the seals, which were said to be located in their bladders.

During the closing performances of the Bladder Festival, the shaman would climb out through the skylight to enter the sea, visit the seal spirits, and request their return. Likewise the inflated bladders were removed through the *qasgiq* smoke hole at the end of the festival and taken to the ice hole. There they were deflated and sent back to their underwater *qasgiq* with the request that they return the following year.

In addition to serving as a passage permitting movement and communication between the worlds of the hunter and the hunted, the central *qasgiq* smoke hole was also a passageway between the worlds of the living and the dead. For example, in the event of a human death, the body of the deceased was pulled through the smoke hole, after first being placed in each of its four corners. By this action the deceased, on the way from the world of the living to the world of the dead, gradually exchanged the mortal sight that it lost at death for the supernatural clairvoyance of the spirit world (Nelson 1899:425). Although both the smoke hole and the ice hole were rectangular rather than round, this does not undercut their significance as spiritual eyes. One variant of the circle-dot motif is, in fact, a rectangle with four small projections, one at each corner, within which was carved a dot surrounded by concentric circles. In fact, the numbers four and five figure prominently in Central Yup'ik ritual, representing among other things the number of steps leading to the underworld land of the dead. The Bladder Festival rituals use four corners and four sets of hunting and boating gear. At one stage in its performance, the bladders were presented with tiny spears, miniature pack baskets, and other tiny tools in sets of four to enable them to capture the food that they were given. Painted bent-wood bowls and incised ivory made for the occasion have spurs that occur in units of four. The reference to square or rectangular holes and the quadrangle functioning like a circle may form a logical symbolic complex with this added sacred dimension.

Not only did the motif of the ringed center connote spiritual vision and movement between worlds but the act of encircling was also performed in various contexts to produce enhanced spiritual vision or as protection from spiritual invasion. For example, during the Bladder Festival, young men ran counterclockwise around the village before entering the men's house bearing bunches of wild celery needed to purify the bladders and "let them see" the gifts of the people. Likewise, when a man hunted sea mammals at certain times of the year, he had to circle his kill in the direction of the sun's course before retrieval. The boat itself was also ritually circled before launching in the spring, both in Alaska and in Siberia (Usugan 1984; Moore 1923:369; Bogoras 1904–9:404ff.). Similarly, on the third or fifth day after the birth of a child in southwestern Alaska, the new mother traditionally emerged from her confinement, marking her return to social visibility by circling the house, again in the direction of the sun's course. Finally, the fifth day after a human death, the grave was circled in the direction of the sun's circuit by the bereaved to send away the spirit of the deceased. All of these ritual acts recall the magic circle reported by Knud Rasmussen (1927:129, 1931:60) from the Netsilik region, where people walked in a circle around strangers who approached their camp so that their footprints would contain any evil spirits that might have accompanied the newcomers.

The performance of an *ingula* dance during the Bladder Festival on Nelson Island continues the image of the ringed center with the connotation of vision as well as movement between worlds. This was a slow, stylized dance by a young bride who appeared with lowered eyes and bedecked in the furs and finery produced for her by her newly acquired mate. This dance often depicted a particularly successful harvesting episode. The *ingula* dance performed on this occasion provided a strong image of the complementarity between the production of game and the reproduction of life. While literally dancing the successful hunt, the bride held her skirt below the waist and rhythmically "fluffed it up to ward off old age and to let her have children." This expansive gesture by a sexually mature woman was in sharp contrast to the rule requiring young unmarried girls to hold their skirts tightly down around their legs when entering or exiting the *qasgiq*. If they failed to do so, it was said that the old men would grab at their vaginal areas "to teach them respect."

When a woman performed an *ingula* dance, she appeared before the audience with studiously downcast eyes. On this occasion, as in other dance performances, her head was encircled with a beaded, wolverine-and-wolf-fringed crown. The effect of this head ornament was simultaneously to restrict her view as well as protect her from supernatural powers. It is possible that the grass masks used by some Kamchatkan peoples, as well as similar grass head coverings occasionally used in southwestern Alaska, also functioned to restrict human sight and protect the dancer from the effects of powerful supernatural vision.

Ugguk *masks collected by Sheldon Jackson at Cape Vancouver. The crescent-shaped eyes and spots on a red background may represent the moon and stars. Sheldon Jackson Museum, IIH2. Used by permission.*

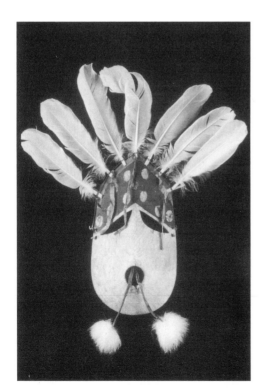

Mask representing the spirit of driftwood, used in dances requesting its abundance in years to come. The black forehead with white dots may represent the upper skyworld with star holes to the next universe. The lower white half represents the human world into which it is hoped the driftwood will come. Collected at St. Michael by Henry Neumann in 1890. Sheldon Jackson Museum, IIG6. Used by permission.

Dance fans (sometimes called "finger masks") featuring the circle-dot motif designated ellam iinga *("eye of Ella," or "eye of the universe"). Sheldon Jackson Museum, IIH45. Used by permission.*

This hand mask has a crescent-shaped cover attached to its edge by baleen. The palm opens to reveal a grinning mouth, goggled eyes, and fingers holding a small carved seal as though offering it to human hunters. Courtesy of the Burke Museum of Natural History and Culture, Catalog #1.2E637. Used by permission.

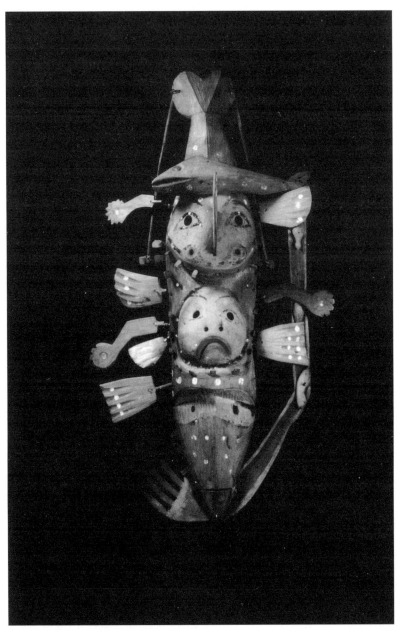

Enormous and complex mask used in a dance at Goodnews Bay around 1912. The body of the mask is a fish with toothy mouth. Looking out from its back are two faces — a smiling land animal on top and a frowning sea mammal on the bottom. Here, as on kayak charm plaques, dance fans, and other two-faced masks, the opposing faces may relate to the complementary relationship between sea and land or sky as well as between women and men. Courtesy of the Burke Museum of Natural History and Culture, Catalog #4528. Used by permission.

The grass and beaded headdresses were not the only paraphernalia used in Central Yup'ik ceremonials. A major focus among Bering Sea Eskimos was masked dancing (Fienup-Riordan 1996). Following the Bladder Festival a ceremony designated *Agayuyaraq* occurred, during which shamanic visions of the spirit world were translated into carved masks, which were used in elaborate dramatic performances. Ritually powerful masks were created representing both the *yuit,* or persons of the game, as well as the *tuunrat,* or shaman's spirit helpers. These large hooped masks are in the oral tradition directly equated with the circle-dot motif described above, and their powerful supernatural gaze directly contrasted to the restricted sight of the other performers.

Like the circle-dot motif, the large hooped masks functioned as eyes into a world beyond the mundane. First the mask was structurally a ringed center. The face of the mask was often framed in multiple wooden rings called *ellanguat* (literally, "pretend cosmos" or "pretend universe"). These concentric rings represent the different levels of the universe, which was traditionally said to contain five upper worlds and the earth (Ray 1967:66). This same heavenly symbolism was repeated in ceremonial activity in which the masked dancer was a key participant. For example, multiple rings, also called *ellanguat* and decorated with bits of down and feathers, were lowered and raised from the inside of the men's house roof during the traditional Doll Festival and were said to represent the retreat and approach of the heavens, complete with snow and stars (Nelson 1899:496; Ray 1967).

The image of the encircling ring can also be seen in the rounded dance fans, fringed with fur and feathers, held in the hands of the dancers. These fans are reminiscent of the mask worn by the central dancer, often having animal or human faces. With their eyes respectfully downcast during the performance, women even now speak of the fan's eye seeing for them while they dance.

Finally, the open-work design of the fans held by Yup'ik dancers is to this day explicitly compared to the pierced hand found as an appendage on many traditional masks. The hole in the hand's center, like the opening in the dance fan, is by some accounts a symbolic passage through which the spirits of fish and game come to view their treatment by humans and, if they find it acceptable, repopulate the world. Thus the dancers, both male and female, holding dance fans and arms extended in the motions of the dance, are like gigantic transformation masks, complete with animal-spirit faces to which the wooden pierced hands are appended.

Given this perspective, one may reasonably contrast the efficacy of the mask's supernatural sight to the lowered gaze of the human performers who dance so that they truly "see," and that the spirits see them. According to one contemporary Yup'ik elder, the traditional application of a white clay base and colored finger spots to the bladders inflated for the Bladder Festival was likewise an attempt to promote spiritual vision on the part of the souls of the seals. The painting of the wooden masks, as well as the painting of the body of the dancer, had a similar effect, allowing the dancer to become visible to the spirit world and in fact to embody the spirit at the same time that its human identity was hidden.

In sum, the Yup'ik universe was traditionally depicted as subject to constant alteration yet ultimate unity in the repetition of reproductive and productive cycles. It is, ultimately, both the alterations and unity that the hooped mask and the performance of masked dances embody. The use of the hooped mask provides a vivid image for the system of cosmological reproduction through which the Yup'ik Eskimos traditionally viewed, and to some extent continue to view, the universe. The same image of supernatural sight that dominates the hooped mask can also be seen in the rounded lamp and the ringed bowl, the hole in the kayak float board and the decorative geometry of traditional ivory earrings, the central gut skylight opening from the men's house and the decorative celestial rings suspended from its ceiling for a dance performance. The world was bound, the circle closed. Yet within it was the passageway leading from the human to the spirit world. Rimmed by *ellanguat* and transformed by paint and feathers, the eyes of the mask, themselves often ringed, looked beyond this world into another.

The Traditional Yup'ik Ceremonial Cycle

After freeze-up in November Yup'ik Eskimos gathered in their winter villages, where they enjoyed a number of public celebrations that marked winter as the ceremonial season. Five major ceremonies were performed during this period, three of which focused on the creative reformation of the relationship between the human community and the spirit world on which they relied. In all three ceremonies (the Bladder Festival, the Feast for the Dead, and the masked dances known as

Agayuyaraq) members of the spirit world were invited into the community, formally hosted, and finally sent back out of the human domain.
This ritual movement effectively re-created the relationship between
the human and spirit worlds and placed each in the proper position
to begin the year again.

The Bladder Festival

The celebration of the Bladder Festival (Nakaciuryaraq) marked the
opening of the winter ceremonial season. At the time of the winter
solstice, the bladders of seals killed that year were inflated and brought
into the men's house. These bladders were believed to contain the
animals' souls, and during their stay in the men's house they were
treated as honored guests. The bladders were hung across the back
wall, comparable to the position of honor in the men's house occupied
by the elders, who were likewise nearing the time of their departure
from this world.

The primary function of the Bladder Festival was to reverse the
separation of body and soul effected at the time of the seal's death.
The Bladder Festival proper was preceded by a ceremony known as
Qaariitaaq in many areas. During Qaariitaaq, the village boys had their
bodies painted and were led from house to house each night, where
they were given food by the women. Through this ritual circuit, the
children opened the community to the seal spirits.

Aaniq (literally, "to provide a mother") was held directly after Qaariitaaq and introduced the Bladder Festival proper. During Aaniq, two
older men, dressed in gutskin parkas and referred to as mothers, led a
group of boys who were termed their dogs around the village. The men
collected newly made bowls filled with akutaq (a mixture of berries, seal
oil, boned fish, and tallow) from the women, a reversal of the usual pattern of women bringing cooked meat to their men in the men's house.
In many areas Qaariitaaq and the Bladder Festival each lasted for five
days, a number that corresponded with the five steps that separated
the worlds of the living and the dead.

During the Bladder Festival, the men's house and its residents were
ritually purified by sweat baths as well as by the smoke from wild celery
plants. Routine activities were set aside, and the days were devoted to
athletic competitions between married and unmarried men, instruction
in and performance of commemorative songs, and the presentation
of special feast foods. All of these activities were performed with the

intent to entertain the seals' souls, residing in the bladders hung along the wall of the men's house.

On the last night of the Bladder Festival, the entire village as well as invited guests from nearby villages gathered in the men's house. Gifts were given by parents to celebrate their children's accomplishments. The wooden dolls of young girls who had come of age were distributed. Finally, a huge village-wide distribution took place, in which large amounts of frozen and dried fish and sealskin pokes full of seal oil were given away. When giving these gifts, each donor was particular to say that everything had been given to him. Giving gifts in someone else's name, particularly that of a deceased kinsman, was a feature of a number of ceremonial distributions. To this day in southwestern Alaska, social ties between the living are both created and maintained through the relationship between the living and the dead.

Finally, at the close of the Bladder Festival, pairs of young men took the inflated bladders along with bunches of wild celery out through the central smoke hole and down to a hole in the ice. There the bladders were deflated and returned to their underwater home, where they would boast of their good treatment and subsequently allow themselves to be taken by the villagers the following season.

The Feast for the Dead

The annual Feast for the Dead (known in some areas as Merr'aq, from meq, "water") was the public occasion on which the spirits of the human dead were invited into the human community to receive the food and clothing they required. It was initiated when men placed stakes at the graveside, effectively opening the village and inviting the spirits to enter as in the ceremonies prior to the Bladder Festival. As in the Bladder Festival, the village was ritually cleansed in preparation for the arrival of the spirits. Moreover, great care was taken during the ceremonial period to limit any human activity (such as sewing or chopping wood) that might injure the souls as they entered the village, or cut their path.

The Great Feast for the Dead, Elriq, was a much more complex and elaborate event. It attracted hundreds of people from the far corners of the Yukon and Kuskokwim Delta and continued for four to six days. Elriq was sequentially hosted by different villages within a single region. Within each village, the feast was hosted primarily by a single individual, aided by his relatives. The major distributions took place on the fourth and fifth days of the ceremony, when first the women and then the men ritually clothed the living namesakes according to the sex of the deceased relative. Gifts were brought into the men's house through the gut skylight, reversing the route they used to remove the human body at death.

The Gift Festival

Another important winter ceremony was the "commercial play" known as *Petugtaq*. This event is usually described as an exchange of gifts between the men and women of one village. Normally the gifts given were relatively small. The men might begin the play by making tiny replicas of things that they desired, such as grass socks, bird-skin caps, or fish-skin mittens. These replicas would be hung from a wand or stick and taken to the women of the village. Each woman then chose one of the images and prepared the item requested. When all was ready, the women brought their gifts to the men's house, where they presented them to the men, who were duty-bound to provide a suitable return.

In some areas at least, enjoyment derived from the pairing of both biologically and socially unlikely couples in the exchange, because no one knew who had made a specific request until the actual distribution. In this context the pairing of cross cousins was considered particularly delightful. In Yup'ik the terms used to refer to cross-sex cross cousins were *nuliacungaq* ("dear little wife") and *uicungaq* ("dear little husband"). Marriage between cross cousins was not traditionally prescribed. However, teasing complete with sexual innuendo characterized their relationship, as distinct from the much more serious and respectful relationship between siblings and parallel cousins, and the proper day-to-day relationship between husband and wife.

The Messenger Feast

Another major ceremony held during the winter season was *Kevgiq*, from the name for the two messengers sent to invite the guest village to the festival. *Kevgiq* was characterized by a mutual hosting between villages, whereby one village would go to another to dance and receive gifts. It was initiated when a host village presented its guests with a long list of wants, and the guests subsequently reciprocated with a list of their own. Besides collecting the articles to be given, each village composed songs describing the desired articles and naming the individual from whom the object was requested.

There was considerable rivalry as to the quality and the quantity of the gifts given during *Kevgiq,* and in some areas the guests were designated *curukat,* or attackers. *Kevgiq* was circumscribed by a calculated ambiguity, as the line between friend and foe was a fine one. Although *Kevgiq* shared common features with the other ceremonial distributions, it stands out as a particularly elaborate display and distribution of the bounty of the harvest, providing a clear statement of respect to the spirits of the fish and game. Two important functions of *Kevgiq* were the redistribution of wealth within and between villages and the expression and maintenance of status distinctions.

Agayuyaraq

The final major annual winter ceremony was *Agayuyaraq* (way of requesting), sometimes referred to as *Kelek* or *Itruka'ar.* This complex ritual event involved the singing of songs of supplication to the animals' *yuit* (their persons) accompanied by the performance of masked dances under the direction of the shaman. Ritually powerful masks were created especially for the event and represented the spirits of the game as well as the *tuunrat,* the shaman's spirit helpers. In the preparations for *Agayuyaraq,* it was the shaman who directed the construction of the masks through which the spirits were revealed as at once dangerous and helpful. Their use, in enactments of past spiritual encounters, had the power to evoke them in the future. As in the Bladder Festival, songs were written and performed by the people of the community to draw the spirit world.

Summary

In sum, at least five major events made up the annual ceremonial cycle in southwestern Alaska. Individually these ceremonies served to emphasize different aspects of the relationship between humans, animals, and the spirit world. The Bladder Festival along with related ceremonies insured the rebirth and return of the animals in the coming harvest season. In the Feast for the Dead living namesakes were ritually fed and elaborately clothed to provision and honor the souls of the human dead. The Great Feast for the Dead (*Elriq*) served the same function within human society as the Bladder Festival within animal society, expressing and insuring continuity between the living and the dead. The intravillage *Petugtaq* and the intervillage Messenger Feast

(*Kevgiq*) played on, exaggerated, and reversed normal social relationships between husband and wife and between host and guest. *Kevgiq* also served important social functions, including the display of status, social control, and the redistribution of wealth. At the same time it provided a clear statement to the spirits of the game that the hunters were once again ready to receive them. Finally, *Agayuyaraq* involved masked dances that dramatically recreated past spiritual encounters to elicit their participation in the future. Together the ceremonies embodied a cyclical view of the universe whereby right action in the past and present reproduced abundance in the future.

References

Bogoras, Waldemar. 1904–9. "The Chukchee." In *The Jesup North Pacific Expedition 7, Memoirs of the American Museum of Natural History.* Leiden and New York (reprinted 1975, New York: AMS Press).

Briggs, Jean L. 1970. *Never in Anger: Portrait of an Eskimo Family.* Cambridge: Harvard University Press.

Brightman, Robert. 1983. "Animal and Human in Rock Cree Religion and Subsistence." Ph.D. Dissertation, Department of Anthropology, University of Chicago.

Fienup-Riordan, Ann. 1983. *The Nelson Island Eskimo.* Anchorage: Alaska Pacific University Press.

———. 1986. "Nick Charles, Sr.: The Worker in Wood." In *The Artist behind the Work,* ed. Suzi Jones. Pp. 25–57. Fairbanks: University of Alaska Museum.

———. 1987. "The Mask: The Eye of the Dance." *Arctic Anthropology* 24, no. 12: 40–55.

———. 1994. *Boundaries and Passages: Role and Ritual in Central Yup'ik Oral Tradition.* Norman: University of Oklahoma Press.

———. 1996. *The Living Tradition of Yup'ik Masks: Agayuliyararpat (Our Way of Making Prayer).* Seattle: University of Washington Press.

———. 2000. *Hunting Tradition in a Changing World: Yup'ik Lives in Alaska Today.* New Brunswick, N.J.: Rutgers University Press.

Fitzhugh, William, and Susan A. Kaplan. 1982. *Inua: Spirit World of the Bering Sea Eskimo.* Washington, D.C.: Smithsonian Institution Press.

Friday, Joe. 1984. Interview, August 7, Chevak, Alaska. 14(h)(1) Site Survey. Anchorage, Alaska: Bureau of Indian Affairs Realty Office.

———. 1985. Interview, February 19, translated by Louise Leonard. San Francisco: Lansburg Productions.

Himmelheber, Hans. 1953. *Eskimokünstler: Ergebnisse einer Reise in Alaska.* 2d ed. Eisenach, Germany: Erich Roth-Verlag.

Hallowell, A. Irving. 1960. "Ojibwa Ontology, Behavior, and World View." In *Culture in History: Essays in Honor of Paul Radin,* ed. Stanley Diamond. Pp. 19–52. New York: Columbia University Press.

Lantis, Margaret, 1947. *Alaskan Eskimo Ceremonialism*. Monographs of the American Ethnological Society 11. New York: J. J. Augustin.

Mather, Elsie. 1985. *Cauyarnariuq*. Bethel, Alaska: Lower Kuskokwim School District Bilingual-Bicultural Department.

Moore, Riley D. 1923. "Social Life of the Eskimo of St. Lawrence Island." *American Anthropologist* 25, no. 3: 339–75.

Morrow, Phyllis. 1984. "It Is Time for Drumming: A Summary of Recent Research of Yup'ik Ceremonialism." *Etudes/Inuit/Studies* 8 (special issue): 113–40.

Nelson, Edward William. 1899. "The Eskimo about Bering Strait." *Bureau of American Ethnology Annual Report* 18:1–518. Washington, D.C.: Smithsonian Institution. (Reprinted with Introduction by William H. Fitzhugh, Classics of Smithsonian Anthropology Series, 1983, Washington, D.C.: Smithsonian Institution Press.)

Rasmussen, Knud. 1927. *Across Arctic America: Narrative of the Fifth Thule Expedition*. New York: G. P. Putnam's Sons.

———. 1931. "The Netsilik Eskimos: Social Life and Spiritual Culture." *Report of the Fifth Thule Expedition 1921–24* 8 (1–2). Copenhagen.

Ray, Dorothy Jean. 1967. "Alaskan Eskimo Arts and Crafts." *The Beaver* (Autumn): 80–91.

———. 1981. *Aleut and Eskimo Art: Tradition and Innovation in South Alaska*. London: C. Hurst & Company.

Schuster Carl. 1951. "Joint Marks: A Possible Index of Cultural Contact between America, Oceania, and the Far East." *Royal Tropical Institute* (Amsterdam), 39:4–51.

Tennant, Edward A., and Joseph N. Bitar, eds. 1981. *Yupik Lore: Oral Traditions of an Eskimo People*. Bethel, Alaska: Lower Kuskokwin School District.

Thalbitzer, William. 1908. "The Heathen Priests of East Greenland." *Verhand Lungen des XVI Amerekanisten-Kongresses, Wien 1980*. Pp. 447–64.

Usugan, Frances. 1984. Interview, July 20, Toksook Bay, Nelson Island, Alaska. 14(h)(1) Site Survey. Anchorage, Alaska: Bureau of Indian Affairs Realty Office.

Images of the Sacred
in Native North American Literature

Franco Meli

Translated by Karen D. Antonelli, Ph.D.

In his book *The Soul of the Indian* (1911), Charles A. Eastman claims that religiosity is the last thing a white man will ever be able to comprehend of the Indian world.[1] Always keeping this warning in mind and never undervaluing its importance, I will attempt to trace the persistence and the importance of the sacred in several of the most significant voices of Native American literature.

Eastman's work is an excellent beginning, not only because temporally it is found at the beginning of the twentieth century, but also, above all, because it betrays a type of splitting, a discomfort felt within distinct realities; therefore, Eastman presents the prototype of the uprooted Indian, the figure which has always been stigmatized by contemporary writers, who have been careful to represent the dilemma of adapting to two cultures.

The Soul of the Indian has an approach which is strongly felt in a moral and civil sense and includes an indignant denunciation of the most iniquitous and hypocritical aspects of acculturation, to which is added the arduous attempt to remove the Indian universe from the archaeo-anthropologic museum in which the invader intends to place it. This intention is implicit in the title, so full of ethic-religious implications: it is provocative at a moment in history in which only a privileged minority is willing to grant the Indian such a principally human attribute as a "soul."

---

1. *The Soul of the Indian: An Interpretation* (1911; Lincoln: University of Nebraska Press, 1980).

Eastman brings us directly to the origins, to a temporal arch and defined space upon which the anguish of the presence of white men has not yet manifested itself in all its corrosive impetus. Eastman aspires to infuse well-deserved life into arid anthropological bones, even amid contradictions and ambiguities that are the results of the politics of assimilation pursued with stubborn determination by the church and the government.

The most appropriate and penetrating condemnation is the moral one, and thus the most centered attack is the reference to the essence of Christianity. In *I letterati e lo sciamano* [*The Writer and the Shaman: A Morphology of the American Indian;* 1969], Elémire Zolla correctly underlines Eastman's great capacity, similar to the early Melville of *Typee* and *Omoo,* to bare the incurable ambiguities and contradictions of Christianity.[2]

In fact, the first chapter ("The Great Mystery") ends with these assertions:

After thirty-five years of experience, I personally believe that what goes under the name of Christian civilization does not exist. I am convinced that Christianity and modern civilization are opposed to and irreconcilable with each other, and that the spirit of Christianity and our ancient religion is essentially the same. (26)

Christianity does not provide the means to give value to the existence of the Indians, and it is far from able to significantly affect even the American society. Only hunger and imprisonment, continues Eastman, convince a portion of the Indians to embrace, without any particular enthusiasm, the Christian word, which is carelessly interpreted as the only glimmer of hope and benevolence.

On the contrary, Christianity reveals itself to be a disintegrating force, the determining cause of the collapse and degradation of Indian civilization; the introduction of the white man's religious and cultural patterns, viewed as abstract and rigid, brings the loss and/or degeneration of the traditional heritage and increases intertribal antagonisms. A systematic operation of destruction and uprooting of the religious beliefs and the social order have irretrievably undermined that delicate weaving of thought, conviction, and socioeconomic organization that make up the necessary cohesion of any culture. Eastman speaks of the

2. Elémire Zolla, *The Writer and the Shaman: A Morphology of the American Indian.*

sacredness of the oral tradition passed on from generation to generation, of the relationship with occult dimensions which are interwoven
with daily happenings: the sacred is inseparable from the ordinary; the
tasks imposed by daily life and those associated with the expression of
the sacred are interlaced and interdependent.

These characteristics of the sacred emerge from the interweaving of
legends and mythologic narrations that, abandoning his bitter initial
criticism, constitute Eastman's central theme. The narrations express
the immense power of the word, at times an enchanting, at times a co-
ercive, force that is identified with reality itself; a mingling of symbols
and vital experiences. The mind and the spirit of the Indian child are
molded by the tales (narrated to young Eastman by his grandmother,
Uncheedah) and by a systematic education, countersigned by an imita-
tive and ritualistic process sustained by a harmony which is not difficult
to find in the "narrations" of the author; his work therefore presents
itself as an inner quest, and the "tale" becomes the substitute for the
ritual.

Eastman was able to select two essential characteristics of the oral
tradition, often used by contemporary writers: a particular perception of
space and a specific attitude toward language. His importance, however,
does not end here: his parable of life indicates a journey, a direction
for the protagonists of following literature — that is a return to the
ancestral land.

Shortly after turning sixty, Eastman leaves New England, the land
of liberalism which in the end had accelerated the disintegration of
the Indian world and thus had become the symbol of shattered hopes.
He finds refuge at Stony Lake in a remote region of Wisconsin. A
return, recurring throughout his life, which now becomes an urgent
need for a "wilderness" seen as the ultimate refuge, the final antidote
to a devastating contamination.

He even abandons his literary activities and appears in public more
rarely. His final two decades of life — he passed away in 1939 —
are years of silence; "narration" gives way to the search for visions.
Agreeing with the most authentic traditions, Eastman's "narration" is
responsibility toward the "word," an itinerary toward the center of all
things. His final silence expresses an availability, an openness to the
harmony of the natural order. The inner voyage brings him back to the
starting point, to the sacredness of the earth, to the silence in which
he was educated; the beginning and the end coincide and unite.

The circularity of the journey refers to the distinctive elements of a literature that continues to assign strong values of sacredness to the word and to the earth:

A word has power in and of itself. It comes from nothing into sound and meaning; it gives origin to all things. By means of words can a man deal with the world on equal terms. And the word is sacred.[3]

The Indian knowledge of the American continent is ancient, and, according to Momaday, the most authoritative voice of the Native renaissance, this has produced a large spiritual investment in a specific space. The natural patterns of this space have developed a harmony out of which a precise cultural identity has been acquired.

The relationship between the Indian world and the earth is usually defined as mystical, but it is more appropriate to speak of moral ties, responsibility, and respect. In fact, the relationship concerns an ethical tie with the environment: the sharing of a defined space develops an understanding of the consequences of abuse, and this results in the assumption of certain responsibilities toward the earth and one's community.

Belonging to a specific people implies, in contemporary Native American literature, an intuitive comprehension and a participation in a ritualism that, even if it may include individual and isolated experiences, translates into expressions of, and continues only in, a tribal context. The individual exists only in a complex system of relationships which, in Leslie Marmon Silko's masterpiece *Ceremony*, finds its own expression in the image of the spider web, with its perfect equilibrium of reciprocal tensions.[4]

The main purpose of ceremonialism is to preserve or reestablish the delicate cosmic balance, within which individuals and the community in its aggregate must integrate. Individual identity, in notable contrast with Euro-American culture, does not come from the activity of the single person; rather, it is received and determined from the belonging to a community. Ceremonialism creates and reinforces this sense of tribal identity, which is absolutely necessary for psychophysical well-being. Therefore, it is therapeutic for the articulation and affirmation

3. N. Scott Momaday, *The Way to Rainy Mountain* (Albuquerque: University of New Mexico Press, 1969), 33.
4. Leslie Marmon Silko, *Ceremony* (New York: New American Library, 1977).

of a besieged Indianness, seemingly nearing extinction, but which, in the end, knows how to take from its deepest soul the strength to affirm its continuity.

Those shreds of ancestral land known as reservations continue to be "home," the only place to which to return, and are still able to transmit a sense of belonging. "Home" is the destination of the Indian refugees in a poem by Louise Erdrich:

> Home's the place we head for in our sleep.
> Boxcars stumbling north in dreams
> don't wait for us. We catch them on the run.
> The rails, old lacerations that we love,
> shoot parallel across the face and break
> just under Turtle Mountains. Riding scars
> you can't get lost. Home is the place they cross.[5]

As Joseph Bruchac emphasizes, this is a particular escape, in direct antithesis to the dominant ethic of the Euro-American society: "It's running home; it's not running away from home."[6]

The "return home" — at times reluctant, at other times decisive, at times symbolic, at other times realistic — cannot be interpreted in terms of defeat and failure. If the Native American, as D'Arcy Mc-Nickle states in his essays, tends to have a self-image that is more tied to his concept of tribalism than to individualism, the return, often motivated by the outrage suffered at the hands of the domineering society, is an attempt to overcome a condition of imbalance, of "illness" caused by the separation from space of vital importance for the sense of identity.

The favor with which Indian writers welcome the return can be read in terms of the tribal dimensions and sacred models to which the protagonists are significantly connected, above all, to parental ties (there is almost always the presence of a decisive relationship with an elderly person) and to the earth. The earth continues to be crucial for the physical and spiritual survival of the Indians. More than merely being a simple aspect of Native literature, one can say that the earth makes it possible, giving it a circular character; the return reveals intentions

5. Louise Erdrich, "Indian Boarding School: The Runaways," in Cinzia Biagiotti and Laura Coltelli, eds., *Figlie di Pocahontas: Racconti e poesie delle indiani d'America* (Florence: Giunti, 1995), 263.

6. Joseph Bruchac, ed., *Survival This Way: Interviews with American Indian Poets* (Albuquerque: University of New Mexico Press, 1990), 76.

and symmetries since it allows the narrated story's beginning and end to coincide.

McMaster is very right stating that "the land is the spiritual, historical, and physical connection that gives Native people their identity."[7] Also enlightening is a quotation from a short story by Sherman Alexie, one of the most interesting voices of the younger generation:

When I got back to the reservation, my family wasn't surprised to see me. They'd been expecting me back since the day I left Seattle. There's an old Indian poet who said that Indians can reside in the city, but they can never live there. That's as close to truth as any of us get.[8]

Broadening the perspective, Momaday has claimed that the Indians live *with* the continent and not merely *on* the continent; Vine Deloria, perhaps the most important Indian intellectual, affirms that to the Indian is due the spiritual possession of the earth, while for the American is reserved *only* the juridical possession, the fruit of violence and deception.

The earth is where the collective memory of Native people echoes and cultural survival seems possible by maintaining a solid bond with the reservations, where traditions, of religious as well as social spheres, tend to be maintained, and thus the collective identity has greater possibilities to stay alive. Deloria warns against incomprehension and simplification; the age-old battle of the Indians (yesterday on the battlefields, today in the court rooms) to defend their lands cannot be identified simply as environmental actions, merely ecological since they possess something of the sacred, of a much greater depth. Environmentalism, disassociated from a spiritual comprehension of the place that human beings occupy in the cosmos, becomes a sublimated version of this same culture which determines its desecration and its destruction.

The return therefore is necessary for a sense of belonging; it is the arrival on authentic, concrete land away from which there is deep loss, an absence of meaning. For this reason, it would be erroneous to interpret it as a return to a past which in fact cannot be restored: Native Americans return not to the past but to the origins; they return

---

7. Gerald McMaster, *Edward Poitras* (Seattle: University of Washington Press, 1995), 76.
8. Sherman Alexie, *The Lone Ranger and Tonto Fistfight in Heaven* (New York: Vintage, 1993), 187.

not to what has already been but to its essence, that which tends to be permanent, even if it is subject to transformations and/or adaptations, in time and in space.

Simon Pokagon's *O-gi-maw-kwe mit-i-gwa-ki, Queen of the Woods* (1890) is commonly considered the beginning of modern Native liter-ature. In the opening scene, the protagonist returns to the reservation where he grew up, after an absence of several years during which he attended government schools. There is an unrestrainable urge to reestablish contact with the uncontaminated forests, far away from the torments of civilization. The return home is narrated as a return to a young girl, Lonidaw, the personification of natural harmony. Beautiful and mysterious, she lives in a mystical relationship with the environ-ment that surrounds her to the point that, at her death, the forces of nature break out into a violent storm. The power and the sacred-ness of the earth are in contrast to the tragedy that consumes the children of Pokagon and Lonidaw, destroyed by the "weapons" of the conquerors: first among them, alcohol.

In *Sundown* (1934), John Joseph Mathews outlines the development of a character from birth to maturity, keeping in evidence tentative redemption, failures and delusions. Chal Windzer attends the school on the reservation and subsequently goes to the university, which he interrupts to enlist in the air force at the outbreak of World War I. Uprooted in ever deeper and irreversible ways, he finally rejects his own Indianness.

After the war, Chal returns to the reservation. His father has died with the bitter knowledge that, having aligned himself with the govern-ment, he contributed irreparably to the betrayal of the traditional life of his people, the Osage. Chal continues, however, to be embarrassed by the "Indian" ways of his mother, by the style of her clothes, by the house in which she insists on living, despite the wealth brought on by the exploitation of petroleum deposits.

If education was the first factor of estrangement, now it is money that morally and psychologically debilitates Chal. Without economic worries, he doesn't know what to do with himself; he spends his time roving about, driving fast cars in the company of various women, and, above all, drinking a lot. The young man, however, senses a vague yet imperious calling; it is the attraction to the open spaces of the wilds, where he senses the presence of mysterious forces. Chal feels ill at ease and a sense of shame blossoms within him because he associates the "call of the forest" with a past which is considered the antithesis of civilization.

Now an adult, in an attempt to recapture a fragment of Indian life and to shake off the apathy that crushes him, Chal participates in a purification ritual that precedes the peyote ceremony. Yet, even this approach to the sacred dimension of the Indian way brings about no spiritual renewal. In an inebriated state, Chal yields to atavistic impulses and begins to dance, sing, and feel Indian again. The ceremony therefore has a cathartic outcome which, however, given that it is an isolated, solitary gesture, cannot pass beyond, in the protagonist's own words, the "extravaganza" — in other words, the wandering outside, without any relation with a meaningful context. Lacking a way out, Chal feels even more empty. He is defeated, and his return to the bottle seems inevitable.

The protagonist's final sleep, preceded by vague ideas of attending Harvard Law School, is contrasted by a nature that immutably continues its course, a symbol of a superior reality that remains intact. Chal's basic failure, to which we can add the defeat and death of his friend Running Elk, is however somewhat mitigated by the choice made by Sun-on-His-Wings, Chal's comrade and friend. Within a precise textual symmetry, to Sun-on-His-Wings is given the role of equilibrator: he becomes, in effect, an active participant in the life of the reservation and adheres to the Native American Church, that is to peyotism. Mathews therefore leaves open the possibility for a significant return to Indian life.

The image of an Indian way, even if confused by the many ways brought about by the invaders, is still visible to and can be followed by the mind and spirit. It characterizes the literature and recurs in the works of contemporary authors. Historically, peyotism has attempted to reduce the catastrophic effects of contact with the Euro-American world and on the other hand, has attempted to preserve certain defining elements of the Native universe.

Economically dependent on the government and forced to endure an assimilation process, the Indians had known a time of great cultural loss and physical decadence (above all in the last decades of the nineteenth century and the first decades of the twentieth century). Peyotism has attempted to hold back the process of acculturation and to produce a new vision that could provide an identity even in the new, tragic conditions of subordination to the invader.

Even while presenting distinctly Native characteristics, in order to
meet the changed conditions, peyotism contains elements of the dominant culture, revealing therefore a more accommodating face compared
with the movement known as the Ghost Dance, with which it has
common threads as well as substantial divergences. In other words,
peyotism's insistence on nonviolence (not only toward whites but also
among Indians), introspection, and meditation, is a sign of reconcilia-
tion and compromise, that is of partial and selective acceptance of the
Euro-American culture.

Integrating Native needs and modalities with elements of religious
and laic visions of the invader, peyotism can offer Native Americans
a religious expression in which they can identify themselves and from
which they can obtain a certain degree of security absolutely necessary
in order not to succumb completely to the political, economic and
cultural superpower of the invader.

The search for a seriously compromised Indianness even animates
D'Arcy McNickle's *The Surrounded.*[9] This work is a milestone in Indian literature, the irreplaceable bridge between the uncertainty of
the first voices and the determination of the post–World War II era.
McNickle bares the significance of the conflict between the two civiliza-
tions and presents a realistic image of the Native encircled by a foreign
and destructive reality that offers no comprehensible and acceptable
solutions.

The theme and drama of the relations among the Indian population and the representatives of government and religious institutions
are modern: the work is therefore out of sync with its own time and
anticipatory in many instances of the Indian rebirth. Interest in Mc-
Nickle, as indicated by the many reprint editions of his book, is not
ambiguously stuck in sentimentality and adventurousness; it should be
remembered, however, that his denouncement is lacking in rhetorical
invective and aggressiveness.

The Surrounded is enriched with flashbacks, mythic tales, historical
facts, lyrical descriptions of Indian land, and pages full of annihilating
violence. Its protagonist is Archilde Leon, son of a Flathead mother and
a Spanish father. The extreme modernness lies even in the selection

9. D'Arcy McNickle, *The Surrounded* (1936; Albuquerque: University of New Mexico Press,
1978).

of a protagonist subjected to biculturalism. In fact, Archilde lives in different worlds, which are at some level discordant, and he therefore faces the need to blend, in a hopefully coherent fabric, fragments of both realities.

After a year's absence spent in Portland, Oregon, where he earned a living playing the violin, Archilde returns to his reservation in Montana. He has made this choice reluctantly and intends it to be completely temporary. The reasons for his return are not immediately clear, even if they include, without a doubt, the desire to see his mother and to "refill his tank" with scenery, sensations, colors, sounds, smells that "were nothing that could be touched and yet they had strength and substance" (25). The Indian land thus seems to be a sort of "supply of life" to better confront the emptiness and alienation of the urban context, to which McNickle often refers in terms of degradation.

Even if in Sniél-emen, the Mountains of the Surrounded, the Salish people described in the novel live in an enclave besieged by hostility and violence, the return to this land arouses in Archilde an involvement in the collective memory of his own people. Through the example set by his mother, Catharine, who achieves full recovery of an Indianness that has been repressed for too long, and through listening to the sacred stories filled with deep meanings narrated by the old people, Archilde undertakes, "despite himself" we could say, a journey of spiritual and social reintegration.

A first sign of change is detectable at the end of a tale told by Modeste, an old, blind, and highly respected chief:

Archilde, listening closely, felt something die within him. Some stiffness, some pride, went weak before the old man's bitter simple words. For the first time he had really seen it happen.... He had heard the story many times, but he had not listened. It had tired him. Now he saw that it had happened and it left him feeling weak. It destroyed his stiffness toward the old people. He sat and thought about it and the flames shot upward and made light on the circle of black pines. (74)

Archilde's mother, had witnessed great changes during the course of her long life, without being deeply touched. Yet while inside her tipi, Archilde senses a feeling of belonging which will reveal itself as decisive for the turn of events narrated in the novel:

Archilde sat quietly and felt those people move in his blood. There in his mother's tepee he had found unaccountable security. It was all quite near, quite a part of him; it was his necessity, for the first time. (222)

Deciding to accompany his mother in what we presume will be her last hunt, following a traditional ritual, Archilde becomes slowly involved in a series of violent and destructive events that will culminate in his arrest and accusation as an accomplice in two homicides. Against the cynical words spoken by Agent Parker, who handcuffs him ("it's too damn bad you people never learn"), is the echo of Archilde's silence, surrounded and innocent, lacking any possibility or will to articulate his defense since he sees no solution.

Communication between the two worlds is not possible, and Mc-Nickle is fully aware that on Indian land there is no dialogue but rather an authoritarian and incontrovertible monologue that obliterates, marginalizes, and excludes the Native voice. This is a central theme, the origin of any type of conflict that develops in the literature through a dialectic that interrupts (interrupted articulation) or never takes shape (inarticulation). The dynamic of dominance is tinged with many strategies for cultural survival which can manifest themselves with unsuspected times and modalities.

For example, Father Jerome, a Jesuit missionary on Salish land, shows no comprehension of or tolerance toward the religious "intemperances" of the Indians, not realizing that Christianity had contributed in a determinative way to the disintegration of a world marked by an integrated religious vision, articulated in accordance with tightly recognized and shared values. He was unable to provide a new, convincing vision, and therefore fragments of songs from ancient traditions can reemerge even during Mass:

It rather got on his nerves that the Indian congregation which sat always at the back of the church still followed its old custom of breaking out into its own prayers and its own songs at odd moments of the Mass. The songs had a pagan wildness. He would rather they had been better disciplined. (263)

In notable contrast to the dominant ethic, the separation from the Native land implies the possible, inevitable return. Archilde again follows the Indian way and accepts down to the very core the implications of his choice; more than a refusal, it is an impossibility of adhesion, of an emotional and cultural separation that distances him from the American dream. Despite the fact that the reservation is held in a terrible stranglehold that leaves no breathing room and offers no other prospects, McNickle suggests that the reservation is the only place where it is possible to preserve and/or reconstitute shreds of the vitality and the dynamic of the Indian way.

With *House Made of Dawn,* N. Scott Momaday has become the most prestigious name in Indian literature and, thanks also to his academic credentials, he is given serious consideration by established critics.[10] Noteworthy are the affinities between the work of McNickle and that of Momaday, which is recognized as the apex of Native American literature. Archilde and Abel, the respective protagonists, are in many ways literary twins whose events overlap on many occasions. For both, the encounter with the dominant reality causes a deep malaise, which in Abel, biblical victim par excellence, assumes the characteristic of a pathology in that he becomes incapable of expressing himself and loses any significant contact with the world, including the Native one.

Both return to the reservation almost instinctively, driven by the hope of regaining, in the only space left them, a reason to live. The healing process is complex and exhausting as well as incomplete, because the external world places its own annihilating stamp even on the remotest Indian lands. If at the beginning of *The Surrounded,* Archilde senses a detachment from and suspicion toward his mother and the model of traditional life, Abel's incomprehension translates, at the moment of his return to Jemez Pueblo, into the inability, because he is drunk, to recognize his grandfather Francisco, the symbol of a Native culture from which he is estranged in consequence of traumas faced during the war and in the Los Angeles ghetto.

But the center of Abel's world isn't lost, it must be regained, and this is a substantial difference between *House Made of Dawn* and earlier works. The path Abel must follow is an arduous search for vision. His family tree already seems to condemn him to oblivion. He doesn't know his own father and his ties with Walatowa, that is the Jemez Pueblo to which he returns, come from his mother through Francisco, her father. The obscure genealogy weakens his sense of identity, as his

---

10. N. Scott Momaday, *House Made of Dawn* (1968; Albuquerque: University of New Mexico Press, 1996).

name, with its unequivocal biblical resonance, emphasizes his tense position between Native culture and the white one.

After his return from World War II, Abel's alienation is sanctioned by the impossibility of his inserting himself into the religious and social models that mark the life of the pueblo. In fact, during a syncretistic ritual, Abel kills an albino Indian, who in his eyes is the personification of the serpent of evil. Believing he can extirpate evil by eliminating it physically with an individual action, he moves away from the Indian vision that seeks, with appropriate ceremonial acts, to preserve or reestablish the precarious equilibrium of good and bad that permits the existence of any form of life. Evil is therefore a primordial ineradicable force which is to be recognized and kept under control, exorcised in a sacred context.

Abel thus comes in contact with Euro-American justice and is tried and imprisoned according to an incomprehensible language and to rules of procedure which are in contrast with Native customs. Following his time in prison, of which he only remembers the immense walls, the young Indian lies on a Los Angeles beach and is compared to a fish out of water (whereas in the pueblo, he had been compared to an eagle in a cage).

Abel is physically and spiritually ill. He cannot "see"; he is stricken with a weakness of vision that is both physical and imaginary and that is worsened by being moved to Los Angeles (this is the result of a government program to relocate young Indians to large cities in order to facilitate their assimilation). For the first time, however vaguely, Abel searches for the origin of the deep malaise that confuses him. The sermons of Tosamah, the Priest of the Sun, provide him with a few hints as to the nature of his affliction.

In his first sermon, Tosamah, through an original exposition of the Gospel of John, puts into strident conflict the attitude of the Indian and the white man with respect to language. The apostle shared with the Indian the sensitivity to the "Word"; he knew its sacredness, but he was also a white man, adds the Priest of the Sun, and as such he obscured reality, weighing it down with words:

> Now, brothers and sisters, old John was a white man, and the white man has his ways. . . . He talks about the Word. . . . He builds upon it with syllables, with prefixes and suffixes, and hyphens and accents. He adds and divides and multiplies the Word. And in all

of this he subtracts the Truth.... Now the white man deals in
words, and he deals easily, with grace and sleight of hand. And
in his presence, here on his own ground, you are as children,
mere babes in the woods. You must not mind, for in this you have
a certain advantage. A child can listen and learn. The Word is
sacred to a child. (87–88)

Tosamah carries out the role that oral tradition has assigned to the
sacred trickster: he is associated with the pleasure of narration, and in
the Indian world, the telling of stories signifies the possibility of "creating," determining, and clarifying a specific reality. The words of the
Priest of the Sun, in fact, take us to the core of Abel's problem. On
the one hand, Abel is inarticulated, disjointed from the ceremonial
"Word" of his people; on the other, he is oppressed by the incomprehensible and hostile sea of the dominant society's words. For example,
at the trial, after having told his version of the story in a simple and
exemplary way, Abel refuses to continue:

That was good, for he should not have known what more to say.
Word by word these men were disposing of him in language, *their*
language, and they were making a bad job of it. (95)

In his second sermon, "The Way to Rainy Mountain," Tosamah
evokes the mythic journey of the Kiowa toward the light of dawn, the
symbol of a new era, of better conditions. During the narration, the
Priest of the Sun appears to recover a new sense of belonging which,
however, he is unable to transmit to Abel. There is no comprehension
and sympathy between the two characters; Abel is repeatedly provoked
and derided; Tosamah labels him a "long-hair," in other words, a traditionalist Indian, a good-for-nothing destined to be victimized in that
horrible jungle that, paradoxically, corresponds to the name of Los Angeles. The Priest of the Sun recognizes his role as spiritual leader in the
desolate city of angels and would like to provide Abel with some defense mechanism, but in fact he cannot help him; he cannot cure him,
no matter how many times Momaday ironically defines him as "doctor."
Tosamah, however, as the Priest of Peyote, is involved in an appropriation of the biblical discussion to support a syncretic Indian spirituality,
a new spiritual order that, despite its emergence in the dark days of the
previous century, is capable of confronting changing conditions. Peyotism, perhaps more than any other form of religious expression, has

been able to adapt itself to the changes brought about by urban civilization, without allowing these changes to overinfluence the vigor of the
cult. For example, Tosamah was able to find alternative places for his
ceremonies, such as rooms or basements in the heart of the metropolis:

> The Priest of the Sun lived with his disciple Cruz on the first floor
> of a two-story red-brick building in Los Angeles. The upstairs
> was maintained as a storage facility by the A. A. Kaul Office
> Supply Company. The basement was a kind of church. There was
> a signboard on the wall above the basement steps, encased in
> glass. (83–84)

Historically, peyotism strengthens with procedures of formaliza-
tion and institutionalization; ceremonial practice is created inside a
"church," the Native American Church, of which Tosamah is the expression. Momaday dedicates ample space to the description of the
ceremony, which appears to be detailed and pertinent, and far from
any type of mystification.

Two particular elements emerge. The first refers to the symbolic traditional universe in that peyotism allows the continuation of the vision
quest, a profound cultural Native feature, particularly of the Plains Indians. In Indian culture there is a strict relationship between "vision"
and "medicine"; because it produces visions, peyote has "power" and
therefore is curative. In a holistic sense, "medicine" has supernatural
connotations. To set out on the peyote road (i.e., initiation into the
ceremonial experience of the consumption of peyote) implies a direct,
immediate, and personal encounter with the spiritual realm.

The second element raised by the author is pan-Indianism, an essential component that has decidedly contributed to the development
of peyotism. It was facilitated by the cessation of the intertribal wars,
by the relative nearness of many reservations, and, as demonstrated by
Momaday's novel, by the "relocation" of many young Indians in major
American cities.

At the ceremony officiated by Tosamah the participants are Cristóbal
Cruz, assigned to the fire; Napoleon Kills-in-the-Timber, assigned to
the drum; Henry Yellowbull; and Ben Benally. The names suggest different tribal origins, but the men see themselves as Indians united
by a destiny of marginalization and the ceremony is presented as distinctly and solely Indian. This confirms the possibility of maintaining
ties with a tradition that is systematically negated and destroyed and

at the same time of receiving an ethical vision and a social-cultural cohesion which are essential to prevent being completely shipwrecked in the oppressive reality of Los Angeles.

If the Priest of the Sun has accelerated Abel's disintegration, Ben Benally is the determining character in Abel's future on the road to a possible recovery. Using a narrative form of incomparable splendor, Momaday is extremely skillful in evoking the various phases of the ceremony, which include prayer, song, peyote consumption, and contemplation.

The ceremony lasts a long time, usually all night, and is demanding because it requires concentration skills, above all in the prolonged contemplation of the ceremonial fire and of "Father Peyote." The ritual is collective, yet it provides answers to individual interventions, each in turn. Prayers, songs, drum sounds, contemplations added to the effects of the peyote, often produce revelations in the form of visions and messages, all coming from "Father Peyote." The spirit of Peyote therefore speaks to the participants, promising redemption for evils committed and the healing of physical and mental illnesses. "Father Peyote" is thus the Celestial Father who takes care of the Indians and leads them on the way to well-being and salvation:

And beneath and beyond, transcendent, was the drum.... The sound was building, building. The first and last beats of the drum were together in the room and the gulf between was growing tight with sound and the sound was terrible and deep, shivering like the pale, essential flame. And then the sound did not diminish but backed away to the walls, and everyone waited. And at the center of the circle, rising and holding over the fetish and the flame, there were voices, one after another. (104)

Benally's vision is indicative of the direction Abel will have to undertake, that is, the return to Jemez Pueblo: "Look! Look! There are blue and purple horses ... a house made of dawn" (105).

Momaday presents the sharp sound of a whistle made from eagle bone, which sanctions the end of the ceremony, as the only sign of sacredness in a context countersigned by a material vacuum:

The Priest of the Sun arose and went out. Far off a juke box began to fill one corner of the night with brassy music, and there were occasional sounds of traffic in the streets. Then in the agony of stasis they heard it, one shrill, piercing note and then another, and another, and another: four blasts of the eagle-bone whistle. In the four directions did the Priest of the Sun, standing painted in the street, serve notice that something holy was going on in the universe. (105–6)

Benally is the Night Chanter who narrates almost in its entirety the third part of the book. It is particularly revealing that Momaday gives him, an Indian on the margins who expresses himself in very poor and basic English, the assignment of singing the fragments of traditional prayers to Abel. Abel and Benally have a common past: they were both born and raised on a reservation and have come to know their Native culture through the voices of their grandparents. This brotherhood enables a comprehension which includes participation on an emotional and spiritual plane. The belonging evoked and shared with Abel in part relieves the anguish experienced by the protagonist in Los Angeles.

"House made of dawn" is the first verse of a Navajo ceremonial prayer — the Night Song which is sung on the third day of the ceremony and, again by the patient, at the rising of the sun on the ninth day, while he takes inside him the breath of the dawn. The ritual resolves upon repelling the bad and attracting the good, thus restoring the cosmic order within the individual, leading him once again on the "Beauty Way":

> *Tségihi*   House made of dawn,
> House made of evening light,
> House made of dark cloud,
> House made of male rain,
> House made of dark mist,
> House made of female rain,
>
> . . . .
> Your offering I make.
> I have prepared a smoke for you.
> Restore my feet for me,
> Restore my legs for me,
> Restore my body for me,
> Restore my mind for me,
> Restore my voice for me.
>
> . . . .
> Happily I go forth.

. . . .
Happily may I walk.

. . . .
May it be beautiful before me,
May it be beautiful behind me,
May it be beautiful below me,
May it be beautiful above me,
May it be beautiful all around me.
In beauty it is finished. (134–35)

The song opens with a precise reference both religious and cultural-geographic. Tségihi is one of the most important divinities in the religious universe of the Navajo, tied to the power of Eagle and Thunderbird. The prayer opens with the description of the space occupied by the god: Tségihi's "house" ends up being the microcosm which encloses all that is animate and inanimate on the earth. Elements of light and darkness are presented, the masculine elements are integrated by the feminine ones, and the animal world and natural phenomena are in equilibrium. Additionally, Tségihi, precisely because it refers to the house of the divinity, is a specific geographic reference that holds an important role in the cultural history of the Navajo. Therefore, the ceremonial words are intertwined with a specific point of the Indian land — the space Abel must find.

The ceremony includes the preparation and ritual lighting of the Sacred Pipe, whose smoke, directed toward the forces of heaven and earth, is the symbol of thankfulness and purification. Then follows an invocation, an invitation to heal the person for whom the ceremony is being held. The initial sensation of tranquillity and harmony is followed by a feeling of pain and suffering, taken away, however, by the divinity which restores happiness and well-being. The journey metaphor, that is the path one must follow on the road to regeneration, is explicit. Having overcome the state of pain and malaise, the reiteration of the word *happiness* intensifies the attainment of an elevated degree of joy, which is expected to endure.

The prayer ends with an invocation, a call to the sacredness of the four directions and to the balancing circularity of the cosmos. The singer again finds himself placed within the totality of the universe, shattered by the appearance of pain and evil, seen as the disintegration of the natural order of things. Benally's contribution, by singing

"House made of dawn" to Abel at night around the fire on a hill above Los Angeles, is essential and anticipates the next decisive step: the protagonist's return "home."

Seven years have passed since Abel's first return to Jemez, and his grandfather Francisco is near death. For six mornings at dawn, the voice of his memory attempts to penetrate his grandson's illness, trying to reassemble the fragments of his story and his soul. Only at dawn on the seventh day, when his grandfather's voice, by now much weaker and more confused, quiets forever, Abel's stiffness and stagnation are transformed into movement and understanding.

Francisco's memories at the point of death are memories of initiation that bind the two existences. Through them Abel sees his own past and the "confusion" that filled it. The aseptic and mechanical noises that had disoriented and frightened him at his point of impact with a reality lived as abstraction seem to disappear when contrasted to Francisco's soft sounds, which place Abel in the proper relationship with things, beginning the reintegration of the physical, emotional, and spiritual sphere.

Now, with his memory soothed, Abel knows "what had to be done." He is finally able to correctly celebrate at a ceremony, the one for his grandfather's death, which will be followed by the Catholic rite led by Father Olguin, a tribute to the invader, which evokes no emotion in the youth:

> He straightened the old man's head and drizzled water on his hair. He shaped the long white hair into a tail and tied strings around it. He dressed the body in vivid ceremonial colors. . . . He took down from the ceiling beams packets of pollen and maize, the sacred feather and the master book. He tied together several spikes of colored grain, placing all of it next to his grand-father after having sprinkled corn flour in the four directions. He wrapped the body in a blanket." (200–201)

Abel's reintegration is quite apparent and ends with his participation in the ceremonial running that is held in Jemez at dawn, in February, shortly before the snow melts. The land of the Pueblo undergoes, on this occasion, an obvious process of being made sacred; in other words, however defined by precise territorial borders, it becomes the image of the entire cosmos through mythologic, ceremonial, and chromatic relationships.

Momaday underlines that the ceremony is an expression of the song; it brings forth in terms of a physical exertion, an intense spiritual harmony. The participants in the ritual run in imitation of the Cloud People, who with their return will fill the irrigation canals with rain, thus bringing new life. Every step outlines the primordial forces that are at the Center of the Earth and in so doing lead to the slow but inexorable passing of all things.

Because of his grandfather's death, Abel covers his torso with ashes and joins the other participants in the ceremonial race. With constant rhythmic movements, at first painfully, then beyond any thought of pain, Abel can finally embrace with a glance the space that surrounds him and place himself at its center. In the closing sentence, in a soft voice Benally's words rise: "House made of pollen, house made of dawn."

Momaday's work ends with a possibility, not with a certainty. One cannot deny, however, that the final symbols are ones of hope, and in part redeem the images of illness, pain, and violence which are present in large segments of the work. Dawn, spring, rain evoke the possibility of regeneration; in addition, the ashes on Abel's torso are dissolving: he is by now the projection/continuation of Francisco's image in a crucial space for his existence. The present is therefore recovered and incorporated in a dimension of continuity and balance.

In Silko's *Ceremony*, the protagonist Tayo's journey ends at sunrise, with a return home to the Indian community at Pueblo Laguna, which, like other pueblos, has its spiritual center in the "kiva," a typical partially buried circular construction.

With "The Rising of the Sun," as with other traditional Pueblo prayers, Tayo's story begins and ends: a cycle that suggests closure and totality. Dawn, which the youth perceives as "an event which in a single moment gathered all things together," is part of a holistic vision of the universe in which reality and myth bind together indissolubly: the story and the events exist independently from a chronologic sequence in that they spring from a mythic understanding from which they obtain tangible meaning.

The first pages of the novel are presented, structurally and thematically, as the preface of the story that is later narrated. Written in a poetic style — it is typical of Silko to blend prose and poetry — these pages introduce the cosmogony of the pueblo and underline the strong magical-religious value of thought and language. They tend to establish a relationship between the word, the story, and the ceremony, a relationship upon which the existence of the Indian people depends because they are the stories and the ceremonies which preserve strength and vitality, and prevent the Native culture from disappearing.

Thought is the source of power for Ts'ist'tsi'nako, Thought-Woman, known also as Mother Creator and Grandmother Spider. Her thought, it is said, generates and gives form to the universe, which creates all the stories and all the ceremonies. And thanks to her that even the story Silko is about to tell exists: the writer thus assumes the role of the carrier of a story that is molded to reflect a contemporary situation but which is ancient, as ancient as the conscience of the Indian people:

> Ts'its'tsi'nako, Thought-Woman
> is sitting in her room
> and whatever she thinks about appears.
>
> She thought of her sisters,
> Nau'ts'ity'i and I'tcts'ity'i,
> and together they created the Universe
> this world
> and the four worlds below.
> . . . .
> She is sitting in her room
> thinking of a story now
>
> I'm telling you the story
> she is thinking. (1)

The temporal paradox enclosed in the opening of the poetic text — Thought-Woman, who thought about her sisters and together they created the world, just by naming it, and at the same time Thought-Woman, who now finds herself in her room and thinks about a story — cancels the distance between past and present and signals that the story which is being narrated is enclosed in the ample breath of mythology:

> I will tell you something about stories,
> [he said]
> They aren't just entertainment.
> Don't be fooled.
> They are all we have, you see,
> all we have to fight off
> illness and death. (2)

"Evil" therefore is not unknown to the Indian world, nor was it recognized only after the arrival of the invader; it existed from the beginning of time as a negative and destructive force that entangles the intricate and delicate theme woven by Thought-Woman:

> The only cure
> I know
> is a good ceremony,
> that's what she said. (3)

The object of ceremonialism is to give life to the conditions that existed at the moment of creation, at the very beginning. The ceremony evokes a spiritual universe and holds an active role in which its force moves toward a healing integration, bringing about balance and harmony in the world.

Within this mythic framework, Tayo's personal story unfolds. A veteran of World War II, he returns to Pueblo Laguna from a Philippine island after a period of time spent in a Los Angeles hospital, where his "illness" was diagnosed as postwar traumatic stress: "The others saw his outline but they did not realize it was hollow inside" (14).

Tayo perceives himself as an empty space, simply an outline; he answers the doctor's questions by referring to himself in the third person.

A psychophysical disassociation overtakes Tayo, and the memories of the past create an entanglement of images that stubbornly and painfully insert themselves in front of the present, forbidding him to organize his own existence. Around him the land is arid, sterile: men and animals appear destined to languish and die. Tayo feels responsible for the drought because while on the Philippine island he had often cursed the rain: "He damned the rain until the words were a chant.... So he had prayed the rain away, and for the sixth year it was dry" (12–13).

Tayo's sense of guilt spreads to include Rocky, his cousin who died under the thick and incessant rain of that Pacific island, and even his uncle Josiah, to whom he had been unable to keep his promise to take care of the Mexican cows, which had vanished from the valley when Josiah died.

Alienation and frustration characterize also other young Indian veterans, who get drunk in the bars on the edges of the reservation to pass the time, waiting for this to end. The stories they tell, at times presented typographically in the same style as the stories from oral tradition, echo a ritual of self-destruction and death: "stories … they repeated them like long medicine chants, the beer bottles pounding on the counter tops like drums" (44).

They damn the land of the reservation; they damn themselves and their Indianness because it excludes them from the illusion of belonging to the American dream. Their exasperation, anger, and bitterness worry the elders of the community, for they see their sons move away, and the mother, the earth, suffers and dries up because such a vital part is uprooted from her womb.

Neither the elder Ku'oosh nor the traditional ceremonies will bring order back to a world overcome by violence and disharmony. The medicine man who guides Tayo on the way to a difficult healing is Betonie, a Navajo mixed-blood from Gallup, a city where Tayo had spent several years of his childhood with his mother, in the riverbank slum inhabited mostly by prostitutes and alcoholic Indians.

Betonie lives at the point where the two cultures meet and clash: in his ravaged hogan there are not only roots, herbs, and typical objects of the traditional medicine man but also old telephone directories, newspapers, calendars, bottles of Coca-Cola, emblems of an America that has penetrated the Indian world. From the heights of the hilltop on which he lives, his view embraces the "ceremonial spaces" and the slum; the sacred and the profane cohabitate and are perceived simultaneously.

Betonie appears to be a positive example of the implicit possibilities of the mixed-blood. This belonging to different worlds and cultures associates him with the protagonist: Tayo, in fact, has an uncertain paternity, and his mother's abandonment of the Native pueblo has provided a significant distance from traditional ways. As an agent of transformation and change within continuity, Betonie is conscious of the need to bring modifications, to adapt the ceremonies to changing circumstances: "things which don't shift and grow are dead things" (133).

In an attempt to mediate tradition and modernity, the writer returns to the myth of the pueblo emergence according to which a migration, from a spot known as "Casa Blanca," in search of the center of the earth began. The destination was forgotten, and disease and death then appeared. Medicine men confronted the situation by creating the "ceremony of oblivion," which "closes" the space of disease and brings the people elsewhere.

The ceremony uses sand paintings which are destroyed at the end of the ritual. Betonie does something similar for Tayo, at the foot of the Chuska mountain, in a place where he "could see no signs of what had been set loose upon the earth: the highways, the towns, even the fences were gone" (146). Betonie draws a chain of white mountains, while his assistant draws a chain of dark mountains, bear tracks, and a large rainbow arched over the mountains. Singing with prayer sticks pressed tightly against his heart, Betonie is determined to provide contrast to the forces that had caused Tayo's sense of detachment and loss.

Betonie is fully aware of the constant metamorphosis of evil and the impossibility of destroying it completely: "But don't be so quick to call something good or bad. There are balances and harmonies always shifting, always necessary to maintain" (137).

In the powerful final image of the book, evil is a vortex of darkness that, after an appropriate ceremonialism, is only momentarily placated: "It is dead for now. / It is dead for now" (274). There is a clear and significant divergence from the victorious mythology of the American continent, according to which "evil" can and must be radically exterminated, through violence. In Vine Deloria's words, violence, "the true lover of America," thus is changed with social utility and an affirmative and regenerative power.

Removing himself from the call of this vision, which at one time is naive and self-justifying, Tayo doesn't kill Emo even though the aberrant and cruel behavior of his comrade-in-arms makes him the symbol of evil. Tayo places himself decisively on the way of healing, and Betonie shows him the stages of this path: "Remember these stars.... I've seen them and I've seen the spotted cattle; I've seen a mountain and I've seen a woman" (160).

Tayo's return home, which is articulated in finding himself, his community, and his space, is even connected with the discovery of love and hope. Through Ts'eh, the woman he meets at the foot of Tse-pi'-na (Mount Taylor), the sacred mountain, Tayo is reintegrated in a vital cycle that is not exhausted but requires care, nourishment, and responsibility in order to return. Ts'eh is the one who brings life back; she is the promise of this return.

Introduced by Night Swan, Josiah's lover, whose eyes are extraordinarily similar to those of Tayo and Betonie, Ts'eh is a feminine figure that contains within herself magical and mythological elements: she is the spirit of Tse-pi'-na, the "Woman Veiled by Clouds," the manifestation of the creative principle, she is the one who looks after the plants and the animals, which are essential to the continuation of Indian life. With Ts'eh's help and the help of the puma, protector of the hunter, Tayo is able to recover the Mexican cows that Josiah had purchased and in which he had placed his hopes. Just like the protagonist they are hybrids and thus resistant, determined to live, blessed with a developed sense of direction and origin which they transmit to their calves.

On the sacred mountain, which the conquerors delusionally believe they have imprisoned and taken possession of with their barbed wire fences, Tayo senses the magnetism that attracts his body and his spirit toward the womb, the center of the earth. Now death and silence no longer arouse terror in him; Ts'eh confirms that death is an integral part of the sacred circle of life and as such must not be feared: "a returning rather than a separation" (210). The deaths of Josiah and Rocky, beloved by Tayo, will not erase their memory.

In the same way that Tayo understands that the notes of a song still flutter around the empty room occupied at one time by Night Swan, so has Ts'eh's love never been lost in time: "He thought of her then; she had always loved him, she had never left him; she had always been there" (267). Tayo's certainty assumes cosmic dimensions since "she" is simultaneously Laura, his mother, victim of an impossible promise of assimilation, the two loved women, the earth, mother of us all.

The traditional role of the "storyteller" who transmits Ts'eh's teachings, assumed by Tayo at the end, highlights the intentions underlying Silko's writings: in the spiritual center of the community of Laguna the telling of his personal story is transformed into a collective experience, an indispensable act for the completion of the ceremony. The words of a song confirm that now Tayo's return home is possible: the mixed-blood who had always lived on the margins of tribal life is now called "a'moo'ooh," an expression filled with profound sentiment and love.

If the emphasis appears to be on the return to the oral tradition and to its rituals as the basis for cultural identity in order to heal painful breaks and overcome the feeling of abandonment and isolation, in effect *Ceremony* portends more of a recovery of the essence of Indian ceremonialism than the reiteration of fixed and immutable forms. The survival of a world vision, entrusted to the memory and creativity of the Indian people, can be guaranteed only by a flexibility and capacity for adaptation to the challenges imposed by constantly changing circumstances.

With three volumes of poetry, a collection of stories (*The Lone Ranger and Tonto Fistfight in Heaven*), and a novel (*Reservation Blues*), Sherman Alexie has become the most original voice of the latest generation of Indian writers.[11]

The ghost of the great bluesman Robert Johnson, who died in 1938, and who, according to legend, had made a pact with the devil in order to gain his exceptional musical gifts, materializes on the Spokane reservation in the company of his magical guitar. He is searching for a woman who lives on a hill, the only one able to dissolve his deal with the "Gentleman" or Papa Leg (an ancient voodoo divinity) and regain his freedom and health.

Thomas Builds-the-Fire, the central character of *Reservation Blues*, is traditionally hospitable and well disposed toward anyone, and therefore accompanies the singer to the foot of the mountain where lives Big Mom, the spiritual leader who chooses her pupils carefully:

> She lived in a blue house on the top of Wellpinit Mountain. She was a Spokane Indian with a little bit of Flathead blood thrown in for good measure. But she was more than that. She was a part of every tribe. . . . "She's powerful medicine," Thomas said. "The most powerful medicine." (199)

Johnson hurries to reach her, leaving the guitar in Thomas's pickup. The instrument, blessed with a life of its own — in fact, it sings and knows how to speak like a human being — becomes the nucleus of the fellowship among Thomas, Victor, and Junior, the characters and narrators also found in *The Lone Ranger and Tonto Fistfight in Heaven*, who reappear in *Reservation Blues* with their backbreaking strength of desperation, humor, and profound humanity.

The Indian universe of the reservation which emerges in all the drama and bitter humor pervasive in the novel is the result, above all, of an imagination which never erases the suffering but helps to bear it. The young Indians, who often search in alcohol for the visions denied by the uncertainty of their identity, confront the absence of opportunity with "welfare checks and commodity food in exchange for [their] continued dependency" (154), with the corruption of the members of the tribal council, and with images of arrogant economic and cultural domination constantly suggested by the mass media.

---

11. Sherman Alexie, *Reservation Blues* (London: Minerva, 1995). Page numbers in text refer to this edition.

To quote Gerald Vizenor, all this produces a type of "tragic wisdom" expressed by Alexie in a basic and colloquial language that, articulated orally in the past and today in written form, constitutes a single and continuous "tale" that struggles against a dark fate of physical and cultural extinction.

In the attempt to preserve fragments of an identity that is strongly weakened but which continues to live in the form of memory and vision, the characters in *Reservation Blues* adapt strategies borrowed mainly from the divine trickster: Coyote, one of his many masks, unifies that which appears to be irreconcilable. "Bricoleur" above all participates in the cosmic circle of metamorphosis and in so doing always manages to survive, overcoming any obstacle.

The trickster acts fundamentally in a reality loaded with comic situations and thanks to his wit and good humor he can, laughingly, reveal "truths" that cannot be stated seriously. Alexie's tricksters are manipulators and creators of language who elaborate and adapt the elements of tradition to the sociocultural conditions of the moment. The result is a picture of a state of siege, both on the reservation and in the urban setting, and this provokes a constant shift between the two cultures.

Alexie depicts a condition in transition in which nothing is definitive: everything appears subject to a process of transformation of events and memories in a single uninterrupted story. Both the structure of the book and the narrative techniques used reflect fractures and imbalances. Even the names of the characters appear abnormal in their tragic comedy, and their reference to the two worlds reveals a precarious identity, the difficulty of being in both realities: Thomas Builds-the-Fire, Lester Falls-to-Pieces, David Walks-by-the-Road, The-Man-Who-Probably-Was-Lakota, Aristotle Heavy-Bundle, and the two sisters Chess and Checkers Warm Water.

The mythologic figure of the trickster, the one who always survives, imposes his own name, reaffirming his creative power to an Indian rock and blues band: Coyote Springs. The band uses the vocal support of Chess and Checkers and begins to play, first, on the reservation and then gets important auditions first in Seattle and then in New York.

If the music appears to be "good medicine" that can redeem the human condition (Indian and non-Indian) — the use of the blues testifies to the flexibility and adaptability of Indian tradition in accepting and translating into its own terms other cultural expressions — Cavalry Records, obviously from New York, represents another attack by a soulless America (show business) launched against the Indian world in order to gain immediate profits.

The American Dream, in terms of success and money, requires too high a price even for the gentleman's guitar ("They don't need to be good. They just need to make money"). The failure of Coyote Springs leads to the band's return to the reservation, which on the other hand had never ceased to wait for them:

> Meanwhile, the reservation remained behind. It never exactly longed for any Indian who left, for all those whose bodies were dragged quickly and quietly into the twentieth century while their souls were left behind somewhere in the nineteenth. But the reservation was there, had always been there, and would still be there, waiting for Coyote Springs's return from New York City. Every Indian, every leaf of grass, and every animal and insect waited collectively. (219–20)

The protagonists of *Reservation Blues* are removed from any kind of stereotyping, they don't bend to the cliché of sacrificial victims, and they vindicate the right, historically denied them, to be active protagonists able to judge and criticize with irony, bitterness, and even comprehension, the dominant way of life. Father Arnold, for example, whose job is to get the Indians on the path of redemption, is presented in all his human weakness and in his basic uselessness. He is strongly attracted to Checkers, and he feels lost: all of his knowledge is useless and his world falls apart.

The most stinging irony is directed at the New Age movement and particularly to Betty and Veronica, the two white girls who join Coyote Springs and whom Victor and Junior use as trophies in a type of revenge against a world which victimizes them. Betty and Veronica comply with the request for Indian music on behalf of the American market and take the place of Coyote Springs at the top of the hits. Inspired by the New Age movement, within the Indian world they search for something they cannot find elsewhere, in other words, something America doesn't have: a vision of harmony, spirituality, and magic. But the harsh reality of the reservation — alcoholism, alienation, and suicides — horrifies them and they leave just taking — according the rapacious eyes of the Cavalry Records people — enough varnish to make them "a more reliable kind of Indian."

Sherman Alexie then speaks of the attempted appropriation of the Indian soul, of its relationship with sacred and occult dimensions that are a priority in the Native universe. Often the characters in Indian literature are bothered by visions, nightmares, recurring sensations of mystery. P. G. Allen, a well-known writer, defines them as the "shadows of the past": the Indian world, destroyed or altered by the invader, can manifest itself in different forms, that is, in oneiric images, visions, magical happenings. The "shadows" can be friendly presences that bring close the Indian world and make it present, transmitting messages, indicating ways to follow.

Alexie narrates the desolation and marginalization of Indian life with no self-pity. His visionary style, at times lyrical, at times brutally realistic, is perfectly adapted to representing pictures of reservation life that desperately attempt to recover a few ancestral patterns which had been deformed and obscured by the imposition of a foreign culture. Through the words of Thomas Builds-the-Fire, one sees that it is necessary to look below the surface because what one sees isn't everything:

Thomas thought about all the dreams that were murdered here, and the bones buried quickly just inches below the surface, all waiting to break through the foundations of those government houses built by the Department of Housing and Urban Development. (7)

The dreams and visions of Father Arnold and Thomas, in their complementarity, reveal on the one hand contradictions and paradoxes and on the other the persistence of a relationship with one's own deep soul. The failure appears to Father Arnold in a dream, almost a confirmation of what the Indians have always known, that the missionaries sent to their lands "were supposed to save souls, not possess them":

In his dream, he stood in front of a huge congregation of Indians. He had come to save them all, his collar starched and bleached so white that it blinded, and was so powerful that he had a red phone at the altar that was a direct line to God. *Listen to me,* Father Arnold said, but the Indians ignored him. They talked among themselves, laughed at secret jokes. Some even prayed in their own languages, in their own ways. Eagle feathers raised to the ceiling, pipes smoked, sweetgrass and sage burned. (163–64)

During one of Father Arnold's sermons, which are always on the theme of redemption, Thomas's eyes cloud over, and he soon finds himself in a different place, dark, dominated by a strong heat. In fact, he is inside the traditional sweatlodge, and he has the pleasing certainty that now, finally, "he could pray aloud, scream and cry, and that would be understood. If he sang, his brothers in the sweatlodge would sing with him" (178).

Alexie vividly demonstrates the attack on Indian spirituality through a sensation Thomas has: "We have to keep our songs private and hidden. There is someone in here now who would steal from us. I can smell him" (178). Even the communion Father Arnold tries to give the Indians can do nothing in the face of the force, the resistance provided by the Native land:

Thomas offered his cupped hands. Father Arnold placed the wafer gently in Thomas's hands. "Amen," Thomas whispered, palmed the wafer, and pretended to eat it. . . . He knelt in the pew again, made a quick sign of the cross. Then he ran outside, crumbled the wafer into pieces and let it fall to the earth. The reservation swallowed those pieces hungrily. Not sure why he even took the Communion wafer in the first place, Thomas felt the weight of God, the reservation, and all the stories between. (180)

The departure from the reservation for Spokane by several members of the musical group is accompanied by the ineradicable force of songs and visions and does not at all preclude their return. The reservation still possesses strength and anger, magic and desperation, joy and pain. All this and the cries of the Indian horses massacred during the previous centuries — "this shadow" flutters above the entire novel — transform themselves, in the closing sentences into a song of celebration and continuance articulated by a rhythmic movement of Big Mom's rocking chair, "back and forth," symbol of the destiny of her children.

Contributors

THOMAS BUCKLEY is Associate Professor of Anthropology and American Studies at the University of Massachusetts, Boston. He has done ethnographic and ethnohistorical research in Native northwestern California since the 1970s as well as applied and advocacy anthropology in this region and elsewhere. Together with Alma Gottlieb, he co-edited *Blood Magic: The Anthropology of Menstruation* (1988). His recent work has focused on the history of anthropology, and he has published a variety of essays on A. L. Kroeber. His summary volume, *Standing Ground: Yurok Indian Spirituality in Time and Ethnology*, is forthcoming.

RICHARD DAUENHAUER is a former poet laureate of Alaska. His publications include three volumes of poetry, many poems and translations in various journals, and many scholarly articles. With his wife, Nora, whose first language is Tlingit and who is a widely recognized Native American writer, he has translated and co-edited three volumes of Tlingit oral texts with facing English translation, including myths, legends, and ceremonial oratory.

ANN FIENUP-RIORDAN is an independent scholar, with a Ph.D. in Cultural Anthropology from the University of Chicago, who has lived, worked, and taught in Alaska since 1973. Her books include *The Nelson Island Eskimo; Eskimo Essays; Boundaries and Passages: Rule and Ritual in Yup'ik Eskimo Oral Tradition; The Living Tradition of Yup'ik Masks,* and, most recently, *Hunting Tradition in a Changing World.* In 1983 she was named Humanist of the Year by the Alaska Humanities Forum, and in 1991 she was named Historian of the Year by the Alaska Historical Society.

TRUDY GRIFFIN-PIERCE is an adjunct professor of anthropology at the University of Arizona as well as an artist. Her *Native Peoples of the Southwest* will appear in the fall of 2000.

JOHN GRIM is a professor and chair in the Department of Religion at Bucknell University, Lewisburg, Pennsylvania. He is the author of *The Shaman: Patterns of Religious Healing among the Ojibway Indians* (2nd edition, 1987). As a historian of religions, Grim undertakes annual field studies among the

Apsaalooke / Crow peoples of Montana and the Swy-ahl-puh / Salish peoples of the Columbia River Plateau in eastern Washington. With his wife, Mary Evelyn Tucker, he co-edited *Worldviews and Ecology*.

JOEL MARTIN teaches in the Department of Religious Studies and the Program in American Studies at Franklin and Marshall College in Lancaster, Pennsylvania. He is the author of *Sacred Revolt: The Muskogees' Struggle for a New World* (1991) and *Native American Religion* (1999), and co-editor of *Screening the Sacred: Religion, Myth and Ideology in Popular American Film* (1995).

FRANCO MELI teaches American literature at the Free University of Languages and Communication (IULM) in Milan. He has been a visiting scholar and Fulbright Scholar at Columbia University in New York and has written on Melville, Thoreau, Steinbeck, and D. H. Lawrence. Toward the end of the 1970s he began introducing into Italy the work of the most prominent writers of the so-called Native American Renaissance and edited the Italian translation of N. Scott Momaday's *House Made of Dawn* and anthologies of contemporary Native American poetry and stories.

WILLIAM K. POWERS has spent over fifty years of research on Lakota culture and language. He resigned as Distinguished Professor of Anthropology at Rutgers University, where he had taught for twenty-four years, to devote his full energies to the editorship of Lakota books. He is the author of twenty-three books, including *Oglala Religion* (1977), *Yuwipi: Vision and Experience in Oglala Ritual* (1982), *Sacred Language* (1986), and *Beyond the Vision* 1987), and several hundred articles.

LAWRENCE E. SULLIVAN is director of the Center for the Study of World Religions at Harvard University and a past president of the American Academy of Religion (1996). Among his publications are *Icanchu's Drum: An Orientation to the Meaning in South American Religions* (1990) and *Native American Religions: North America*.

INES TALAMANTEZ is Associate Professor of Native American Religious Studies at the University of California, Santa Barbara, and managing editor of *New Scholar: An Americanist Review*. She has done extensive fieldwork in the Southwest and has directed the Society for the Study of Native American Religious Traditions. Her book *Isnaklesh Goral: Introducing Apache Girls to the World of Spiritual and Cultural Values* is in press.

Index

Aaniq (pre-Bladder Festival) ritual, 202
Aberle, David F., 128, 137, 139
Absaroke/Crow people
  ceremonies, 60, 68, 73, 76–82
  Christianity and, 82–84
  clan system, 56–60, 66–67
  history, 61–65, 69, 78
  language, 13, 53, 64, 84
  migration story, 12–14, 55, 62, 66–67,
    76–77
  myths, 59–62, 65
  oral tradition, 12–13, 53, 57, 73, 84
  prayer, 55–56, 59, 62–63, 76–78, 81–83
  ritual dance, 60, 68, 78–82
  sacred pipe and tobacco, 55–56, 61, 66–68
  shamanism, 69–70, 73–74
  thought, power of, 11, 70, 75, 79, 82
  Tuckabatchees, 17, 100–101
Absaroke Pentecostal Christianity, 76
adoption, ritual, 14–15, 60, 68, 71, 114–15
Alaska Native Brotherhood (ANB), 173–74
Alaska Native Sisterhood (ANS), 173–74
alcohol, 25, 173, 176, 214, 233, 235
Alexie, Sherman, 30, 213, 233–37
Allen, P. G., 236
Amiotte, Arthur, 7
Antonio, Willetto, 22–23, 145–54
Apache. *See* Mescalero Apache people
Arapooish (Crow Chief), 14, 76–77
Arndt, Katherine L., 172
Ashkisshe. See Sun Dance
asi: celebration, 95–96
assimilation
  Absaroke/Crow resistance to, 62–65, 69, 78
  Creek/Muskogee resistance to, 99–100, 103
  in fiction, 220, 222, 232
  government policies of, 18, 209
  Lakota resistance to, 18, 104–5
  into Native American cultures, 8–10, 93
  peyote use and, 215–16
  resistance to, in fiction, 215–16
  Tlingit resistance to, 25, 168–70, 175–78
Athabascan/Navajo. *See* Navajo people
Axtell, James, 9–10
Ayugutaar, myth of, 185–86

Bakhtin, Mikhail M., 40
Balzer, Marjorie Mandelstam, 177
Baptist Church, 15, 17, 64, 101, 103, 170. *See
  also* Christianity
Barnyards, Timothy, 59
Barreiro, José, 5
Bartram, William, 92, 94–95, 97
Bataille, Georges, 86
Bataille, Gretchen M., 8
Beaver Dance, *Baasshussuua*, 68. *See also* ritual
  dance
Beckwith, Martha W., 108
Begishe, Kenneth Yazzie, 132
Bell, Amelia R., 86, 98, 101–2
Bering Sea Eskimos, 200
Berkhofer, Robert F., 69
Big Day, Heywood, 80
Big Day, William, 80
Bitar, Joseph N., 185
Black, Lydia T., 171–72
Black Codes, 93
black-drink, 95–96
Blackgoat, Roberta, 5
Bladder Festival, 28, 188, 194–96, 201–3, 205
Blitz, John H., 89–90
Blue-eyes, George, 137
Bogoras, Waldemar, 189, 196
Bolt, Christine, 8, 10
Bowden, Henry Warner, 69
Bowers, Alfred, 67
Boyd, C. Clifford, Jr., 88
breath, 26–27, 92, 118, 125–26, 188. *See also*
  soul
Briggs, Jean L., 181
Brightman, Robert, 184
Brown, James A., 89–91, 111
Bruchac, Joseph, 212
Buckley, Thomas, 10–12, 38–39, 47
Burgess, Stanley M., 172
Busk (green corn, *póskita*) ceremony, 85–86,
  96–97, 101, 103

Campbell, Robert, 77
Catholic Church, 15, 64, 84, 117, 167. *See
  also* Christianity
Catholic Kateri Tekakwitha Societies, 84

ceremonialism
  in *Ceremony* (Silko), 231–32
  as creative critical reflection, 14–16, 19–21,
    60
  language and, 11–12, 22, 28–31, 47–48
  Navajo chantways and, 123, 131–32
  peyote use and, 78–79, 215–16, 221–23
  as restoring balance, 3–4, 28–31, 124–25,
    145, 162, 211, 230–31
  ritual specialists, 74, 105, 109–13. *See also*
    medicine men/women; shamanism
  self-torture, 80, 115–16, 189
  tobacco use and, 55–56, 61–62, 66–68, 74.
    See also sacred pipe
ceremonies
  asi: celebration, 95–96
  Bladder Festival, 28, 188, 194–96, 201–3,
    205
  Busk, 85–86, 96–97, 101, 103
  Doll Festival, 200
  Feast for the Dead, *Merr'aq,* 28, 203–5
  Gift Festival, 28, 204
  Great Feast for the Dead, *Elriq,* 28, 203,
    205
  green corn. *See* Busk
  'Isánáklésh Gotal, 21–22, 145–46
  Making of Relatives, *Hunka,* 114–15
  Memorial Feast, *Wokiksuye Wohanpi,* 113–14
  Messenger Feast, *Kevgiq,* 28, 204–5
  Night Song, 224
  peyote use in, 78–79, 103, 215–16, 221–23
  póskita. See Busk
  rites of passage, 21–22, 142–45, 156–59,
    189–90, 194–96
  Sun Dance. *See* Sun Dance
  sweat lodge. *See* sweat lodges
  way of requesting, *Agayuyaraq,* 28, 205
  Wiping the Tears, 18, 106
  Yuwipi Sing, 116
  See also rituals
Ceremony (Silko), 29–31, 211, 227–33
Chanar, David, 181
Changing Woman, 20, 126, 144
chanting, 20–24, 73, 125–26, 129–33, 143,
  156. *See also* oral tradition
Child of Water, 22, 143
Christianity
  Absaroke/Crow people and, 76, 82–84
  Absaroke Pentecostal, 76
  Creek/Muskogee people and, 16–17, 91, 99,
    101, 103
  Lakota and, 117
  syncretism and, 15, 173–75, 218

Tlingit people and, 24–25, 160–61, 163,
  167–73
Yup'ik Eskimo and, 209
  See also specific denominations, e.g.
    Presbyterian Church
Churchill, Ward, 7
circle-dot motif, 27–28, 185–86, 189–90,
  194–96, 200
clan systems
  Absaroke/Crow, 56–60, 66–67
  Creek Muskogee, 90–91, 94, 98, 101–3
  Tlingit, 164–67, 172, 174–77
Clarke, Katherine, 35
Collier, John, 69
Constitution, U.S., 8
conversion experiences, 8–10, 93
corn, 85–86, 89, 96–97, 102–3, 226–27. *See
  also* Busk (green corn, *póskita*) ceremony
Corn Mother, 89
Coyote Old Man (trickster), 60, 70
creation myths, 21–23, 106–8, 123–25,
  129–30, 135–37, 142–46
Creator, *Acbadadea,* 54–56
Creek/Muskogee people
  assimilation, 99–100, 103
  ceremonies, 85–86, 95–97, 100–101, 103
  Christianity and, 16–17, 91, 99, 101, 103
  clan system, 90–91, 94, 98, 101–3
  divinities, 89, 92
  hunting, 88, 98–99
  maxpe, the sacred, 12–15, 54, 69–71, 84
  mounds, 88–91, 94
  religious transformations, 87–96
  stomp grounds, 17, 85, 94–95, 101–3
  women, 94, 97–98, 101–2
Crow Allotment Act of 1920, 83
Crow people. *See* Absaroke/Crow people
Crummett, Michael, 80–81
Curley, Slim, 129
Curtis, Edward S., 70
Curtis Act of 1898, 86
Custer, George Armstrong, 104–5
Cygnaeus, Uno, 168

dance. *See* ritual dance
dance fans, 195
d'Ans, André-Marcel, 5
Dauenhauer, Nora Marks, 162–63, 167, 172
Dauenhauer, Richard, 23–26, 162–63, 167,
  172
Davis, R. P. Stephen, Jr., 88
Dawes Allotment Act of 1887, 65, 86
de Laguna, Frederica, 164, 167
De Smet, Father Pierre-Jean, 62–63

de Soto, Hernando, 86, 91
death
  end-of-the-world myths, 119
  funeral customs, 25, 88–91, 94, 165–66,
    173–75
  and mourning, 59, 72, 82, 95, 113–16
  potlatch, 25, 165–66, 173–75
  rebirth cycling, 26–28, 182–87, 195–96,
    203–6
  as reincorporation of life force, 131
  soul, four aspects of, 117–18
debate. *See* world renewal discourse
Deerskin Dance, 37, 41, 44–45. *See also* Jump
  Dance; ritual dance
Deloria, Vine, Jr., 3, 9, 213, 231
Deloria, Vine, Sr., 7
DeMaillie, Raymond J., 7, 107, 111
Denig, Edwin Thompson, 82
Densmore, Frances, 111
dialogue. *See* world renewal discourse
Diné, The. *See* Navajo people
divinities
  Be'gochidi, One Who Created People, 5
  Child of Water, 22, 143
  Corn Mother, 89
  Coyote Old Man (trickster), 60, 70
  Creator, *Acbadadea*, 54–56
  diyin dine'é, The Holy People, 20, 126, 128
  Double Woman, 107, 110
  Failed-to-Speak Ones, 126, 128–30, 133
  Holy Wind, 19–21, 123, 126
  'Isánáklésh, Our Mother, 21–23, 142–46
  Maker of Breath, 92
  Papa Leg (The Gentleman), 233
  Something That Moves, *Takuskanskan*, 105
  Talking God, 125, 134
  trickster, 60, 70, 106, 220–21, 234
  Tségihi, 224–25
  White Buffalo Calf Woman, 18, 108–9, 111
  Woman Veiled by Clouds, *Tse-pi'-na*, 231
  See also myths
diyin dine'é, The Holy People, 20, 126, 128
Doll Festival, 200
dolls, 192, 200, 203
Dorris, Michael, 5
doubling, 70, 107, 110
Duncan, Father William, 171
Durkheim, Émile, 38
dwellings, gender segregation in, 26–28,
  187–88, 194

Eastman, Charles A., 29, 208–10
Emerging from the Chrysalis (Lincoln), 143
Emmons, George T., 164, 167, 172

environmentalism, 145, 213
Episcopal Church, 103, 117, 171. *See also*
  Christianity
Erdrich, Louise, 30, 212
Eskimo people, 27–28, 166, 189, 200. *See also*
  Yup'ik Eskimo people
evil, nature of
  Lakota view, 107, 110, 131–32
  Navajo view, 110, 131–32, 220, 229, 231
  Yurok view, 10, 34
eye contact, 27–28, 186, 188–89, 196
eyesight, 186, 189–91, 195–96. *See also*
  circle-dot motif

Farella, John, 129
Farrer, Claire R., 8
fasting, 34, 54, 69–72, 80–83, 113
Feast for the Dead, *Merr'aq*, 28, 203–5
Feather Dance, 41. *See also* ritual dance
fertility rituals, 27, 97, 142–44, 182, 187, 196
Fienup-Riordan, Ann, 26–28, 181–84,
  186–87, 189–90, 192, 194, 200
fire, holy, 85, 96–97, 103
firemen, 112. *See also* medicine men/women
Fitzhugh, William, 185
fixing the world ritual, 10–12, 33–35, 41–51
forty-day parties, 25, 173, 175
Fourth Russell Tribunal, 6
Frey, Rodney, 58–60, 70–71, 82
Friday, Joe, 182–83, 188
Frisbie, Charlotte J., 129, 138
funeral customs, 25, 88–89, 113–14, 165–66,
  173–75. *See also* death

Galloway, Colin G., 64
Garrett, Paul D., 172
Ghost Dance, 19, 117, 216. *See also* ritual
  dance
Ghost-Keeping, *Wanagi Wicagluhapi*, 113–14
Gifford, Edward W., 36–37, 39, 45–46
Gift Festival, *Petugtaq*, 28, 204
Giono, Jean, 35
Gold, Peter, 130
Goodwin, Grenville, 142
Great Feast for the Dead, *Elriq*, 28, 203, 205
green corn ceremony, 85–86, 96–97, 101,
  103
Griffin-Pierce, Trudy, 19–21, 122, 124, 127,
  130, 134–36, 138–39
Grim, John, 1, 12–16

Haas, Mary R., 85
Hallowell, A. Irving, 182
Hamayon, R., 162, 166

Harjo, Joy, 85–86
Hawking, Stephen, 12
Hawkins, Benjamin, 96
head ornaments. See masks
Healing Blanket ceremony, 25, 176
Heffner-McClellan, Kathy, 35, 40–41, 43, 48
Himmelheber, Hans, 189
Hinckley, Ted C., 172
Hoijer, Harry, 143–44
Holiness Pentecostal Church, 15–16, 83–84.
    See also Christianity
Holy People, diyin dine'é, 20, 126, 128
Holy Wind, Nílchi, 19–21, 123
Holy Wind, 19–21, 123, 126
Horseshoe Bend, Battle of, 16–17, 86, 100
House Made of Dawn (Momaday), 30, 211,
    219–27
Howard, James H., 103
Hoxie, Frederick E., 65, 69
Hudson, Charles, 88, 90–91, 96–97
Hughes, J. Donald, 77
Hunka, Making of Relatives, 114–15
hunting
    Creek/Muskogee, 88, 98–99
    Lakota, 105, 115
    Mescalero Apache, 162
    Navajo, 139
    Yup'ik Eskimo, 182–92, 193–97, 206
Hupa people, 36–37, 41, 44–45, 48
Hurley, Robert, 86

ice holes, 190, 194–95
illness, 86, 110, 131–32, 212. See also medicine
    men/women
impersonators, sacred, 18
"Indian Boarding School: The Runaways"
    (Erdrich), 212
Indian Reorganization Act of 1934, 83
individualism, 37–38, 54, 69–70, 81, 146,
    162–64
Invasion Within: The Contest of Cultures in
    Colonial North America, The (Axtell),
    9–10
'Isánáklésh, Our Mother, 21–23, 142–46
'Isánáklésh Gotal, 21–22, 145–46

Jackson, Andrew, 16–17, 86, 100
Jackson, Sheldon, 24–25, 169, 197
Jaimes, Annette, 7
jish. See medicine bundles
Joe, Jennie, 131
John, Paul, 188

Johnson, Robert, 233
journeying, 32, 123, 130, 188, 210–11, 225.
    See also migration stories
Jump Dance, 11, 33–36, 40–51
Kan, Sergei, 164, 167, 171–72, 175

Kaplan, Susan A., 185
Kelly, John E., 89, 91
Kerber, Richard A., 89–91
Kiowa, 221
Kista, R. C., 78
Knight, Vernon James, Jr., 90, 94
Krause, Richard A., 90
Kroeber, A. L., 36–42, 44–47

Lakota people
    adoption, ritual, 114–15
    assimilation, 18, 104–5
    Christianity, 117
    death, 117–19
    divinities, 18, 105, 107–11
    on evil, 107, 110, 131–32
    hunting, 105, 115
    marriage, 107
    prayer, 106, 111, 115–18
    religious life, 17–19, 104–5, 111–19, 146
    ritual dance, 105, 115–16, 118
    sacred pipe, 18, 108–9, 116–18
    Seven Fireplaces, 17–18, 104
    Seven Sacred Ceremonies, 111–16
land
    ancestral, 210, 212–13
    history and the, 63–65, 77, 86–87
    as identity, 213, 217–18
    as metaphor, 12–14, 29–32, 65–66, 226
    as sacred, 76–77, 121, 145, 213
    sound and, 12–13
    See also reservations
Lang, Julian, 34
language
    Absaroke/Crow, 13, 53, 64, 84
    Athabascan/Navajo, 123
    ritual, 11–12, 22, 28–31, 47–48
    Russian Orthodox use of Tlingit, 24
    sacred words, 29–32, 210–11, 220–21
    See also oral tradition; world renewal
        discourse
Lankford, George E., 97
Lansing, J. Stephen, 145
Lantis, Margaret, 181
Larocque, François, 53, 61–62
Lena, Willie, 103
Lincoln, Bruce, 143

literature, Native American
Ceremony (Silko), 29–31, 211, 227–33
House Made of Dawn (Momaday), 30, 211, 219–27
"Indian Boarding School: The Runaways" (Erdrich), 212
Lone Ranger and Tonto Fistfight in Heaven, The (Alexie), 213, 233
O-gi-maw-kwe mit-i-gwa-ki, Queen of the Woods (Pokagon), 214
Reservation Blues (Alexie), 233–37
Soul of the Indian, The (Eastman), 29, 208–10
Sundown (Mathews), 214–16
Surrounded, The (McNickle), 216–19
Survival This Way (Bruchac), 212
Writer and the Shaman, The (Zolla), 209
See also storytelling
Little Big Horn (battle), 105
Little Big Horn College, 14, 58, 66
Lone Ranger and Tonto Fistfight in Heaven, The (Alexie), 213, 233
Looking Horse, Arval, 7
Lowie, Robert, 58–59, 64, 67–68, 70, 75
Lutheran Church, 167–68. See also Christianity
Lyons, Chief Oren, 14

Mails, Thomas E., 64
Maker of Breath, 92
Mallery, Garrick, 108
Manning, Allen, 132
marriage, 24, 102, 114, 165, 168, 204
Martin, Joel W., 16, 92
masks, 145, 196–201
Mather, Elsie, 181
Mathews, John Joseph, 30, 214–15
matrilineal societies, 13, 59, 94, 98, 101, 164, 166
Mauss, Marcel, 38
maxpe, the sacred, 12–15, 54, 69–71, 84
McAllester, David P., 138
McCleary, Timothy P., 59, 83
McClellan, Catharine, 167
McGinnis, Anthony, 64
McMaster, Gerald, 213
McNeley, James K., 123
McNickle, D'Arcy, 30, 212, 216–19
McPherson, Aimee Semple, 82–83
medicine
functions of, 16, 99, 167
herbal, 98, 137, 144, 156, 163
objects, 83, 96, 163
vision and, 71–73, 109–12, 201, 222
See also medicine men/women

medicine bundles, 15, 54–55, 62, 70, 73, 129, 131
Medicine Crow, Joseph, 53, 58, 65, 82
Medicine Fathers, Iilapxe, 14–15, 70, 81–82. See also medicine men/women
medicine men/women
Absaroke/Crow, 14–15, 69–70, 73–74, 81–82
in fiction, 230
Lakota, 109–13, 117–19
Yup'ik shamans, 27–28, 188–90, 195, 200, 205
See also shamanism
Medicine, Beatrice, 7–8
Meli, Franco, 29–31
memorial ceremonies, 113–14, 175, 203–5
Memorial Feast, Wokiksuye Wohanpi, 113–14
menarche, 114–15, 142–45, 156–57, 189–90
Mescalero Apache people
divinities, 21–23, 142–46
hunting, 162
oral tradition, 22, 145–46
prayer, 22–23, 34–35, 41
rites of passage, 21–22, 142–45, 156–59
shamanism, 27
women, 22–23, 143–45, 155–59
Messenger Feast, Kevgiq, 28, 204–5
Methodist Church, 17, 101, 170. See also Christianity
migration stories
Absaroke/Crow, 12–14, 55, 62, 66–67, 76–77
Creek/Muskogee, 17, 86–87, 100–102
Navajo, 230
Milanich, Jerald T., 91
Mississippian religious formation, 87, 89–92
Mitchell, Mike, 126, 128
Moccasin, Harry, 13, 65
moieties, 24, 165. See also clan systems
Momaday, N. Scott, 30, 211, 213, 219, 221–24, 227
Mooney, James, 105
Moore, Riley D., 196
Morrison, Kenneth M., 10
Morrow, Phyllis, 181
mounds, 88–91, 94
mourning rituals, 59, 72, 82, 95, 113–16
Mousalimas, S. A., 169, 172
Muir, John, 169
Mullen Sands, Kathleen, 8
Muskogee/Creek people. See Creek/Muskogee people

myths
Ayugutaar, 185–86
boy who went to live with seals, 186, 194
clan system, origin of, 59–60
creation. See creation myths
end-of-the-world, 119
hunting, 162, 185–86, 190, 194
Kiowa, 221
tobacco in, 61–62
See also divinities

Nabokov, Peter, 60, 68, 72
naming conventions, 182
Native American Church, 19, 76–79, 103, 117, 221–23
Native American Graves Protection and Repatriation Act of 1990 (NAGPRA), 25, 175–77
Navajo people
Athabascan language, 123
ceremonies, 123, 131–32, 224, 230–31
chanting, 123, 125–26, 129–33, 138
constellations and, 137–40
divinities, 19–20, 123, 126, 128–30, 133
on evil, 110, 131–32, 220, 229, 231
hunting, 139
migration story, 230
prayer, 124, 125, 129–30, 140, 223–26, 231
religious practice, 19–20, 123–26, 129–40
są'a naagháii bik'e hózhó, 19–20, 123–26, 130–37, 140
sacred pipe, 225
sandpainting, 132, 134, 136, 137
storytelling, 232
thought, power of, 129, 131, 228–29
Neihardt, John G., 111, 113
Nelson, Edward William, 181, 189, 192, 195, 200
Newcomb, Franc Johnson, 139
Neumann, Henry, 197
nucleated circle. See circle-dot motif
numbers, symbolic, 86, 112, 118

O-gi-maw-kwe mit-i-gwa-ki, Queen of the Woods (Pokagon), 214
odyssey motif. See journeying
Oklahoma statehood, 86
Old Coyote, Barney, 82
Old Man Coyote, 60, 70
Oleksa, Michael, 169, 172
oral tradition, 12–15, 29, 145–46, 210, 220–21, 232. See also chanting; language; migration stories; sound, sacred; storytelling; world renewal discourse

Orthodox Church in America (OCA). See Russian Orthodox Church

Page, Suzanne, 126
Papa Leg (The Gentleman), 233
Paredes, J. Anthony, 103
Parks, Douglas R., 7, 17
Pentecostal movement, 25, 76, 83–84, 117, 172. See also Christianity
peyotism, 76, 78–79, 103, 215–16, 221–23
phratries, 59–60, 67. See also clan systems
Pickett, Albert James, 101
Pierce, Richard A., 172
Pilling, Arnold R., 43
pipe. See sacred pipe
Pokagon, Simon, 214
pollen
blessing, 124, 125
cattail, 30, 142, 148, 156–57
corn, 135, 226–27
póskita ceremony, 85–86, 96–97, 101, 103
potlatch, 25, 162, 165–66, 173–75
Powers, Marla N., 8, 106, 108, 111, 114–15, 117
Powers, William K., 17–19, 104–6, 108, 112, 114–15, 117
prayer
Absaroke/Crow, 55–56, 59, 62–63, 76–78, 81–83
dance as, 12, 44–45, 47, 81. See also ritual dance
Lakota, 106, 111, 115–18
Mescalero Apache, 22–23, 34–35, 41
Navajo, 124, 125, 129–30, 140, 223–26, 231
peyote use as, 78–79, 223
Pueblo, 226
Tlingit, 164, 169, 172–74
Yurok, 34–35
Presbyterian Church, 24–25, 169–71. See also Christianity
Prewash, Francis Paul, 69
property ownership, 165
prophecy, 19, 83, 119
puberty, 190. See also menarche

Qaariitaaq (pre-Bladder Festival) ritual, 202

Rasmussen, Knud, 196
Ray, Dorothy Jean, 189, 200
Red Cloud, 19, 104, 119
Reichard, Gladys A., 128
Removal. See migration stories
Reservation Blues (Alexie), 233–37

reservations, 15, 65, 213, 219, 234. *See also* land
Ries, Julien, 2
rites of passage
  Mescalero Apache, 21–22, 142–45, 156–59
  Yup'ik, 189–90, 194–96
ritual dance
  Beaver, 68
  Deerskin, 37, 41, 44–45
  Feather, 41
  Ghost Dance, 19, 216
  Hupa, 37, 41, 44–45
  ideal forms, 40, 44–51
  Jump Dance, 11, 33–36, 41–51
  Sun Dance. *See* Sun Dance
  Yup'ik Eskimo, 195–96, 200–201
  Yurok women and, 33–34
ritual specialists. *See* medicine men/women; shamanism
rituals
  Aaniq (pre-Bladder Festival), 202
  adoption, 14–15, 60, 68, 71, 114–15
  circles, 195. *See also* circle-dot motif
  fertility, 27, 97, 142–44, 182, 187, 196
  fixing the world, 10–12, 33–35, 41–51
  Ghost-Keeping, 113–14
  for healing, 25, 83, 116–17, 131–34, 176, 230
  mourning, 59, 72, 82, 95, 113–16
  Qaariitaaq (pre-Bladder Festival), 202
  sacred dance. *See* ritual dance
  Throwing the Ball, *Tapa wankaiyeyapi*, 114
  tobacco use in, 55–56, 61–62, 66–68, 74. *See also* sacred pipe
  vision quest, 105, 110–13, 222
  See also ceremonialism; ceremonies
Robbins, Lester E., 102
Robert's Rules of Order, 25, 173–74
Russian Orthodox Church, 24–25, 163, 168–69, 171. *See also* Christianity

sq'a naagháii bik'e hózhǫ́ (Navajo), 19–20, 130–37, 140
sacred pipe
  Absaroke/Crow, 55–56, 66–68
  Lakota, 7, 18–19, 108–9, 116–18
  Navajo people, 225
  See also tobacco, sacred use of
sacred sound. *See* sound, sacred
Salvation Army, 171–72. *See also* Christianity
sandpainting, 132, 134, 136, 137
Sands, Kathleen Mullen, 8
Sandy Bar Bob, 43, 47
Sawmill Jack, 43

Say, Kee, 5
scarification, 189
Scarry, John F., 90
Schlegel, Alice, 8
Schlesier, Karl, 68, 79
Schnell, Frank T., 90
Schnell, Gail S., 90
Schroedl, Gerald F., 88
Schuster, Carl, 189
Second, Bernard, 1
self-torture, 80, 115–16, 189
Seven Fireplaces, *Oceti Sakowin*, 17–18, 104. *See also* Lakota people
Seventh Generation, doctrine of the, 119
shamanism
  Absaroke/Crow, 69–70, 73–74
  Creek/Muskogee, 88, 96
  Mescalero Apache, 27
  Tlingit, 25–26, 164–67, 169–71, 175, 177–78
  Yup'ik, 27–28, 188–90, 195, 200, 205
  See also medicine men/women
Silko, Leslie Marmon, 29–31, 211, 227–33
Sioux, 3, 104. *See also* Lakota people
Sioux Indian Religion: Tradition and Innovation (DeMaillie and Parks), 7
Sitting Bull, 105
Smirennikov (Aleut elder), 169
Smith, Charlie, 143
Smith, John L., 116
smoke holes, 190, 194, 202
Social Organization of the Western Apache (Goodwin), 142–43
Something That Moves, *Takuskanskan*, 105
Soto, Hernando de, 86, 91
soul, 26–27, 117–18, 182–85, 188–90, 201–3
Soul of the Indian, The (Eastman), 29, 208–9
sound, sacred, 13–15, 23–24, 33–34, 223, 235. *See also* oral tradition
Spencer, Katherine Halpern, 129
Spider, Emerson, 7
Spott, Robert, 46
square grounds. *See* stomp grounds
Stead, Robert, 7
Steinmetz, Paul B., S.J., 117
Steward, Julian, 38–39
Stewart, Nellie, 82–83
Stewart, Omer, 78
stomp grounds, 17, 85, 94–95, 101–3
storytelling, 30, 57, 145–46, 221, 230, 232. *See also* oral tradition
Sturtevant, William C., 85
Sullivan, Lawrence E., 5

Sun Dance
  Ashkisshe (Absaroke/Crow), 60, 73, 76,
    79–82
  Wiwanyang Wacipi (Lakota), 105, 115–16,
    118
  See also ritual dance
Sundown (Mathews), 214–16
Surrounded, The (McNickle), 216–19
Survival This Way: Interviews with American
    Indian Poets (Bruchac), 212
Swan, Caleb, 85, 95
Swanton, John, 162, 164, 167
sweat lodges
  Creek/Muskogee, 103
  Crow, 15–16, 74–76, 84
  in fiction, 237
  Lakota, 105, 111–12, 118
  Navajo, 132
  Yup'ik men, 27, 34, 187, 202
Sword Bearer, 64
syncretism, 15, 83–84, 105, 173–75

Talamantez, Inéz, 8, 21–23, 27, 146
Talking God, Yéii Bicheii, 125, 134
tattoos, 189–90
Taylor, Lyda Averill, 98
Tecumseh, 16, 99
Tennant, Edward A., 185
Theisz, R. D., 107
Thetis, Reuben Gold, 63
Thompson, Lucy, 34, 38–40, 42, 48
thought, power of
  Absaroke/Crow view, 11, 70, 75, 79, 82
  Navajo view, 129, 131, 228–29
  Tlingit view, 23–26, 162–63
  Yup'ik Eskimo view, 183–85, 201, 206
Three-Wolves, 75
Three Worlds of Bali (Lansing), 145
Throwing the Ball, Tapa wankaiyeyapi, 114
time, Creek/Muskogee sense of, 99
Tinker, George E., 63
tiyospaye, 113–14
Tlingit people
  assimilation, 25, 168–70, 175–78
  Christianity and, 24–25, 160–61, 163,
    167–73
  clan system, 164–67, 172, 174–77
  individualism, 162–64
  marriage, 160, 165, 168
  potlatch, 25, 162, 165–66, 173–75
  prayer, 164, 169, 172–74
  Robert's Rules of Order, 25, 173–74
  shamanism, 26, 161–67, 170, 177–78
  thought, power of, 23–26, 162–63

To the American Indian (Thompson), 34, 38
tobacco, sacred use of, 55–56, 61–62, 66–68,
  74. See also sacred pipe
Toelken, Barre, 131, 133
totem poles, 161
trickster beings, 60, 70, 106, 220–21, 234
Trimble, Stephen, 131
Trudeau, Jean Baptiste, 53
Trujillo, John, 80
Tségihi, 225
Tuckabatchees (Crow warriors), 17, 100–101
Two Crows, 39
Two Leggings, 72–73
Two Men, 59

Ubelaker, Douglas H., 92
Udall, Stewart L., 77
Uncheedah (Eastman's grandmother), 210
Usugan, Frances, 196

Van Gennep, Arnold, 143–44, 158
Veniaminov, Ioann (John), 24, 164, 168–70
Verano, John W., 92
vision quest, 105, 110–13, 222
vision (spiritual), 71–73, 109–12, 201, 222
Vizenor, Gerald, 234
Voget, Fred W., 59, 70, 80

Walker, J. R., 106, 111, 113
Walters, Harry, 134
water, 190, 194–95
Water, Bitter, 135–36
way of requesting ceremony, Agayuyaraq, 28,
  205
Welch, Paul D., 91
Werner, Oswald, 132
Wheelwright, Mary Cabot, 129
White, Richard, 93
White Buffalo Calf Woman, Ptehincalasanwin,
  18, 108–9, 111
white-drink, 95
Wilbert, Johannes, 9
Wildschut, William, 70, 72–73
Winters, Howard D., 89–91
Wiping the Tears, Istamniyan pakintapi, 18, 106
Wissler, Clark, 110
witchcraft, 46, 73, 167
Witherspoon, Gary, 129–30
Woman Veiled by Clouds, Tse-pi'-na, 231
women, roles of
  Creek/Muskogee, 94, 97–98, 101–2
  Mescalero Apache, 22–23, 143–45, 155–59
  Yup'ik Eskimo, 26–27, 187–96
  Yurok, 33–34

Woodland religious formation, 87–89
world renewal discourse, 11–12, 33–37,
  39–51. *See also* fixing the world ritual;
  oral tradition
Wounded Knee massacre, 18–19, 105–6,
  116–17
Wright, Robin M., 5
*Writer and the Shaman: A Morphology of the
  American Indian, The* (Zolla), 209
Wyatt, Victoria, 172
Wyman, Leland C., 128–29, 132
Yellowtail, Thomas, 1, 12–13, 55–58, 74, 80,
  82

Young, S. Hall, 169–70
Yup'ik Eskimo people
  animal-human relationships, 182–87
  Ayugutaar, myth of, 185–86
  ceremonies, 27–28, 188, 194–96, 201–5
  circle-dot motif, 27, 185–86, 189–90,
    194–96, 200
  death, 26–28, 182–84, 195, 203–5
  eye contact, 27–28, 188–89, 196

eyesight, 186, 189–91, 195–96
  hunting, 182–87, 188–97, 206
  marriage, 204
  masks, 196–201
  rebirth cycling, 26–27, 182–87, 196,
    205–6
  rites of passage, 189–90, 194–96
  ritual dance, 195–96, 200–201
  shamanism, 27–28, 188–90, 195, 200, 205
  soul, 26–27, 182–85, 188–90, 201–3
  tattoos, 189–90
  thought, power of, 183–85, 201, 206
  vision (spiritual), 201
  women, 26–28, 187–96
Yurok people
  on evil, 10, 34
  fixing the world ritual, 10–12, 33–35,
    41–51
  ritual dance, 11, 33–37, 41–51
  ritual language, 47–48
  women, 33–34

Zolla, Elémire, 209